The Women, Yes!

Marie B. Hecht
Joan D. Berbrich
Salley A. Healey
Clare M. Cooper

HOLT, RINEHART AND WINSTON, INC.

New York · Chicago · San Francisco · Atlanta · Dallas · Montreal · Toronto · London · Sydney

Executive Editor: Clifford L. Snyder

Managing Editor: Robert deVilleneuve

Photo Editor: Myra Schachne

Designer: Ruth Riley

The Women,
Yes!

Contents

to our mothers
who began and
our sisters who
continue . . .

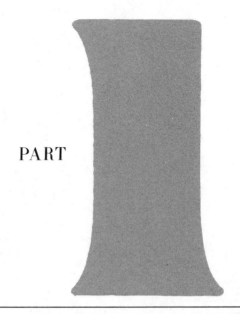

PART

What Is A Woman?

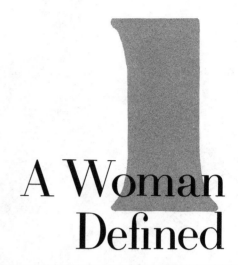

A Woman Defined

wom·an (wŏŏm'en) *n., pl.* **women** (wĭm in). 1. An adult female human being. 2. Women collectively; womankind: *Woman is fickle.* 3. Feminine quality or aspect; womanliness. Often preceded by *the: brought out the woman in him. 4.* A maid-servant. 5. A mistress; paramour. 6. *Informal.* A wife.—*adj.* Female as opposed to male. [Middle English *wumman, wimman,* Old English *wīfmann : wīf,* WIFE + *man(n),* person, MAN.]

The American Heritage Dictionary of the English Language, 1969.

What is a woman?

Is she a mother? a wife? a romantic object? a worker? an intellectual? a drone? Is she, as a sex, superior, inferior—or equal? Is she man's conscience, man's servant—or man's peer?

What is a woman?

Millions of puzzled males have asked this question, and many have tried to answer it. Only recently have women broken their long silence—some to answer the same question, some to comment on male commentary.

Quotations cannot give answers, but they do reflect commonly held opinions—even contrasting opinions. They isolate attitudes and dramatize prejudices. They mirror the deepest desires, the most repressed fears, the innate needs of the human animal. Above all, they suggest the complexity and the vital nature of the relationship of the two sexes.

So once again—what *is* a woman?

On Woman's Purpose

The fact of the matter is that the prime responsibility of a woman probably is to be on earth long enough to find the best mate possible for herself, and conceive children who will improve the species.

NORMAN MAILER
(American author), 1963.

HELMER: *Before all else you are a wife and mother.*
NORA: *That I no longer believe. I think that*

BELLES OF ALL NATIONS

before all else I am a human being, just as much as you are—or, at least, I will try to become one.

HENRIK IBSEN
(Norwegian dramatist), 1879.

On Romance and Chivalry

These chicks are our natural enemy . . . It's time to do battle with them. They are unalterably opposed to the romantic boy-girl society that Playboy *promotes.*

HUGH HEFNER
(owner of *Playboy*), 1970.

The man over there says women need to be helped into carriages and lifted over ditches, and to have the best place everywhere. Nobody ever helps me into carriages or over puddles or gives me the best place . . . and ain't I a woman? Look at my arm! I have ploughed and planted and gathered into barns, and no man could head me . . . and ain't I a woman? I could work as much and eat as much as a man—when I could get it—and bear the lash as well! And ain't I a woman? I have borne thirteen children, and seen most of 'em sold into slavery, and when I cried out with my mother's grief, none but Jesus heard me . . . and ain't I a woman?

SOJOURNER TRUTH
(feminist and orator), 1851.

On Marriage

Marriage is "that sphere for which woman was originally intended, and to which she is so exactly fitted to adorn and bless, as the wife, the mistress of a home, the solace, the aid, and the counsellor of that ONE for whose sake alone the world is of any consequence to her."

GEORGE BURNAP,
Sphere and Duties of Woman, 1854.

I'd rather be a free spinster and paddle my own canoe.

LOUISA MAY ALCOTT
(author), 1832–1888.

On Motherhood

Biologically and temperamentally, I believe women were made to be concerned first and foremost with child care, husband care, and home care.

BENJAMIN SPOCK
(doctor and author), c. 1968.

We must start with the realization that, as much as women want to be good scientists or engineers, they want first and foremost to be womanly companions of men and to be mothers.

BRUNO BETTELHEIM
(psychologist), c. 1968.

If Bruno Bettelheim says that women want first and foremost to be good wives and mothers, it is extremely likely that that is what Bruno Bettelheim wants them to be.

NAOMI WEISSTEIN
(psychologist), c. 1968.

On Fools

Three things have been difficult to tame: the ocean, fools, and women. We may soon be able to tame the ocean; fools and women will take a little longer.

SPIRO AGNEW
(U.S. Vice-president), c. 1969.

Mrs. Poyser's immortal saying about the women being fools because God made them to match the men, is proving itself true.

ALICE STONE BLACKWELL
(feminist), 1929.

On Intelligence

Women, then, are only children of larger growth: they have an entertaining tattle, and sometimes wit; but for solid, reasoning good sense, I never knew in my life one that had it, or who reasoned or acted consequentially for four and twenty hours together.

LORD CHESTERFIELD
(English author), 1748.

Mind has no sex.

HANNAH CROCKER
(American author), 1818.

If American men intend always to keep women slaves, political and civil, they make a great mistake when they let the girls, with the boys, learn the alphabet, for no educated class will long remain in subjection.

MARY CLAY
(feminist), 1884.

On Leadership

If you are a man, it is assumed you are competent until you prove you are incompetent. For a woman it's just the other way around.

POPPY NORTHCUTT
(NASA mathematician), 1970.

This world taught woman nothing skill-ful and then said her work was valueless. It permitted her no opinions and said she did not know how to think. It forbade her to speak in public and said the sex had no orators. It denied her the schools and said the sex had no genius. It robbed her of every vestige of responsibility and then called her weak.

CARRIE CHAPMAN CATT
(feminist), 1902.

On Successful Careers

There is no career more exciting or exacting for a woman than marriage to a great man.

GEORGINA BATTISCOMBE,
Mrs. Gladstone, 1957.

If you ask me what offices they (women) may fill, I reply—any. . . . Let them be sea-captains if you will.

MARGARET FULLER
(editor and feminist), 1845.

From the time guys are old enough to put pants on, Mama and Papa start asking, "What are you going to do with yourself?" With a daughter nobody ever says one word, except that hopefully she'll get married and get off her parents' back before her inlays go.

JANE TRAHEY
(agency executive), 1970.

I loved working on the magazine because it's full of women. Really, I mean it. I found I loved working with women because they do serious things lightly.

JEANNE MOREAU
(French actress; guest editor of *Paris Vogue*), 1970.

On Self-Identity

I know it's old-fashioned, but I do feel that women just are inferior to men in almost every way. So women should concentrate on being just that—women—and leave the rest to men. I'm sure everybody would be a lot happier.

JANET PEARCE
("Pet of the Month"), 1969.

We live in a masculine society owned and operated by a masculine power structure and—just as in a black and white society—the ruling elite will define the reality, even the identity of those whom it rules. Therefore, what women think of women is pretty much what they have learned from men to think of women.

KATE MILLET
(author and feminist), 1969.

There are differences between men and women and I am not denying that. But we will not know what those differences are until women have begun to spell their own names and define themselves in the human dimension more than they've been able to do in the past.

BETTY FRIEDAN
(author and feminist), 1969.

"His" and "hers" should not divide the world, which is "ours."

MARY CALDERONE
(physician), 1970.

DISCUSSION TOPICS

1. A refutation of _____'s quotation (any name)

2. An evaluation of the quotations from a chronological point of view

3. An evaluation of the quotations from a sex point of view

SUGGESTED ACTIVITIES

1. Ask twenty people who are not taking this course to answer the question; "What is a woman?" Record their answers on audio tape. See if you can detect a pattern of attitude.

2. Watch three different types of continuing series on television (e.g. situation comedy, western, adventure, soap opera). Describe all female characters depicted.

3. Describe in detail the personalities and/or characters of three women you know. Then study your descriptions. Do nonphysical characteristics vary from description to description or are they similar in all three selections? If the latter, are the similarities real or the result of unconscious stereotyping?

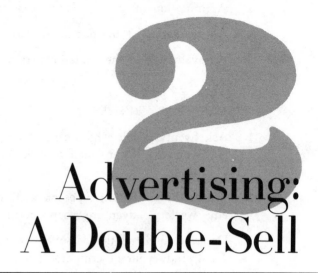

Advertising: A Double-Sell

In this age of mass media, advertising is a two-way street. It reflects present behaviors and attitudes, and in doing so, reinforces and perpetuates them. It starts out by telling us what we are and ends up by telling us what we ought to be.

Consider the typical approach and result. Some Americans have two new cars in a suburban garage. Picture a good-looking healthy male and a beautiful, loving female. Picture two clean, well-dressed, laughing children. Picture two gleaming cars and a just-painted garage. Now display this picture in all media as often as possible. The message is obvious: *all* Americans, if they desire to be healthy, happy, and attractive, should have (and should want) two new cars in a suburban garage.

Anyone who doesn't want two new cars and a suburban garage is—obviously—not quite normal. Anyone who cannot afford two new cars and a suburban garage is—just as obviously—being deprived; and being deprived not only of cars and a garage, but of health, beauty, and the pursuit of happiness.

Of course, the ad does more than sell cars. It sells a whole bushelful of concepts: that a man should be strong and masterful; that a woman should be affectionate and admiring; that children, endowed with the proper physical possessions, will grow up to be praiseworthy citizens. Two new cars in a suburban garage becomes the magic formula to family togetherness and worldly success.

A few advertisers are content to sell a patio roof or a lawnmower, but many advertisers today are selling not just a product, but a way of life. They are exploiting the needs, fears, and hidden dreams of the average person. They are implanting new needs and new desires. They are constructing models to be emulated; and anyone who dares to reject the model is threatened with failure and social ostracism.

This philosophy of advertising is especially injurious to women. Most advertisers and manufacturers are male; the image of woman that they project is *their* image. Unfortunately, their image of woman is often a collage of clichés:

A man thinks; a woman feels.

A man is strong; a woman is weak.

A man is interested in the world; a woman is interested in her house.

225.
(a) Riding habit. (1888.) (b) Tennis costume. (1888.)

CYCLING COSTUME, c. 1892

The so-called womanly image has always been a male creation—even in the Gay 90's.

A man gives orders; a woman obeys them.

A man wants to make his mark on life; a woman wants to make her mark on a man.

A man is straightforward; a woman is devious.

To a man, love is one aspect of life; to a woman, love *is* life.

Men have many varied ambitions; women have one ambition—to get a man.

And finally:

A man chases a woman until she catches him.

Through constant repetition, these generalizations (opinions only) begin to masquerade as fact. The result is a double-sell: A product is sold; so is woman.

Some Magazine and Newspaper Ads

1. "There's no pushing or pulling with the self-propelled Hoover Dial-A-Matic vacuum cleaner with Power Drive. Just a touch on the handle and it goes..."

   HEADLINE: "All it needs is a woman's touch."

2. "I don't want to be liberated... I love being a woman tenderly cared for by a man. Wearing soft, furry, feminine things from Penn Fifth Avenue Furs."

3. Ad for *Family Circle,* a monthly magazine: "You become a woman one day when you walk instead of run, when you smile instead of laugh.

   "You become a woman one day when you begin to think about hairdos and recipes. Later on you'll be thinking about home decorating and your family's health and Thanksgiving dinner."

   HEADLINE: "When does a woman become a woman?"

4. Ad for Field & Stream Pipe Tobacco:

   "If your girl doesn't like the great autumn day aroma of Field & Stream ... *start playing the field.*"

5. Ad for Emeraude Perfume by Coty:

   "Want him to be more of an man? Try being more of a woman."

6. Ad for Flying Dutchman Pipe Tobacco:

   "Lead women around by the nose."

7. "SpeakEasy Mouthspray when you know he's going to be close."

8. Ad for Ambush Perfume by Dana:

   "There are a lot of things for a guy to think about. Make sure you'll be one of them."

9. Ad for Betty Crocker Chocolate Fudge Frosting Mix:

   "When he compliments you on your homemade frosting, why bother him with unnecessary details?"

10.

She	He
"They say the Kenmore self-cleaning oven even gets the corners clean. You just set the dials... The automatic timer on the oven's great, too. It'll cook dinner even if I'm out shopping or something."	"That stove's really put together right. And another good thing, you can sure depend on Sears service. Honey, you're about to own a new stove."

   HEADLINE: "It's designed for you, but built for your husband."

Television Commercials

In recent years television commercials have become a major target of Woman's Rights groups. One leader in this new battle is Frankie (Franchellie) Cadwell, president of the Cadwell

Davis Company, an advertising agency. In 1970, Ms. Cadwell said: "Television ads perpetuate the image that women are stupid clowns. They show women looking ga-ga at giants in their washing machines or having a nonsensical conversation with a dove about softer hands. Women aren't idiots and it's time ads stop depicting them that way."

In an attempt to prove that the "average" woman is rebelling against slanted and degrading advertising, Ms. Cadwell had a poll conducted in California. Over six hundred women were asked: "What TV advertisement can you recall that you find particularly demeaning or objectionable?" The ten most-hated ads included those for Right Guard deodorant, Axion pre-soak, Ultra Brite toothpaste, Crest toothpaste, Bold detergent, Dove dishwashing liquid, Colgate 100 mouthwash, Punch detergent, Ajax Liquid cleaner and Scope mouthwash. Several critics quickly pointed out that these ads all show women as stupid, servile, or unattractive. In several, a male (or a male voice) gives advice, rescuing some inept woman from near catastrophe. In others, women are depicted as basically unattractive: only with a certain mouthwash or toothpaste or deodorant can a woman hope to win a kiss from the man she loves. "Advertisers must think that women are stupid," commented Ms. Cadwell, "if they are to believe that a toothpaste will bring sex appeal."

The Latest Gambit

The latest gambit in the women-and-advertising war is the use (or abuse) of women's struggle for equality.

1. Slipstick, a product of Liquid Paper Corporation, can help a secretary to correct errors. But its advertisement promises much more. Under the banner headline, *Liberation*, it eulogizes:

   "Those marvelous new dimensions you're discovering in yourself were there all the time, waiting to be liberated. Like our new Slipstick."

A few sentences follow, explaining how Slipstick works; then the ad concludes: "These new freedoms have been declared for you by Liquid Paper, the people on your side."

2. Carnation Slender proclaims "the Liberated Line" as 34–22–34.

3. And Virginia Slims highlights an attractive model circled by the slogan: "Rosemary . . . For President." Underneath the slogan is the succinct comment, "Someday." The ad goes on to comfort women for their lack of political power by promising, "Meanwhile you've got Virginia Slims. The taste for today's woman. You've come a long way, baby."

Women's rightists are not particularly happy with the latest technique. Joan Nicholson of NOW describes the Virginia Slims approach as "a ripoff of the movement because it implies that the only advancement women have made is to get their own cigarette . . . They say, 'You've come a long way, baby.' We haven't come no place. We're still segregated from men. We have a separate—but equal—cigarette."

Lee Walker, also of NOW, is even more bitter. "This is a human-equality movement that they're making jokes about . . . They're abusing the movement."

Among the few "liberation" ads that have won applause from women's groups are those for Tiparillo, the little cigar. One of these ads features the following short dialogue:

QUESTION: "Do you think we'll ever have a lady president?"
ANSWER: "No, a woman president."

The Future

What about the future? How will women and advertisers resolve their differences? Here are some comments from advertisers and activists in the movement:

LEE WALKER (of NOW): "If you're selling silver polish, show the husband and wife polishing the silver together. If you're selling Slender, show them both drinking Slender."

DR. ROBERT WACHSLER (a psychologist on the staff of the Batten, Barton, Durstine, and Osborn advertising agency): "In advertising we will have to show women less as women and more as people."

GEORGE REICHART (vice-president of advertising for the General Cigar Company): "If we're not going to support women's lib in so many words, let's at least take the psychology of it and go along with it today."

FRANKIE CADWELL (president of the Cadwell Davis advertising agency): "Some advertisers act like women have brain damage. This has to change. Women are tired of insults."

COLLEEN BUTLER (employee of the J. Walter Thompson Company, an advertising agency): "Some (people), still in school, or social workers, accuse me of selling out. Maybe I'm unrealistic in the credit I give the vast public, but I don't see them as a bunch of slobs who will be manipulated one way or the other."

LUCY KOMISAR (a journalist, radio producer, and activist in Woman's Rights): "How can women get . . . companies to change? 'Boycotts,' answer the ad women in unison. Women are 85 percent of the retail market; they could end degrading advertising tomorrow if they refused to buy products that use such methods. Even written complaints to companies would have an effect."

In the last few years some advertisers have become sensitive to women's feelings and attitudes. Some changes have been made. However, sexist ads still appear in every medium. Education will help; so will complaints. But as Lucy Komisar indicated, little real improvement can be expected until women become militant with money. The hand that shuts the wallet may rock the world!

DISCUSSION TOPICS

1. A picture of the American Female as advertisers see her

2. A picture of the American Male as advertisers see him

3. An analysis of popular advertising techniques

SUGGESTED ACTIVITIES

1. From a newspaper or a magazine, clip three ads that are selling an image, a value, or a concept as well as a product. Explain why you selected each.

2. Draw up an annotated list of ten TV commercials. Include the product, the story line, the characters, the approach, and the mood. Include also a brief evaluation of *what* is being sold.

3. Develop a story board for one TV commercial that a woman might find demeaning. Be sure it is detailed enough so that anyone who studies it will be able to detect the advertiser's message(s).

4. Select an ad (from any medium) that a woman might find objectionable. Using the same techniques and approach, prepare a comparable ad that men might find objectionable. Present both ads to your group. Evaluate the reactions of females and males to each ad.

3 Facts And Figures

The moment you were born, you became a statistic. When you started school, you became another statistic. Every time you buy a car, find a job, lose a job, get sick, or drive through a red light, you add another number to some set of statistics.

The American Heritage Dictionary defines statistics as "the mathematics of the collection, organization, and interpretation of numerical data; especially, the analysis of population characteristics by inference from sampling." Part of the time you are an actual number in a computer; part of the time you are a representative number in a poll. Either way, your life in twentieth-century America is the raw material for a numbers game.

Sometimes numbers have a reputation for honesty greater than they deserve. If someone says that 364,972 women are currently involved in trying to overthrow the government of the United States, people are inclined to believe the speaker—not because his statement is true, but because the specific number has such a solid, factual *ring* to it. An apparent intellectual once admitted that peo-

ple admired his fantastic memory because whenever a problem arose, he solved it by quoting a statistic: a statistic that he *made up*. Few will take the trouble to check; besides, statistics *sound* true.

Statistics contribute to dishonesty in another way: through careless interpretation or deliberately deceptive interpretation. A set of numbers is only as good as the interpreter's objectivity.

When all the pitfalls have been listed, however, it remains true that statistics are a valuable aid in spotting trends and in suggesting causes as well as effects. Consider the following chart:

1. Marital Status of Women in the Civilian Labor Force

	% of Female Pop. Working	Single	Married	Divorced or Widowed
1940	27.4	48.1	16.7	32.0
1960	34.8	44.1	31.7	37.1
1970	42.6	53.0	41.4	36.2

* Figures in all charts are from the U.S. Bureau of Census, *Statistical Abstract of the United States*, 1970, 1971.

This particular group of numbers indicates that from 1940 to 1970 the percent of the female population working has increased, the percent of single women working has increased, the percent of married women working has increased, and the percent of divorced or widowed women working has (with conditions) increased. This is all we actually *know* from this statistical chart. We do not know whether *more* women are working, simply that a larger percentage are.

However, we do know, from other sources, that the actual population (both female and male) of this country has increased from 1940 to 1970, and so we can *deduce* that *more* women are now working than were in 1940. We can make the same deduction about single women and married women.

The problem arises when someone, after studying the chart, announces: "More divorced women are working than ever before." This is not necessarily true. First, the statistics do not separate divorced women from widows, so there may be more widows and fewer divorcees working; second, to arrive at this conclusion, the reader has conveniently omitted the 1960 figure; third, the interpreter is also assuming that the pre-1940 figures would reflect exactly the same trend. On the basis of the numbers given in the chart, the statement simply is not warranted.

The problem becomes even more complex when emotionalism enters the picture. Someone who is leading a campaign against women working might reach a conclusion like this: "Since over 40 percent of the married women are now working compared to 17 percent in 1940 and since we know there are more divorces now than there were in the past, we may conclude that any married woman who works is deliberately sabotaging her marriage."

Again, this statement is not valid. Before coming to this conclusion, one would have to know why 17 percent of the married women were working in 1940, how working affected (if at all) their marriages; and why married women are working in 1970. One would also have to know whether attitudes toward marriage and toward married women working have remained the same. And one would have to analyze both the ostensible and real causes of divorce over the last thirty years. Without additional knowledge in all of these areas, the conclusion is worthless.

If the problem of interpretation of statistics is so complex, why use statistics at all? The answer is that, used properly, they can be extremely valuable. They are excellent raw material for thinking and deduction; they can indicate a pattern or lack of pattern; they can detect a trend; they can provide an overall view of a particular situation.

Even the small chart with which we started, "The Marital Status of Women in the Civilian Labor Force," proves conclusively that more women are working in 1970 than were working in 1940. This is important data for employers, economists, marriage counselors, and students of modern society.

Here is another chart:

2. **U.S. Population by Sex**

	Male	*Female*
1820	4,897,000	4,742,000
1860	16,085,000	15,358,000
1900	38,816,000	37,178,000
1940	66,062,000	65,608,000
1970	98,882,000	104,284,000

Some interesting (and valid) facts can be found in this chart. In 1820 when much of America was still frontier, there were more males than females. This was true in 1860, at the beginning of the Civil War, and in 1900. It was still true in 1940, at the beginning of World War II. But in the thirty years between 1940 and 1970, the balance changed. There are now more females than males, and the numerical difference is not a small one: it is over five million! This is meaningful knowledge for every economic and governmental leader in the country as well as for sociologists.

Far more fascinating are the questions posed by this set of numbers. Why has the numerical edge shifted from male to female? Is the cause biological, sociological, or totally unknown? What changes can be expected to occur in a country in which this shift has occurred What changes have occurred in the last thirty years? Which of these changes *might* be the result of the shift? Is the Woman's Rights movement a cause or a result of the shift Serious thinking about any one of these questions can lead to further research and a deeper understanding of today's society.

Educational Statistics

The next chart deals with educational statistics. People talk glibly about the educational opportunities for male and female. What is the truth?

3. High School and College Graduates, by Sex

	High School	
	Male	Female
1900	38,000	57,000
1940	579,000	643,000
1970	1,439,000	1,467,000
	College	
1900	22,000	5,000
1940	110,000	77,000
1970	456,000	328,000

There is enough significant material in Chart 3 to settle many old arguments and to start as many new ones. It is interesting to observe that from 1900 to 1970 there were always more female than male *high school* graduates, but that during the same time period there were always more male than female *college* graduates. Does this indicate that more women than men are educable, but that more men than women are *highly* educable? Are there economic or social causes for this strange combination of figures? It is possible that males are either stupid or bright, while females are usually of "average" intelligence? (Please note that these are questions, not conclusions. All the chart really gives us is the number in each category.)

Another interesting observation can be made about Chart 3. In the high school category, the female-over-male edge has decreased dramatically. In the college category, the male-over-female edge has decreased almost as dramatically. Are the two sets of figures correlated in some way?

A third observation is possible. Note that the total number of high school graduates in 1940 is not much higher than the total number of college graduates in 1970. This may seem an irrelevant comparison, but is it? Has the value of the high school diploma remained the same from 1900 until 1970? Is a college degree worth as much in the 1970s as it was in 1900? The position of the President (one office) is significantly greater than the position of the senator (100 offices) which, in turn, is greater than the position of the representative (435 offices). Must the value of something *decrease* as the number of people who achieve it *increases*? It is a provocative question for and about human nature, and it is a question that any "rights" group might well ponder.

In the world of the '70s, the education that really seems to matter is education beyond high school—education at the college level, preferably at the graduate level. A question important to any consideration of the position of women is—how are women doing at the bachelor's level, at the master's level, at the doctorate level? How are they doing in specific major fields? Chart 4 carries on with the next level of educational statistics.

It takes only a reading, not an interpretation, of Chart 4 to realize that more males than females earn bachelor's, master's, and doctoral degrees and that while the male edge is not very large for the first degree, it is exceedingly large for the final degree. The figures do not, of course, explain why this is true. Is it true because women do not want higher degrees, are unable to earn them, or are prevented from earning them? The figures do suggest one thing, however. If so few women

A COLLEGE THROUGH THE YEARS

PROCESSION OF STUDENTS OF MOUNT HOLYOKE COLLEGE ON THE WAY TO DRAPE MARY LYON'S TOMB.

4. Earned Degrees Conferred—1969

All Fields	Male	Female
Bachelor's and 1st		
Professional degrees	446,933	322,750
Master's	121,881	72,533
Doctorate	22,753	3,436
Specific Fields		
English and literature		
Bachelor's	17,539	36,820
Doctorate	799	352
Education		
Bachelor's	36,562	116,686
Doctorate	3,859	970
Library Science		
Bachelor's	64	936
Doctorate	12	5

are earning the highest degree, the top positions in most professions must be barred to them.

The figures listed under "Specific Fields" are even more worthy of note. More than twice as many females as males take a bachelor's degree in English and literature, but only half as many take a doctoral degree in the same field. One can expect then to find many female teachers of English, especially at the high school level, but few female professors of English at the college level—and that, indeed, is the case. The same disparity exists to an even greater extent in the fields of Education and Library Science. In each case, females receive enough education to become workers while males receive enough to become leaders. Females are prepared for positions in which they follow policy, males for positions in which they make policy.

To conclude that this is a consciously conceived male plot is ludicrous—there must be half a dozen causes, perhaps more—but the results are obvious. If women hope to attain equality in top positions, they must work to bring about a shift in these figures that will result in a more equitable balance of power.

Crime Statistics

One of the major concerns in the United States in the '70s is the crime explosion. Chart 5 shows the number of homicides committed by males and females from 1930 to 1968.

5. Homicides Committed

	Male	Female
1930	8,373	2,100
1950	6,089	1,853
1967	10,236	3,189
1968	11,523	3,163

After studying these statistics, one is inclined to question Kipling's statement that "the female of the species is more deadly than the male." However, that, too, would be oversimplification; to be fair, one must study the social conditions of each age. Was it (and is it) easier for a man to commit murder than for a woman? Or are men simply more prone to violence? Also—why were there fewer murders committed by both men and women in 1950 than in 1930 or again in the late 1960s? And—is the very small decrease of female murderers (26) from 1967 to 1968 significant? The number is so small that it might be the result of chance; but it might be the beginning of a new trend. If so, what has caused this change?

Other crime statistics are just as interesting. In 1930, 14,319 men and 4,004 women committed suicide. In 1968, 15,379 men and 5,993 women committed suicide. For both sexes the number of suicides has increased at almost the same rate.

Employment and Income Statistics

Employment opportunities and income are two items that concern almost all adults. Chart 6 provides some fascinating figures for analysis and discussion.

6. Employed Persons by Major Occupation Group and Sex (April, 1970. Add three 000's to each number)

	Male	Female
Professional and technical workers	6,890	4,431
Managers, officials and proprietors	6,896	1,301
Clerical workers	3,497	10,337
Salesworkers	2,724	1,990
Craftsmen and foremen	9,737	290
Operatives	9,539	4,272
Nonfarm laborers	3,499	115
Private household workers	26	1,559
Other service workers	3,185	4,954
Farmworkers	2,692	472

Add to the above information these further facts: that in 1960, of the college presidents, professors, and instructors, 140,000 were male, 39,000 female; of the lawyers and judges, 206,000 were male, 8,000 female; of the physicians and surgeons, 214,000 were male, 16,000 female.

The sets of figures together suggest that a woman will have little difficulty in getting a job as a clerk or as a maid, but that if she hopes to be a craftsman (craftswoman?), a manager, or a college president, she had better be prepared for a long hard battle that will almost surely end in defeat.

How does this employment picture affect salaries? The median income for male employed civilians in 1968 was $7,080; the median income

Teaching, particularly at the primary level, has been, and still is an acceptable career choice for women.

7

for female employed civilians in the same year was $3,380. Quite a difference. One reason, undoubtedly, is shown in Chart 6—women work in lower-paying jobs. What, then, about men and women who work in the same jobs? In 1968, in professional and technical fields, males earned $9,960; females $5,598; in sales, males earned $7,367, females $2,248; in clerical work, males earned $7,034, females $4,002.

These figures round out the picture nicely. Women, in general, work in lower-paying jobs, hence receive lower salaries. The few who do manage to get into higher paying jobs still receive lower salaries than their male counterparts. Either way they get less money—and money, quite often, means power, mobility, and prestige. The statistics paint a picture; they cannot, unfortunately, offer a solution.

Miscellaneous Statistics

Each of the following items is interesting in itself—and often provocative. They are offered without further comment.

In 1969, 4,891,343 males were arrested; in the same year, 725,496 females were arrested.

In 1968, 287,601 males were arrested for driving while intoxicated; in the same year, 19,630 females were arrested on the same charge.

In 1966 there were 281,336 male lawyers, 8,068 female lawyers.

In 1971, the Long Island Lighting Company had 1,100 women among its 5,500 employees. Of 1,200 management-level positions, only 35 were occupied by women.

1969–70. According to a survey taken by the Education Commission of the United States, of 80,000 persons in four age groups: 9, 13, 17, and young adult (20–35) —girls and women are more skilled in writing than boys and men.

In 1960, 30 percent of the wives of professional men worked; in 1970, 41 percent of the wives of professional men worked.

In Virginia, 21,000 women were rejected for college entrance during a period when not one man was rejected.

In 1969, men made up only 12 percent of the elementary teachers, but accounted for 78 percent of the principals of elementary schools.

In 1970, a Harris poll revealed that women oppose capital punishment by 46 percent to 39 percent while men favor it by 56 percent to 37 percent.

In 1971, budgetary cutbacks in New York State necessitated some decrease in the number of people employed by the state. Senator Samuel Greenberg of Brooklyn, N.Y. quoted some statistics: "Less than half the state labor force—44.2 percent—is female; more than half those fired—51.8 percent—were female. Women in the most responsible positions suffered the greatest. Almost 50 percent more women in grades 31 to 38 were fired than their share of employment justified. . . . Three of the four women heading state agencies at the start of 1971 are no longer there. One quit, one retired, and one acting director was returned to her old position. All three were replaced by men."

A questionnaire sponsored by the American Association of University Women discovered that 67 percent of the women and 68 percent of the men believe males resent a female boss.

Eleven percent of all U.S. families are headed by females—single, widowed, or divorced.

DISCUSSION TOPICS

1. An analysis of some ——————— statistics (Basic, Educational, Crime, Employment, and Income)

2. Twisting statistics

SUGGESTED ACTIVITIES

1. Do a statistical sex-ratio study of a school. How many males and females are in the student body? How many of the last five valedictorians were females? males? of the last five salutatorians? Consider student organization officers, class officers, editors of the school newspaper and yearbook, members of the dramatic group. How many males have been absent in the last month? how many females? How many males have cut classes in the last month? how many females? When you have acquired as many statistics as possible, present them to the group for analysis.

2. Do a statistical sex-ratio study of one block of stores in your community. Who owns each store, a man or a woman? how about the sales people? Who plans the advertising? Who establishes the prices? Are most purchasers men? or women? When you have acquired as many statistics as possible, chart them and present them for analysis.

3. Take a recent copy of a general magazine such as *Time* or *Newsweek*. Do a statistical sex-ratio study of the articles. How many are about men? about women? about both? about other subjects? Present the results in the form of a chart and/or essay.

4. Do a statistical sex-ratio study of ten books you have read. Are the authors male or female? Are the major characters male or female? Ask twenty females and twenty males to rate each of the ten books as enjoyable and/or informative on a one-to-five scale (with one being the highest score). Chart both sets of statistics and study them to determine possible correlation between the two sets.

5. Do a statistical sex-ratio study of the faculty and administration of the schools in your district. How many teachers in the elementary school are male? female? in the junior high? in the secondary school? in all the schools combined? in the nearest college? Present these figures to the group for analysis.

Famous Distaffs

In an open-air colonnade on the New York University campus is the Hall of Fame for Great Americans. From 1900, when it was established, until 1970, 95 persons were found worthy of election to this elite group. Of these, 85 are male, 10 female.

The women who have been honored were primarily social reformers and educators:

1905— *Mary Lyon (1797–1849)*. Educator; founded Mount Holyoke Seminary for Women.

1905— *Maria Mitchell (1818–1889)* Astronomer; director of the observatory at Vassar College; discovered a comet in 1847.

1905— *Emma Willard (1787–1870)*. Educator; founded Troy Female Seminary; influenced education for women in the United States and Europe. Poet and translator.

1910— *Harriet Beecher Stowe (1811–1896)*. Author of *Uncle Tom's Cabin*; active in anti-slavery movement.

1910— *Frances Elizabeth Willard (1839–1898)*. Educator; dean of Women's College of the Northwestern University; president of Woman's Christian Temperance Union and of World's Christian Temperance Union.

1915— *Charlotte Saunders Cushman (1816–1876)*. Distinguished actress.

1920— *Alice Freeman Palmer (1855–1902)*. Educator; president of Wellesley College; director of the World's Columbian Exposition.

1950— *Susan B. Anthony (1820–1906)*. Leader of Woman Suffrage Movement; active in anti-slavery and temperance movements.

1965— *Jane Addams (1860–1935)*. Sociologist; established Hull Settlement House in Chicago; interested in city reform, woman suffrage, and the peace movement.

1970— *Lillian Wald (1867–1940)*. Social worker and nurse; president of the Henry Street Settlement, New York; worked for public welfare.

Apparently it was possible to accept a woman as eminent only when she worked in "womanly" fields, although the star-studded list does include an actress, an author, and an astronomer.

More noteworthy though are the omissions.

The poets *Bryant* and *Whittier* and *Lanier* made it; *Emily Dickinson* did not.

The lawyer *Rufus Choate* made it; *Belva Lockwood* did not.

Dr. Walter Reed made it; *Dr. Elizabeth Blackwell* and *Dr. Mary Walker* did not.

The artist *James Whistler* made it; *Mary Cassatt* did not.

James Fenimore Cooper and *Oliver Wendell Holmes* made it; *Louisa May Alcott* and *Edith Wharton* did not.

The Puritan preacher *Jonathan Edwards* made it; the Puritan rebel *Anne Hutchinson* did not.

So it goes.

In recent years feminists have been calling for *her*story instead of *his*tory. The answer to the question—"Have women been treated fairly in history books?"—is complex. Until the twentieth century not many women were leaders. Denied advanced education, accused of being "unladylike" if they sought independence, barred from most jobs and professions, they settled for the only role considered proper: wife and mother. The few women who did make it were extraordinarily determined, daring social ostracism, poverty, and the mocking jeers of colleagues.

Another by no means inexplicable tendency has kept women out of the history books. Sometimes women who had initiative and imagination did lead the way—founded new institutions, organized movements, and did the work required—and then, in this male-oriented society, stepped back to give the titular leadership to a man. The most dramatic example of this tendency is the U.S. Sanitary Commission.

The primary purpose of this Commission was to help the wounded during the Civil War. It was originated, organized, and operated by women. Yet its first president was Henry W. Bellows, a Unitarian clergyman who could provide the male prestige that was thought necessary.

As the wounded increased, the women's *auxiliaries* raised most of the money and did most of the nursing; yet almost every unit was headed by a male. Under this interesting system, males naturally received the credit.

In New England in 1840 when the male-dominated government was unable to find the money to complete the Bunker Hill Monument, the women launched a campaign. Through fairs and donations they quickly raised the amount needed. But "it was woman stuff and it was not to be taken seriously. In fact, the money raised was turned over to the committee of men who managed the construction of the monument and it was accepted on the condition that the ladies not be given any credit for what they did."*

A third factor that decreased the woman's role in this country's formal history is the emphasis placed on war and military leaders. William T. Sherman, who burned his way through Georgia, is in the Hall of Fame; Clara Barton, who helped clean up the mess, is not. Accused of knowing nothing about war, Ms. Barton retorted: "I wish men didn't either. The war side of war could never have called me to the field. Through and through, thought and act—body and soul—I hate it! The side of the picture which history never shows belongs to those who must follow the track of conquering armies, faces bathed in tears and hands in blood."

A fourth factor that militated against women is that most historians have been male. Male labor leaders have been written about extensively; female labor leaders have been relegated to the footnotes or to oblivion. Male lawyers have been quoted; female lawyers have been "overlooked." Reforms of industry (male-led) have been extolled and credit given to the reformers; reforms of penal institutions and educational systems (female-led) have been described in general terms, with credit seldom given to the reformers.

These four factors taken together account for the absence of women from today's history books. Women have made history; they simply have not been given credit for it.

The women described in each of the following sets of four statements deserve to be well-

---

* Ferguson: *The Male Attitude*, pp. 222-223.

Joan of Arc and Molly Pitcher both took the initiative in time of crisis.

8-9

Betsy Ross and George Washington—Women have made history, they simply have not been given credit for it.

known; yet most people (including women) are not able to identify them.

1. ———— (1830–1930)

   a. When she was more than fifty years old, this woman became a union organizer.

   b. She traveled on foot across much of the country, organizing miners in several states.

   c. She worked for the child labor law in Pennsylvania at a time when it was unpopular.

   d. Her slogan was "Pray for the dead and fight like hell for the living." Who is she?

2. ———— (1802–1887)

   a. In 1841, after recovering from tuberculosis, she gave up teaching and started a second career—this time as a social re-

former. For the next 48 years she worked for the improvement of asylums, hospitals, and prisons.

   b. Through her efforts 32 new hospitals were built in this country, and six others enlarged. Several hospitals for the mentally ill were completely reformed, and a model asylum created in New Jersey.

   c. Not content with bettering the life of the underdog in the United States, she traveled to Scotland and there won improvements in that nation's asylums. Next she went to Rome, saw Pope Pius IX, and persuaded him to build an asylum which would be a model for the entire world.

   d. During the Civil War she was named Superintendent of Nurses, and later Superintendent of Army Nurses. She was the first woman to fill an executive post for the federal government. Who is she?

3. _____ (1830–1917)

a. This woman was tutored in law because the National University of Law in Washington refused to accept her for formal study. In 1873, her diploma was signed by President Grant who did not realize it belonged to a woman.

b. She drafted a bill that guaranteed equal pay for equal work in the federal civil service, then shepherded it through Congress. She drafted another bill that permitted *any* lawyer who "had practiced before the highest court of any state . . . for the space of three years" to practice before the United States Supreme Court, and this bill, too, was enacted into law.

c. She led the battle against court discrimination in Virginia, secured an award of five million dollars for the Cherokee Indians, and sponsored the first Negro lawyer to appear before the Supreme Court.

d. In 1885, she drew up and presented to Congress a bill "advocating an international court to preserve the peace of the world." This was the *first bill in history* that favored an international peace league. In 1884 and again in 1888, she was nominated for President of the United States by the National Equal Rights Party. Who is she?

4. _____ (1821–1910)

a. When this woman decided to study medicine, she applied to medical schools in Philadelphia and New York, but was rejected because she was female. Undaunted, she applied to the Geneva Medical College (New York), and was accepted, and in 1849 received her M.D. She was the first woman in the United States to receive a medical degree.

b. In 1857, she established in New York City a hospital entirely staffed by women. Eventually this hospital provided a full course in medical education for women. She also founded the first training school for nurses in the United States.

c. During the Civil War, she called a meeting that eventually resulted in the uniting of thousands of Ladies' Aids into a strong Women's Central Association that trained nurses for war work and moved into military camps with food, clothing, and medicine. This New York group, against the wishes of the army, expanded into the U.S. Sanitary Commission that had the power to inspect and enforce good sanitary practices in camps and in hospitals. The U.S. Sanitary Commission, in turn, was the forerunner of the American Red Cross, the U.S. Department of Public Health, and other agencies.

d. Her pioneer work here done, she moved to England where she supported the establishment of the New Hospital for Women and the London School of Medicine for Women. In the latter institution she accepted the chair of gynecology and served for years on its governing council. In 1871, she organized the National Health Society of England to promote health among all classes of the population. In her spare time she wrote (and had published) almost twenty books or pamphlets dealing with health, medicine, and morality. Who is she?

5. _____ (1903–   )

a. This woman, when she was sixteen, flew in an airplane over Buffalo throwing out handbills for women's rights. When she was twenty, she worked with the National Women's Party and was an active crusader for equal rights for women. In 1936 she wrote a play, *The Women*, which ran for 657 performances and which savagely attacked the so-called feminine vices.

b. Early in World War II she spent months in Asia and the Mideast and wrote a lengthy analysis of the military situation there that awed Churchill and stunned the Joint Chiefs of Staff. The articles, expurgated and abridged, were later published by *Life* magazine. Incidentally, she was a congresswoman from Connecticut from 1943–1947.

c. Her wit and crystal-like perception (into herself as well as others) is already legendary. When she was converted to Catholicism, Father Sheen asked her to choose a priest to hear her first confession. The lady replied: "Bring me someone who has seen the rise and fall of empires!" She was also the U.S. Ambassador to Italy.

d. She played a major role in inspiring President Roosevelt to establish the National Recovery Act and was strongly influential in the development of the Trieste treaty and the Marshall Plan. Who is she?

(*Answers:* 1) Mary Jones, also known as Mother Jones; 2) Dorothea Dix; 3) Belva Ann Lockwood; 4) Elizabeth Blackwell; 5) Clare Boothe Luce.)

Barbara Frietchie waved the United States flag in defiance of Confederate forces under Gen. "Stonewall" Jackson when they entered the city of Frederick, Md.

11

More Famous Women: A Catechism

1. Q. In 1892 who set a record by going around the world in 72 days, 6 hours, and 11 minutes?

   A. A woman—Nellie Bly.

2. Q. Who broke the above record in 1936?

   A. A woman—Dorothy Kilgallen.

3. Q. Who wrote the *first* anti-slavery book published in the United States?

   A. A woman—Lydia Frances Child: *An Appeal in Favor of the Class of Americans Called Africans*, 1833.

4. Q. Who suggested the annual Thanksgiving Day and persuaded President Lincoln to proclaim it?

   A. A woman—Sarah Josepha Hale.

5. Q. Who founded the kindergarten movement in the United States?

   A. A woman—Elizabeth Peabody.

6. Q. Who was the first American dramatist to write about American themes?

   A. A woman—Mercy Otis Warren.

7. Q. What American historian wrote the first history of the American Revolution?

   A. A woman—Mercy Otis Warren.

8. Q. Who created the system of public school nursing?

   A. A woman—Lillian Wald.

9. Q. Who was responsible for winning the West for the Union and who also presented the military strategy that saved the North after Bull Run?

   A. A woman—Anna Ella Carroll.

10. Q. Who invented the first "skeleton tooth" or cap?

    A. A woman—Elizabeth Morey of New York City.

11. Q. Who wrote an article that was published in the *Atlantic Monthly* in January, 1863, that was a factor in swinging England's favor from the Confederacy to the Union?

    A. A woman—Harriet Beecher Stowe.

DISCUSSION TOPICS

1. Evaluate the following quotation: "The study of history is useful to the historian by teaching him his ignorance of women; and the mass of his ignorance crushes one who is familiar enough with what we call historical sources to realize how few women have ever been known."—Henry Adams

SUGGESTED ACTIVITIES

1. Choose five women who are (or were) important in their own right and look up their accomplishments. Then compose sets of statements for each of the five. Try them out on your friends.

2. Construct a Hall of Fame for your town. Choose historical candidates (by questioning oldest residents, checking local newspaper files, etc.) and contemporary candidates. Look beyond elected offcials; look for the unpublicized "doers" behind progress.

5

Some People Are More Equal ...A Legal Ana

By marriage, the husband and the wife are one person in law; that is, the <u>very being or legal existence of the woman is suspended</u> during her marriage, or at least, is consolidated into that of her husband under whose wing, protection and cover, she performs everything.
Sir William Blackstone: <u>Commentaries</u> (1723-1780)

Did you know that: according to New York law, a girl of sixteen, but not a boy of the same age, can be kept in an institution until she is twenty-one if she is "a habitual truant, incorrigible, ungovernable or habitually disobedient and beyond the control of a parent"?

Did you know that: according to Alabama, Florida, Indiana, North Carolina, and Texas law, a woman cannot sell *her own* property without the consent of her husband?

"The law's the law—it's the same for everybody!"

That's what is said—but it just isn't true, as even a cursory survey of the law codes will indicate. George Orwell once wrote: "All animals are equal, but some animals are more equal than others." In the law courts all persons are equal, but men are more equal than women.

This unequal equality, this unjust justice, is the result of the double standard, a system of female-male relationship which began several thousand years ago and which—possessing remarkable longevity—continues into the present. Today the double standard operates primarily under two euphemistic masks:

Mask I:
The Sanctity of the Home

a. To preserve domestic bliss: In Kentucky a man may divorce his wife because she drinks to

excess, but she may divorce him for the same cause *only* if his actions jeopardize the economic health of his family. In Arkansas *she* may be imprisoned for three years for habitual drunkenness; *he* remains free to go on drinking. (Apparently overzealous consumption of alcohol threatens the sanctity of the home only when the practitioner is female.)

b. To ensure marital fidelity: In Texas a man has the right to kill his wife's paramour if he catches them together. But if *she* tries the same procedure in reverse, she can be charged with murder.

c. To foster togetherness: In Louisiana a married woman may possess only one legal residency—that of her husband. If she sets up a separate apartment, it is "illegal" and she loses all rights related to residency. (Among the rights related to residency are the right to vote, the right to receive welfare assistance, and the right to hold or run for public office.)

d. To maintain stability: In Florida when a man becomes a prisoner of war, his wife is forbidden to sell the family car or home. In case of disaster such as fire, insurance payments are not made. This law was modified in 1971. Now a wife is considered capable of handling transactions that involve less than $5,000. If a transaction involves more than $5,000, however, she must still get the permission of the state circuit court.

Mask II: Protective Legislation

a. To "protect" women from overexertion: In Utah a woman may not be hired for a job that

Women have always been "protected," for "their own good" of course.

requires her to carry anything that weighs more than fifteen pounds. (How much does an eight-month-old baby weigh?)

b. To "protect" women from difficult situations: In Ohio a woman is forbidden by law to be a truck driver, an electric or gas meter reader, a bellboy, or a crossing guard.

c. To "protect" women from moral hazards: In Michigan a woman may work as a barmaid but not as a bartender. (The latter position, apparently, would endanger her morals; it certainly would increase her pay check.)

d. To "protect" women from mental strain: The United States Congress has enacted legislation to prevent prejudice against any minority in the area of college admissions. It continues to "protect" women by permitting absurdly low quotas for this majority of Americans.

e. To "protect" women from financial stresses: In California, Florida, Nevada, Pennsylvania, and Texas, a married woman cannot go into business for herself without the approval of the court. In Kentucky she cannot co-sign a loan without her husband. In Georgia she cannot borrow money, using her own property as collateral, without his permission.

Referring to the above laws, Washington State Representative Catherine May, commented: "Protective legislation, in fact, protects women out of the better paying jobs."

Why haven't these laws been changed? Where are the woman lawyers and the woman judges who could initiate and shepherd reform legislation? The answer for today and a hope for change lie in the following figures for 1970–71:

	Total	Male	Female
Graduate lawyers	324,318	315,215	9,103
Students enrolled in law schools	82,041	75,104	6,937
Students taking Law School Admission Test	104,408	90,517	13,891

A word of caution: That last line of figures means less than it seems to mean. According to the Educational Testing Services which administers the test, the average scores of women, in general, have been higher than those of men yet the proportion of women actually admitted to some law schools is smaller than the proportion taking the test. Obstacles persist.

Obstacle: Acquiring an education in law

As has already been seen, being accepted by a law school is a major problem for a woman. In 1970, 54 of the approximately 150 law schools in the United States kept female enrollment below 20 percent . . . frequently well below 20 percent. The University of California Law School, for example, in 1970 had 1,171 male students, only 82 female students.

Once she has been accepted by a law school, a woman faces still another problem: she has few if any models to emulate. According to a spokesman for the Association of American Law Schools, about one-half of the law schools in this country have no women at all on their faculty. Of the other half, most have one woman faculty member; only a few have more than one. Professor Daniel G. Collins of New York University Law School gave this reason: "One problem is that faculties looking for new members look for people who've been law clerks to judges. But many male faculty members won't recommend a woman for a clerkship, no matter how high she ranked in her class. It's all part of the closed system that operates against women."

If the female student manages to survive without models, she soon discovers a third problem: until recently, *there were no courses that concentrated on the law as it applied to women.* Yet "women have a separate legal status that is reflected in all legal disciplines—employment law, education law, criminal law, media law, family law, constitutional law, tax law, etc." (Anne Freedman, third-year law student at Yale, 1970). This situation is changing: New York University, Yale, and several other law schools now offer courses in women and the law.

Obstacle: Finding a job

Equipped at last with a law school diploma, a woman quickly learns that her troubles are only starting. Many law firms won't hire women at all. Barbara Bowman, who now teaches a course on women and the law at Georgetown University Law School, tells about one experience she had. She applied for a summer job in a New York firm (note: she was third in her class). She was told that, although she had an enviable record, one that many men would envy, they were in a "downtown cycle" in hiring women. Ms. Bowman adds wryly: "I asked if that meant that they had hired too many already, and was told that no, they had never hired any. Some cycle."

Not all law firms are so blatant in their rejection of woman lawyers. Some are happy to employ women for the work men aren't interested in. As Professor Frederica Lombard of Wayne State University Law School put it, "If law firms do hire women, they still shunt them into estates and trusts. They tell us we're good at working with widows and orphans."

Prestigious law firms have some fascinating reasons why they do not hire women. Women are obviously not suitable for corporate law work, they claim, since such work demands out-of-town trips and all-night meetings in hotel rooms. In situations like these, the partners' wives might object to the presence of woman lawyers! Other firms fear that women—frail creatures that they are—may collapse under the strain of litigation. And a few hide behind their clients, insisting that *they* will not accept a woman.

Here, too, the situation is changing. Because of alleged discriminatory hiring practices, some major law firms have been barred from campus recruitment and are now the target of legal proceedings instituted under federal and state equal employment opportunity laws. If these laws are enforced, the job market for woman lawyers should soon show a marked improvement.

Obstacle: Breaking into trial law

Women earned the right over 100 years ago to act as trial lawyers, yet today even the best-qualified woman trial lawyer soon discovers that she must prove her right to be in a courtroom. Kathryn Emmett, a trial lawyer in Bridgeport, Connecticut, noted that when she enters a courtroom, she is usually asked whether she is a secretary or the defendant. Once when she wished to visit a client in jail, she was forced to wait 2½ hours while her credentials were checked. An official of the jail called her office and complained. "There's a woman here who claims she's an attorney."

Prejudice against the woman trial lawyer is varied, and lacks subtlety. Eleanor Jackson Piel, a former deputy attorney general of California, experienced one barbaric attack that masqueraded as a compliment. As she finished summing up her case, the judge turned to the jury. He hoped, he said, that in arriving at a verdict, they would not be misled by Lawyer Piel's "beauty and charm." How many times, one wonders, has a judge warned a jury not to be misled by some male lawyer's handsome face or stalwart physique?

The woman trial lawyer has endured more than her fair share of difficulties. She has been prohibited from seeing clients; has been told her voice is too shrill and that juries do not like her; has been publicly insulted; and has been treated unjustly by judges who still feel that a woman's place is in the kitchen, not in the courtroom.

Obstacle: Obtaining a judgeship

If you are a woman defendant, you have very little chance of ever being tried before a woman judge; if you are a woman lawyer, you have even less chance of ever becoming a judge. Out of the 5,000 judges in this country at Federal, state, and local levels, only about 150 are women. Nor is the situation improving with any great rapidity. In 1968 when the New York State Legislature created 125 new judgeships, only two of them went to women. In 1971 when President Nixon had the opportunity to nominate two members for the United States Supreme Court, he chose to nominate two men. He did tentatively suggest the name of one woman who was deemed unqualified, but he did not put forward the name of any one of the ten highly qualified women submitted to him by the National Women's Political Caucus. Patricia Roberts Harris, a black woman lawyer who served as President Johnson's ambassador to Luxembourg and as the dean of Howard University Law School, was one of the ten. Asked why women have not been nominated as justices for the Supreme Court, Ms. Harris said: "We have generally not been permitted to achieve the external signs of eminence that are considered qualifications for the Supreme Court. We are not part of the little group that is asked to publish. We are not partners in the large law firms from which Secretaries of State are drawn. Women haven't been considered—so they aren't considered."

Mr. Nixon's 1971 nominations produced a barrage of criticism, including the following comments:

Senator Birch Bayh of Indiana: "I think the time has come to nominate a woman to the Supreme Court, but the President apparently thought otherwise."

Senator George McGovern of South Dakota: "I am sorry the President did not take the great opportunity he had to end the 200 years of injustice and name a woman to the Supreme Court."

The National Women's Political Caucus: "His choices, by omission, are an insult to the competence of women lawyers, judges and professionals . . . We can only conclude that the imagination of Mr. Nixon or that of his advisers is limited, that their estimation of the intelligence of women is low and that their understanding of the democratic institutions they have been elected to serve is misguided."

Prognosis: Poor.

The Supreme Court Record

In 1894, Belva Lockwood applied for permission to practice law in Virginia. She was denied entry and her case went to the Supreme Court. The Supreme Court issued this statement:

> *It was for the Supreme Court of Appeals to construe the statute of Virginia in question, and to determine whether the word "person" as therein used is confined to males, and whether women are admitted to practice law in that Commonwealth. Leave denied.*

By that simple statement the United States Supreme Court determined that a female was not necessarily a "person"; a woman lawyer thereby became a "non-person."

In the decades since 1894 the Supreme Court has done little to improve its anti-woman record. In 1908 it declared that women were not equal competitors with men and that, therefore, "protective legislation" was constitutional. In 1948 it announced that a distinction between the sexes in the area of job opportunities is permitted and therefore a state (Michigan, for example) can legally permit women to work as barmaids but prohibit them from working as bartenders. In 1961

it agreed with a Florida law that said that women might serve on juries only if they requested it. The grounds for this decree? A "woman is still considered the center of the home."

If these decisions of the Supreme Court had been based on the male desire to protect the "weaker sex," women would still object but might sympathize. It is worth noting, however, that in the 1948 decision, Justice Frankfurter who stood with the majority referred with nostalgia "to Shakespeare's bawdy barmaids." Implicit in such a statement is the equation of the United States Supreme Court and any male locker room in a derogatory attitude toward 51 percent of the citizens of this country: women.

Outlook for the future

Women who are working for equal *legal* rights are placing their faith not in the Supreme Court and not in Congress. They are watching with interest the EEOC (Equal Employment Opportunity Commission) which is empowered to hear complaints, investigate charges, and institute proceedings against businesses, schools, etc. that allegedly practice discrimination in hiring or promoting. They are educating women into greater awareness of their legal rights and of the need for additional legislative reform. They are keeping a sharp eye on inadequate quota systems in colleges and on unfair staffing practices in businesses. They are drafting new laws and lobbying for their passage. They are, in short, placing faith in themselves.

DISCUSSION TOPICS

1. American law: A male preserve

2. Protective legislation: A double-edged sword

3. The following statement was made by Justice Frankfurter in *Law and Politics*:

> *To be sure judicial doctrine is one thing, practice another. The pressure of so-called great cases is sometimes too much for judicial self-*

restraint, and the Supreme Court from time to time in its history has forgotten its own doctrines when they should have been most remembered.

Analyze several Supreme Court decisions as they may be related to the above quotation.

SUGGESTED ACTIVITIES

1. Investigate laws in your state applicable to teenagers, girls and/or boys. Are working conditions as specified in working papers the same for girls and boys? Can girls be newspaper carriers at the same age as boys? If inequities exist, write letters to your representative and senators requesting corrective legislation. Write letters to newspapers exposing these inequities. Write letters to political candidates suggesting that they incorporate needed reforms into their platforms.

2. Conduct a poll among men and women of all ages. Ask each: "Do you consider _____ a serious crime for men? for women? for both?" Insert in the blank the following crimes: theft, murder, child abuse, drunkenness, assault, adultery. Record the answers and analyze them. Is there a pattern? Does the double standard still exist? Present your conclusions to the class.

3. Investigate the legal position of women in ancient Greece, ancient Rome, the medieval period in Europe, and Victorian England. Chart the high and low points of women's struggle for legal equality. What political, economic, or social factors caused changes from one period to another? Why is this struggle especially strong now, in the second half of the twentieth century? Present your findings orally or in writing.

Daughters Of Eve

She took of the fruit thereof, and did eat

Some 5,000 years ago Eve reached forth one hand and plucked a piece of fruit from the tree of knowledge. For that act of initiative, the daughters of Eve have been paying ever since.

What exactly had Eve done? She had, it is true, disobeyed God. She had also made a decision —the first real decision ever made by a human being. Advised by the serpent that the forbidden fruit would give her a knowledge of good and evil, she chose to hazard all for what seemed to her a greater good. Her decision brought exile from Eden and distress for herself and her descendants; but it also brought moral responsibility, moral freedom, and moral self-reliance for all humanity.

The Gates of Paradise had barely closed when Adam took a second look at the glittering new toys Eve had discovered: decision-making, initiative, intellectual curiosity, and ambition. While Eve was busy bearing Cain and Abel, Adam —with a boldness he had not formerly known— pre-empted these fascinating playthings and declared them henceforth to be male prerogatives.

There is a kind of ironical innocence in the Judaic-Christian pattern as it has evolved in the thousands of years since that first D-Day. Males—who admire decision-making, initiative, intellectual curiosity, and ambition—have embraced these traits as specifically male, hence inappropriate for females. With Alice-in-Wonderland logic, they have deemed women incapable of initiative, although a woman was the first to display initiative; they have deemed women devoid of ambition, although a woman gave birth to ambition. And women also have forgotten that Eve was the first activist and have allowed themselves to be brainwashed. Too many of them for too many years have swallowed the "natural law"—that females are passive.

Today, some people accept the Eve-Adam story literally, some accept it symbolically, and some accept it not at all. Yet its influence on the female-male relationship continues to operate in our time.

The Past

The most dramatic and enduring influence of the Eve-Adam story is the male depiction of woman as the wicked temptress. The artist found this an especially rich lode. Did not woman dazzle men with beauty, making him mindless of her real self: to wit, a gaunt and ugly skeleton? (See "Gateway to Death," a painting by Abraham Bloemart.) Did not she strip man of his strength (see "Samson and Delilah" by Turchi); decapitate him when he proved immune to her wiles (see "The Dancer's Reward" from *Salome* by Beardsley); turn him against his brother through her fickleness and his jealousy (see 1896 lithograph by Edvard Munch)? The artist knew. As Eve tempted Adam, so all women tempted all men, turning them (if men are to be believed) from their natural goodness and virtue.

The theologians were not far behind. Was man evil? Eve had made him so. Was he treacherous? She had seduced him. Was he a fool? She had addled his wits. All of the major religions of the last two millennia have warned men to control her, or she will control him. The orthodox Jew reminds himself every morning when he prays, "Blessed art Thou, O Lord our God, King of the Universe, Who

has not made me a woman." In *Ecclesiasticus*, the Bible reader learns: "All wickedness is but little to the wickedness of a woman." Paul, in his letters to the Corinthians, teaches men to keep their women silent in church and teaches women to subject themselves to men, their natural lords. In Mohammedan countries, many mosques bear the sign: "Women and dogs and other impure animals are not permitted to enter." And John Knox, in a tract entitled *The First Blast of the Trumpet Against a Monstrous Regiment of Women* (1558) ranted against placing women in positions of authority for it is, he cried, repugnant to nature "that the foolish, mad and frenetic shall govern the discreet and give counsel to such as be sober of mind. And such be all women, compared unto men in bearing of authority."

The writers followed. Milton, sure that all of his woes came from women, wrote: "Wisest men have erred, and by bad women been deceived." Kipling concluded: "The female of the species is more deadly than the male." And G. B. Shaw, the misogynist, wailed, "Women upset everything."

The second trend can be summarized by a couplet written in the seventeenth century by Samuel Butler:

The souls of women are so small,
That some believe they've none at all.

What had happened, of course, was that while some men continued to equate Eve and evil, others found women delightful. Finding her so, how could they take to their hearts an evil being? How could they accept, as the mother of their children, the source of all evil? Eve was not really evil, these men decided; she was simply weak, unable to think clearly, a victim of passion and whim—in short, inferior.

This second theory beautifully simplified life and all its problems. Man could embrace woman, cherish her, even admire her greater sensitivity—and at the same time keep her firmly "in her place." Obviously that place was not in the pulpit. In synagogues and churches she was wel-

Women have tradition-
ally been cast as the
temptress, in both art
and theology.

come, but in a subordinate position. She must sit apart from the worthy (the males); sit with covered head; listen to male interpretation of Scripture.

It was this view of women that led to one of the great paradoxes of the Middle Ages in Europe. Men knelt at the feet of the Virgin Mary, and at the feet of the noble ladies of the realm, resting in the hands of women their very lives; then went home, clasped their own wives into chastity belts and wedded their daughters to land-rich scoundrels. It made sense—to them.

Judaic law counselled: "If thy wife does not obey thee at a signal and a glance, separate from her." New Testament law counselled: "The head of every man is Christ; and the head of every woman is man."

But that was in the Mideast and in Europe. Surely it was not also true in America—the land that opened its arms to the oppressed of all kinds?

Anne Hutchinson found that it was indeed true, even in America. Forbidden by law to comment on the Scriptures or even to ask questions about them within the church building, Anne began to invite women to her home to discuss each Sunday's sermon. Amazingly, these women (inferior though they were) were interested, did care about religious teachings. The meetings were so lively and provocative that men requested permission to attend and received that permission. Anne Hutchinson talked of divine revelation, of the love and mercy of God, but the Puritanism of her time talked only of authority. Soon both men and women who were burdened with problems they could not solve were coming to her for advice. And that, naturally, was intolerable.

The Rev. John Wilson and Governor Winthrop considered the giving of advice a monopoly of their own. They took Anne to court, but moved the court to Cambridge since the female rebel was so popular in her native Boston. Winthrop himself acted as her prosecutor and judge. He listened sternly to the evidence against this "dangerous" 47-year-old woman who had borne fifteen children and who was pregnant again. He denied her a trial by jury, choosing to sit instead in lone righteousness. What was the accusation against her? Winthrop refused to say, but he found her guilty, convicted her, and sentenced her to exile. Later, at a church trial, her guilt was put into words: "You have been rather a husband than a wife, and a preacher than a listener, and a magistrate than a subject." It seems an innocuous charge today—no charge at all, really—but it was damning enough in seventeenth-century America. Anne Hutchinson had dared to challenge male supremacy in churchly matters; clearly she had to be chastened and restrained.

Footnote: Today a bronze statue of the "dangerous rebel" presides on Beacon Hill in Boston. Anne would have enjoyed that. Times have changed.

The Present

Yes, times have changed.

In Flushing, New York, in May 1971, the Temple Beth Sholom retained Hilda Abrevaya as cantor, the first woman cantor in New York State.

"I've always felt a woman should pursue whatever talent she has," Ms. Abrevaya said, ". . . the womanpower of this nation is being wasted." At least one worshiper at the reform temple liked the change and commented, "She has brought me back to the synagogue."

A few months later, woman delegates from the National Federation of Temple Sisterhoods charged American Reform Judaism with neglect. It is time, they insisted, that men and women share equally in the policy-making decisions of the Reform Movement. On behalf of the sisterhoods, Mrs. David Levitt of Great Neck, New York, demanded a position "commensurate with our talents and numerical strength." Mrs. Calvin Weiskopf of Chicago said, "We refuse to be restricted to serving tea and cookies. Women should be totally involved, even to removing the Torah from the Ark and reading from it."

The call for total involvement has had results. In March 1972, Naomi Bronheim Levine was appointed executive director of the American Jewish Congress. This appointment made history: never before had a woman held the top position in a major Jewish organization of both men and women. In June of the same year came another first: Sally Jane Priesend of Ohio was ordained the first woman rabbi in the United States, probably only the second in the history of Judaism. Rabbi Alfred Gottschalk who presided at the ordination called it an historic occasion. "It attests," he said, "to the principle of reform Judaism long espoused—of the equality of women in the congregation of the Lord."

The Lutherans had already proclaimed this kind of equality. In November 1970, Elizabeth A. Platz was ordained as the first woman Lutheran pastor in the United States. A few months earlier at a national convention, the Lutheran Church in America (one of three Lutheran branches in the United States) had changed one word in the list of qualifications for ordination: they had changed "man" to "person." When interviewed, Ms. Platz replied that she believed she could bring a new kind of sensitivity to the needs of the people.

In May 1971, in Minneapolis, Ruth Rohlfs was elected president of the one and a half million member American Baptist Convention. Ms. Rohlfs was elected, at least in part, because a year earlier the American Baptist Women had announced that if a woman was *not* elected, the Convention officials would be faced with a resounding floor fight.

The Episcopalians met the problem of women and ordination with traditional caution. The first Anglican Council met in Kenya in March 1971, and decided by a 24 to 22 vote that a woman could be ordained as priest under certain conditions. This ruling did not force any province to accept a woman for ordination; it simply permitted a province to do so.

The ruling was happily accepted by some—and strongly protested by others. Bishop C. Kilmer Myers of California, for example, insisted that "the male image about God pertains to the divine initiative in creation. Initiative is in itself a male rather than a female attribute . . ." The Bishop should re-read *Genesis*.

The Bishop of Hong Kong, however, the Right Rev. Gilbert Baker, found the new ruling a logical step forward. In November 1971, he ordained Jane Hwang Hsien-yuan and Joyce Bennett, the first women to enter the church's priesthood with full recognition. The American church is still debating the issue although some dioceses—including the Episcopal Diocese of New York—have already endorsed this change in church rules.

The Presbyterians, who for some time have had woman ministers, took an even more daring step. The Rev. Margaret Howland, in late 1971, became the first woman pastor. She was elected to the position by the parishioners of the Woodside Presbyterian Church in Troy, New York. The Rev. Howland stated that a woman pastor can contribute meaningfully in two areas: in empathizing with the parishioners in times of grief or joy and in encouraging men to become active in church work.

Some of the sharpest controversy regarding women's role in religion has developed among Catholics. With a large varied membership and a fairly conservative hierarchy, forward and backward steps have sometimes been taken almost simultaneously. In 1967 Pope Paul VI appointed Rosemary Goldie as Undersecretary of the Council on the Laity, the first woman ever to hold a post in the Curia. But at about the same time, the Vatican refused to accept Elizabeth Muller as a member of the diplomatic mission from Bonn. (The Vatican does, however, employ women as typists and clerks.)

Pope Paul acted again in 1970 when he bestowed on St. Teresa of Avila and St. Catherine of Siena the title, "Doctor of the Church," a title until then reserved for men. The honor was a trifle tardy. Catherine of Siena had shown both initiative and firmness in 1376 when she persuaded the Avignon pope to move the papacy back to Rome, something that many "superior" males had attempted in vain to do.

In the fall of 1971 the National Conference of Catholic Bishops appointed the Committee of Organizations Concerned with the Status of Women in the Church (COCSW). Among the proposals it considered was open enrollment in all Catholic seminaries and universities "so that women may be eligible for professional and academic theological degrees on the same basis as men, including studies for the diaconate and the priesthood."

By mid-1972 the cause had gained considerable momentum. The National Coalition of American Nuns (representing 1400 sisters) met in Chicago and issued a Declaration of Independence for Church Women. They wanted, they said clearly, full equality and that meant proportional representation on all policy-making boards *and ordination.*

But the end of the summer brought a temporary end to the quest. In September, Pope Paul announced that not only were women barred from the priesthood; they were also barred from all formal roles in the ministry. "In accordance with the venerable tradition of the Church," the 74-year-old pontiff declared, "installation in the ministries of lector and acolyte is reserved to men."

Only a little more than a year had passed since Virginia Finn of Milwaukee had composed a "Mass for the Equality of Women in Religion." It was offered at St. Thomas Aquinas Church by the Rev. David Braun. It included a reminder of equality in creation: "God created man in His image. In the image of God He created him. Male and female He created them"; St. Paul's statement: "There is neither Jew nor Greek; there is neither slave nor freeman; there is neither male nor female"; and the repeated statement by the women in the congregation: "We have chosen. It shall not be taken from us." The latter refers to Jesus' praise of Mary when she turned away from Martha's domestic role and chose instead to listen and learn about God.

The Future

Within the last few decades the position of women in most churches has changed radically, but many of the women involved feel that the changes that have already taken place form only the tip of the iceberg. The really important reforms are still submerged. Perhaps the major concern in the next two decades will be with the sex—or lack of sex—inherent in the concept of God. Is God male—is God female—or is God truly universal?

Esther Woo, a doctoral student at Fordham University in 1971, thinks God should be feminized and suggests a new Trinity of Mother, Daughter, and Holy Spirit. Episcopalian Penelope Chen is thinking along similar lines. "How much better," she suggests, "to conceive of God the creator as pregnant with the world, giving birth to it and nourishing it, rather than as the divine watchmaker who never has to intervene in the machinery."

Other woman theologians are less extreme. Some, like Dr. Elizabeth Farians, believe that emphasis should be placed on the humanity rather than on the maleness of Christ. Some, like Dr. Mary Daly, are concerned with the reworking of "the basic myths and symbols of theology in light of the new awareness of how women have been exploited."

No proposed change in theology—not even ordination for women—is as shocking for most people as a proposed change in the concept of God. Yet it is not a new idea. For decades the Christian Scientists have prayed to a "Father-Mother" God, confident that God included the female as well as the male. And in the early years of this century when Emmeline Pankhurst and a friend found themselves in jail for feminist activism, Ms. Pankhurst comforted her companion with these words: "My dear, you must pray to God and *She* will help you."

DISCUSSION TOPICS

1. God—male, female, or universal?

2. Theology, the last frontier

3. Do you agree or disagree with the ideas expressed in the following quotation:

Women would bring a different quality to the ministry; the presence of women in the ministry would express and convey the fuller human and spiritual richness of the entire People of God.
John J. Begley, S.J. and Carl J. Armbruster, S.J.

SUGGESTED ACTIVITIES

1. Check the churches and synagogues in your community. Do women take any part in leading the services? Are women active in the writing of prayers? What roles do they play? What kind of work do they do? After you have collected relevant data, analyze to determine the theological status of women in your locality.

2. Listen attentively to four sermons delivered in the church you attend. After each one, ask yourself the following questions: Was it directed toward men, toward women or both? If it was directed toward women, was it meant for married women or for all women? Next, probe your own memory and the memories of friends and relatives: Do you *ever* remember hearing a sermon that pertained to single women and/or working women? Finally, after thinking about the answers to the above questions, what conclusions can you reach about the way churches regard women? Present your conclusions to the class orally or in writing.

3. Select any church in your community. Then, through talking to church officials and checking newspaper files, find answers to the following questions:

    a. Who (person or group) started the movement that culminated in the founding of that particular church?

    b. Who drew up the architectural plans? Who had final approval of the architectural plans?

    c. Who raised the money for the actual construction?

    d. Who contributed the money needed? Who persuaded the contributors to contribute?

    e. Who planned the opening ceremonies? Who carried out the plans? Who officiated at the opening ceremonies?

4. For the religion of your choice, draw up a calendar of woman-related events. Include as many firsts as you can, e.g. first woman deacon. Include also official church pronouncements on the status of women, duties of women, rights of women, etc. Present your findings in outline form.

Sports: An All-Male Preserve?

Riddle

Q. What is man's first love, his most enduring passion, and his most jealously guarded preserve?

A. Sports. All sports. Any sport.

Steal a man's wallet, his dog, even his car, and he will bear the loss with equanimity; but steal his football trophy from high school or his favorite iron and he is a creature bereft and unmanned. From the time he chortles at the baby-blue boxing gloves dangling above him in his crib to the time he adds up his final golf score, he savors the world of sports as an all-male domain—and heaven help the woman who violates that sanctum.

In the past, few women challenged a man's supremacy on the field or in the arena. In the present, *just* a few are beginning to do so. But already the chorus of outraged male voices is heard in the land. The litany they chant is the nightmare music of any sports-minded female.

Women aren't strong enough, they say.

Perhaps. Certainly *most* women are shorter, lighter, less muscular than *most* men. But the average woman today is stronger than her counterpart of a generation ago. And what about the un-average woman? If girls received the same physical training, encouragement, and opportunities that boys receive, would there be as many woman athletes as man athletes?

VERDICT: insufficient evidence.

Women can't stand the tension, they say.

Hard to believe. A woman surely endures more tension in the last 24 hours before her baby is born than a football player does in his entire professional life.

VERDICT: perjurious charge.

Women will cry, they say.

So they cry. Is that worse than starting a riot, or punching someone in the jaw?

VERDICT: irrelevant and immaterial.

Women will lose their femininity, they say.

What *is* femininity? In the past, man defined it; women were supposed to be frail, timid, and dependent. Today women are re-defining it.

VERDICT: rules no longer applicable; case thrown out of court.

The final verdict lies in the future. It will be several generations before anyone can say with certainty that women can or cannot compete equally with men in most sports. Meanwhile, however, women are breaking barriers. The litany goes on, but as the following random survey indicates, *this* all-male preserve will never be the same.

Baseball

Poole could bat, throw, and field better than most of the boys in the Little League in Haverhill, Massachusetts. Poole played in two games, batting in the winning run in the first and covering center in the second. Then suddenly Poole was declared ineligible and the two victories were erased from the record. What was Poole's crime? Her name is Sharon.

But maybe—just maybe—injustice may breed justice, and Little League baseball may soon be co-ed in Haverhill.

Footnote: Jack Smith, columnist for the Los Angeles *Times*, noted that women want to be priests. Mr. Smith commented: "I agree with the women. I see no earthly reason—physiological, psychological, or theological—why women shouldn't be admitted into the hierarchies of organized religion. *But not baseball. Baseball's sacred.*" [Italics added.]

Basketball

Eleven-year-old Amy Smolens of Great Neck, New York, has been an enthusiastic basketball fan for years. She knows how to handle a basketball, too. So when the New York Nets and Converse Rubber Company sponsored a Run, Dribble, and Shoot Contest for *youngsters* between the ages of 9 and 12, Amy naturally figured she was eligible and entered the contest.

The contest operators were appalled. A *girl* basketball player? At first they tried to turn her away; then they decided that the fastest and easiest way to eliminate Amy was to let her compete. So Amy dribbled, ran, and threw foul shots with more than 100 boys. She finished *third*.

Did Amy make the semi-finals? She did not. After the quarter-finals, it was decided that the contest was really for boys only. As a consolation prize, Amy received a couple of tickets for a game, a basketball, and a letter from Jim Garvey, contest coordinator for the Nets. "You have enlightened Converse and the Nets," he wrote, "and *perhaps next year* [italics added] you will be able to compete. We offer our apologies."

Boating*

The United States Power Squadron is a nation-wide *men's* social and educational organization. For the seafarer, the group offers all kinds of courses, including courses in yachting, weather, and engine maintenance. After a first course is successfully completed, a diploma is given—but the diploma a woman receives is just a little different. It says: "The granting of a woman's certificate confers on the holder neither the right to fly the ensign of the United States Power Squadron nor any rights of membership whatsoever."

That "little difference" means, among other things, that when a business meeting is being

* Quotations from "Is the All-Male U.S. Power Squadron Running Against Tide" by Richard Severo in *The New York Times*, Feb. 9, 1971.

held, the female diploma-holder is not welcome, though she is encouraged to serve coffee and tea to the yachtsmen *after* the meeting. Now women are rebelling.

Lisa Kasak of Westchester refuses to accept auxiliary status. "We take the same course, the same exams and we have the same responsibilities on a boat," she declares. "We ought to be treated the same way."

Dean Fuller, an instructor with the New York Power Squadron, agrees: "It is a nineteenth century Rotary attitude. It is tribal and it is nonsense."

But change is not imminent.

Edward Dakin, a lieutenant in the Power Squadron, believes that discrimination on the basis of sex should be continued. "Men are interested in the product result," he says, "but women go for personalities." Then he added, "They (women) like to take an order from the male skipper."

Dr. George Hodell, a Texas physician and the national commander of the Power Squadron, is equally traditional. "Much of the strength of the USPS lies in our ability to mold our activities to fit those of this changing world," he wrote recently. When asked if his changing world included changing the rules about admitting women, he reneged: "We are a men's club. Some squadrons have auxiliaries but this is as far as it is going to go."

Football

Women (including the Kennedy women) have played touch football for years, but not until 1970 did a woman actually invade the gridiron. In Orlando, Florida, Patricia Palinkas (wired for sound so that the listening world would not miss her slightest gasp) ran out to hold the ball for her husband's extra point attempt. The first snap from center she fumbled, to the everlasting glee of the male spectators. A 235-pounder promptly barreled into her. "I tried to break her neck," swore Wally Florence. "She's out here prancing around making folly with a man's game."

Before it was over, Pat succeeded twice in holding the ball for successful conversions. It was a gimmick appearance, of course—not even tokenism on the gridiron—but even this mild "violation" was enough to anger a hefty linebacker into telling the truth!

Horseracing

In 1968, when Kathy Kusner announced that she wished to participate in the Sport of Kings, she was denied a jockey's license. No woman could ride professionally, she was told. When a short time and a court decision later, Penny Ann Early made the same attempt at Churchill Downs, she had a proper license and that helped her not at all: male jockeys stopped her by threatening to strike if she rode.

Why are some male jockeys so fervently against female jockeys? Their reasons are instructive:

John Choquette: "If you let one woman ride one race, we are all dead."

Bobby Ussery: "I don't think a girl can be tough enough."

Bill Hartack: ". . . a female cannot compete against a male doing anything. . . . They might weigh the same as male jockeys, but they aren't as strong. And as a group, I don't think their brains are as capable of making fast decisions. Women are also more likely to panic. It's their nature."

An anonymous jockey: "A woman's place is in the kitchen."

Since then, the girls have proved they are indeed "tough enough." In 1969, Diane Crump rode at Hialeah, Barbara Jo Rubin at Aqueduct, and Tuesdee Testa at Santa Anita. In 1970, Robyn Smith brought home three winners at Hialeah, and in 1971, she was riding regularly on the Belmont-Aqueduct-Saratoga circuit. In May 1972, *four* women rode at Belmont on the same day.

Bill Hartack made two other comments about woman jockeys. He implied that after a broken collar bone or two, they'd grow discour-

LUCY WATSON!

THE BEST EQUESTRIENNE IN AMERICA,

WITH G. F. BAILEY & CO'S QUADRUPLE COMBINATION!

16

aged. In 1971 Mary Bacon, who prefers the smaller tracks, took a fall that smashed her collar bone, bruised her ribs, and gave her a concussion. Thirteen days later she was riding again.

Hartack also said (in December 1968): "I still doubt you'll ever see a female riding in the Kentucky Derby." Four months later, in the spring of 1969, Diane Crump did just that.

Horseracing should be rechristened: it's no longer the Sport of Kings; it's now the Sport of Royalty.

Swimming

Look at the record.

In Australia at the 1956 Olympics, the U.S. women's swimming team won *one* gold medal.

In Mexico City at the 1968 Olympics, the U.S. women's swimming team won *seventeen* gold medals. Incidentally they also set ten Olympic records.

What caused the sudden increase in champions? Something women have been clamoring for

—*training*. Two California men, Sherman Chavoor and George Haines, have been giving American girls the opportunity to excel, and the girls have been making good use of the opportunity. Here is Chavoor's daily schedule for the "frail" mostly teen-age girls training with him: up at 5:30 a.m., three two-mile swims and a few 1,000-yard sprints for a total of two hours of hard labor; school; then a repeat of the morning's exercise.

Special note: Debbie Meyer, in 1968, was the first swimmer, man *or* woman, to win Olympic gold medals in three individual events.

Second special note: In July 1972, Lynne Cox, a fifteen-year-old from Los Angeles, swam the English Channel in 9 hours and 47 minutes, bettering the *men's* record by 26 minutes!

Tennis

The racquet-smashed tennis ball is hardly new to distaffs. For decades it has been a "respectable" sport, even for the well-bred, carefully nurtured debutante. The most feminine maiden might bandy balls a bit with her white-flanneled, blue-blazered escort. Naturally she didn't bandy them too hard or too fast, and above all she didn't expect any real financial compensation for her efforts.

Then tennis began to change. The woman player became rougher and tougher; she served, lobbed, and returned with and to the best of the male players. She switched to more comfortable clothing, forgot her hairdo, sweat instead of per-

spired, asked for and received no handicap. But one thing remained the same. She still couldn't expect any real financial compensation.

Now even that is beginning to change. In 1970, a group of tennis players who happened to be women boycotted the U.S. Lawn Tennis Association tournament. Their reason? Absurdly small purses. One result of that boycott was the Women's Pro Tour, a series of tournaments set up in 1971. Another result? For the first time in history a woman athlete—Billie Jean King—earned more than $100,000 in one year. For that money, Ms. King won 18 tournaments out of 24 .

In today's world, money *is* king. Suddenly Billie Jean found that she was famous: manufacturers of tennis racquets, dresses, socks, and shoes wanted her endorsement; condominiums and camps wanted her presence. And the endorsements and appearances brought in still more money.

Some people claim that athletes should play for love not for lucre. Not so, says Billie Jean King. "Money is everything in sports," she explains. "It has made me a star. I am hitting the same shots that I did five years ago. But now I'm finally getting some recognition out of it."

If money breeds recognition and prestige, flamboyance breeds fame. Until recently, woman athletes were demure and docile. When they broke records, they did so with becoming modesty. When they disagreed with decisions, they spoke with gentle charm and proper tenderness. Such conduct seemed necessary in the male-dominated arena of sports. Better to blend into the background, even if that meant blending into obscurity.

In the 1970s, women don't blend quite so easily. In September 1971, when Billie Jean King and Rosemary Casals disagreed with an action of the LTA (Lawn Tennis Association), they strode huffily off the court. Raucous comments followed: "Unbecoming behavior"—"Poor sports"—"Suspension." The two women shrugged off the comments and the threat. Their unprecedented action was right for the times. It won them respect, admiration, and—most important of all—publicity. A Joe

Namath gets it by shaving or not shaving; a woman athlete has to work harder.

Track

"Records are falling to a China doll" announced one *Life* magazine headline. *Time* called her the "Taiwan Flash." The object of the near hyperbole is Chi Cheng, a 26-year-old Taiwanese woman who has so many specialties that sports writers hesitate to isolate one. Out of 121 races, she won all but two; she takes the hurdles like a thoroughbred; and more than holds her own in long jump and sprints. Chi Cheng came to the United States in 1963 for special coaching. By 1970, she had set all kinds of records and was being called the world's leading female track star.

Across the globe from Taiwan is the Bedford-Stuyvesant ghetto in Brooklyn. Here several dozen young girls, mostly black, make up the Atoms Track Club under the martinet-like training of coach Fred Thompson. Begun fairly casually in 1964, the Atoms have developed amazing esprit de corps and track power. Girls who had run only in the streets discovered they could break records, be leaders, go to college. In 1970 in Los Angeles, the Atoms stunned the sports world by breaking a world record while winning the mile relay. In the final heat they did even better.

For the girls who have been Atoms, life will never be the same. They themselves describe it best:

Shelley Marshall: "Track used to be just something to do on your own. Now people say, 'Wow, you run for the Atoms,' and we feel like leaders."

Pat Hawkins: "Track made me raise my standards and hold myself higher. This team breeds college material."

In golfing, fencing, and skating there are a few women who are champions and thousands of others who are enthusiastic amateurs. There are women skilled in judo and karate, woman wrestlers, and female fisher*men* (note the semantic bias!). In school gyms, girls are playing basketball and volleyball, tennis and badminton, softball and ping pong. On the streets, girls clad in denim rather than in organdy are practicing on pogo sticks and balancing on uni-bikes. The sports mania is growing; it has infected females, too.

Where will it end? Will men and women, boys and girls, some day compete in the same meets and contests? Will women ever be players on a major league team? Will Jane Doe instead of John Doe run the fastest, throw the farthest, jump the highest? The Olympic records *suggest* answers.

Swimming—100 Meter Free Style

In 1896 the male record was 1 minute, 22.2 seconds; in 1972 it was 51.22 seconds.

In 1912 the female record was 1 minute, 22.2 seconds; in 1972 it was 58.59 seconds.

Swimming—200 Meter Breaststroke

In 1908 the male record was 3 minutes, 09.2 seconds; in 1972 it was 2 minutes, 21.55 seconds.

In 1924 the female record was 3 minutes, 33.2 seconds; in 1972 it was 2 minutes, 41.71 seconds.

Track and Field—100 Meter Dash

In 1896 the male record was 12 seconds; in 1972, it was 10.14 seconds (but in 1968 it was 9.9 seconds).

In 1928 the female record was 12.2 seconds; in 1972, it was 11.07 seconds (but in 1968 it was 11 seconds).

Track and Field—Discus Throw

In 1896 the male record was 95 feet, 7½ inches; in 1968 it was 212 feet, 6½ inches; in 1972 it was 211 feet, 3½ inches.

In 1928 the female record was 129 feet, 11⅞ inches; in 1968 it was 191 feet, 2½ inches; in 1972 it was 218 feet, 7 inches.

Note that both the male records and the female records have improved over the years, though to varying degrees. The males have been at it longer, have had more training, have been *expected* to improve. These factors undoubtedly have contributed to their greater speed and power. If so, as male records plateau, female records may rise to meet them—or surpass them. It depends—are the differences innate, or the products of conditioning?

Neither history nor science can yet provide the answer.

VERDICT: unknown.

DISCUSSION TOPICS

1. Have a round-table discussion about athletic contests that admit only male contestants.

SUGGESTED ACTIVITIES

1. After doing some research, write a biographical essay about one of the following woman athletes: Babe Didrickson Zaharias, Florence Chadwick, Gertrude Ederle, Peggy Fleming, Tenley Albright, Billie Jean King.

2. Take a poll of 50 people (25 females, 25 males). Ask each one the following questions:
    a. Do you participate at the present time in any form of athletic activity?
    b. If the answer to "a" is yes, do you expect to continue to participate in this activity?
    c. Do you admire athletes of the opposite sex? of your own sex?
    d. Who is your favorite athlete?

    Chart the results, weigh them, and explain any possible conclusions.

3. Study the style and format of your favorite television sports announcer. Then prepare and tape your own five-minute "spot" for a real or imaginary local TV station. Be sure to include the athletic achievements of girls and boys, women and men. Check on "minor" sports like bowling and archery as well as on "major" sports like football and hockey. (An interesting tangential topic: why are some sports "major" and some "minor"? Does the "gate" affect the "degree," or does the "degree" affect the "gate"? Is sexism involved?) After the tape is completed, play it for your group and ask for comments or reactions.

8

The Great Debate: Do Women Belong In The Arts?

Years ago when the world was young and a Muse was a miss not a myth, the Nine Muses perched on Olympus directing shafts of inspiration upon a few fortunate mortals. Sharing divinity, these charming goddesses apparently supervised the birth and the development of the Fine Arts.

Each Muse had her own empire. Together they directed the course of love poetry (Erato), lyric poetry (Euterpe), epic poetry (Calliope), hymns or psalms (Polyhymnia), tragedy (Melpomene), comedy (Thalia), and dance (Terpsichore).* Feminine they seemed, and feminine—to some extent—they seemingly have remained. But the younger arts—painting, architecture, and especially film—had no Muse and wanted no women. Was it simple coincidence, or cause and effect?

Neither.

The Nine Muses did not supervise; they inspired. Like a basket of apples, they served as

* The other two areas, no longer included among the arts, were history (Clio) and astronomy (Urania).

the focal point of an artist's eye, as the object-to-be-acted-upon by an artist's brush. They might help to create the creator, but never, never to share in the creation of ART.

For the arts—like every other important aspect of life—have been masculine, are masculine. When women have entered, they have entered through the back door. When they have served, they have served as the servants of men. When they have demanded equal consideration, they have been met by absurd *dicta* and turned backs.

Emily Dickinson was one of the women who slipped through the back door. Intrigued by her domestic imagery and by her tender pity, male critics nodded approvingly at this woman who knew her woman's place and established her as a minor poet in their anthologies and critical histories. Then awareness came. That tenderness was blunted bitterness; that pity, the cold ash of burned-out violence. No minor poetess this, but a major poet whose strength exposed the flabbiness of Longfellow and Lowell, whose taut power challenged the sprawling verbosity of Whitman. The offensive has already begun: she has been accused of plagiarism, of hypocrisy, of superficiality. One waits with amusement for the day when, all else having failed, someone suggests that it was really General Grant who built her exquisite barbs!

Another woman who slipped through the back door was the Philadelphian, Mary Cassatt. Always a "lady," always willing to acknowledge her debt to Degas, she lived in Paris, painting mothers and children. The art critics smiled. Then her brush strokes grew more confident, her style more individualistic. Finally breaking away from the impressionists, she plunged into printmaking, and in this field achieved a sharpness of definition unrivaled. The critics must have been uncomfortable; but they need not have worried. A reporter put her in her proper place when she returned to the United States for a visit. The talented artist was greeted with this announcement: "Mary Cassatt, sister of Mr. Cassatt, president of the Pennsylvania Railroad, returned from Europe yesterday. She has been studying painting in Paris, and owns the smallest Pekinese dog in the world." One wonders what Degas' sister was doing, and whether he had any interesting pets.

The most fascinating example of back-door entry is the French artist, Constance-Marie Charpentier. Her portrait of Charlotte du Val d'Ognes was widely hailed as a masterpiece when, in 1917, it was sold for $200,000. This *seems* to prove that when a woman creates a really fine work of art, it will be recognized. But there is a catch. When the painting was praised and appraised, it was believed to be the work of Jacques-Louis David, a neoclassicist and a *male*. About fifty years passed before the truth came out. Today in the Metropolitan Museum of Art, Charpentier receives credit. But would the painting be considered a masterpiece if it had not first been attributed to the illustrious David?

Back-door entry is possible only for a few unusual women. More common is entry through service. For 2,000 years, women were barred from the stage on the grounds they could not act, would destroy morale, probably would destroy morality. Then, as male playwrights grew weary of the lisping youths who warped their Cleopatras, they decided that women *could* act. The doors opened, and the theatre has never been the same. The men may have had a two millennia headstart and the choice roles, but they had a hard time holding their own. A Sarah Bernhardt, an Eleanora Duse, a Kit Cornell, a Katharine Hepburn yields to no man when it comes to dynamic presence and dramatic forcefulness. The female body, it was discovered, could be at least as expressive as the male, the voice as vibrant, the perception of character as keen.

A similar situation occurred in opera. Men composed the music, wrote the librettos, designed the sets and costumes. But it made good artistic sense to have an alto to set off a baritone, a soprano to complement a tenor. So women were permitted to sing—and performed so effectively that they soon outshone many of their male colleagues. The tradition that includes Kirsten Flagstad, Helen Traubel, and Lily Pons continues today with Leontyne Price and Joan Sutherland. Nor do their magnificent voices negate the equally magnificent voices of Lauritz Melchior and Ezio Pinza. On the contrary; the counterpoint of male and female voices has produced a richness lacking in the other arts.

What was true of the theatre and the opera house is true everywhere; but in most of the arts, service limits rather than expands opportunity. In painting and sculpture, the woman is welcomed as a model; in writing, as a secretary or proofreader; in architecture, as a draftsman. She is even praised as long as she is content to serve. Should she attempt to move ahead, however, she will find that massive barriers spring forth as if by magic, their source all too often in her former "master."

The newest of the arts, the film, has aped the theatre, but suffers from hyperbole. The stripling cinema has a Pygmalion complex: it considers woman not just as object, but as formless protoplasm that it alone has the skill to make over into a "glamour girl." It then places her in story after story in which woman is the pretty but dumb creature whose existence dramatizes the hero's intelligence and courage. In recent years, the picture has grown even dimmer with woman disappearing altogether. In movies like *Easy Rider* and *Carnal Knowledge*, the males rejoice in male preoccupations in an all-male world. The only females who wander onto the set are blurred menials, or—as Betty Friedan noted—non-persons.

If service and entry through the back door provide only limited access, one hardly dares to consider the situation of the woman who chooses direct confrontation. Every artist must be a rebel, but the rebellion essential to the woman who *demands* entry into the arts somersaults the comprehension. She must rebel not only against home, society, and country, but against her own inner being as it has been conditioned through the years. Where the male rebel will find comfort from other rebels, the female rebel will find only angry stares. No, not stares only. She will learn (if she hopes to survive) to close her ears to jeers and insults, to stiffen her spine against contempt, and to keep her mind clear in spite of the *absurd dicta.*

Philharmonic orchestras seem to be especially sexist in their attitudes. The Los Angeles Philharmonic has seventeen women members—mere tokenism, but even seventeen appalls conductor Zubin Mehta. Seeking desperately for a rationale for barring women, Mehta came up with this brilliant if absurd *dictum:* "They become men. Men treat them as equals; they even change their pants in front of them. I think it's terrible." Michele Saxon, who plays with the New York Philharmonic (*five* women, one hundred two men), shrugged off that remark. "I've seen men zillions of times in their underwear," she quipped. "You see it all the time in the fashion ads. And some of our Philharmonic men look better than those male models."

Another absurd *dictum* is trotted out with weary regularity by concert management companies trying to find a reason to reject a qualified musician: the wives of the male performers, they claim, dislike having their husbands travel cross-country with woman pianists! Users of this cliché-alibi have one thing in their favor: it's so ludicrous it's almost impossible to refute.

A woman cannot conduct an orchestra. So men have said. Twenty-odd years ago Deems Taylor explained why. First, he noted, a woman is not strong enough to stand the strain; second, her shoulder muscles aren't quite right for the job; third, she lacks the kind of leadership necessary to persuade a group of people to want to carry out her intentions, and fourth . . . "any woman who tries to conduct an orchestra runs up against a fearful barrier of male prejudice. Don't ask me why, but as a rule men bitterly resent taking orders from a woman. . . ." The truth, at last. But women are beginning—Margaret Harris, the musical director of *Hair,* has conducted Chicago's Grant Park Symphony Orchestra; she survives, and civilization has barely trembled.

The woman novelist has both a harder and an easier time of it. If she writes Gothic stories for girls, that's fine. Or if she writes high-class mysteries, as Mary Stewart does, that's fine too. But if she even considers the *serious* novel, she soon finds unexpected barriers. For one thing, the literary critics are male. The most derogatory statement they can make about a novel is that it is "feminine" or sounds as if it has been written by a woman. Why it is wrong for woman writers to write like women, or for woman readers to enjoy womanly observations, literary critics have failed to make clear. They have dominated the modern Parnassus so long that they admit no need to explain anything. Note the critic or college professor who comments smugly that few women can appreciate the genius of James Joyce, especially in the Molly Bloom soliloquy. He will also add that Molly Bloom is the finest depiction of woman in all literature. Let a woman suggest, ever so meekly, that the latter is not true and he will approach apoplexy. Let her add that if his first statement is true, then it is probably also true that there are nuances of feeling in Virginia Woolf that no man can fully appreciate. He will find this illogical, irrational, and inconvenient.

Some of the finest novelists have been women, from the Brontë sisters in the nineteenth century to Willa Cather and Edith Wharton and

Mary McCarthy in the twentieth. Novels by these women appear on reading lists, but they are damned as "minor classics." As long as male criteria are the sole criteria used in judging novels, they will indeed be "minor." The kitchen range must become as important a symbol as the automobile jack; the housedress must appear as romantic as overalls; the death of a child must loom as large as the death of a fellow soldier. Today the smothered sob is feminine and sentimental, while the cursed obscenity is masculine and aggressive. A dichotomy like this, which labels the first "inferior" and the second "superior," results necessarily in something less than great writing. When women have taught men and men have taught women, then indeed there may be a real renaissance of great fiction.

Meanwhile, the highest praise a critic can give a woman novelist is to say condescendingly that she writes "like a man." But women must be patient. They have made some progress since 1853, when a critic for *The New York Times* pontificated: "No female writer can be said to have finished her literary labors before producing a Cookery Book."

Still, one asks, why haven't women overcome these hurdles and proved that they too possess genius? The answer lies in the Six Commandments of Art, propounded by men, supported by men, and passed down from male generation to male generation:

1. Thou shalt teach females to vary their interests, not to concentrate on one consuming interest. (This provides adaptable, pleasant housewives who are experts in nothing.)

2. Thou shalt forbid females all specialized education in the arts. (This permits superficial education so that a wife can play sweet airs on a piano or scribble love poetry. It simultaneously bars her from sketching live models which might lead to professional proficiency.)

3. Thou shalt teach all females that they may choose a career *or* marriage but that any attempt to merge the two will destroy both. (Naturally this should be accompanied by full-scale conditioning that persuades every female that she will be less than complete, less than human, if she does not marry and have children.)

4. Thou shalt remind all females frequently that they can create babies, and therefore have no need to create anything else. (This is especially effective: it goads men to work harder and lulls women into passiveness. It also causes a guilt complex in the woman who doesn't bear children, causing her to dissipate her energies in frantic efforts to prove that deep inside she really *is* maternal.)

5. Thou shalt warn all females that placing an interest in a career above an interest in men will destroy their womanliness. (This is akin to #4. Women have been warned so often of the dreaded consequences of losing their womanliness that the most poised, successful, and apparently confident woman, when faced with such a threat, will pause automatically to smooth her hair, or check her lipstick, or look to see if her slip is showing. On occasion, such a woman will remark fiercely that she *likes* being a woman, a defense tactic that no man ever feels the need to employ.)

6. Thou shalt greet each female's first artistic creation with a pat formula: your work is "feminine." (This will cause inner confusion; most women think it's natural for a woman to write, paint, or compose like a woman; it also reemphasizes her slight worth, implying —ever so gently—that she might better use her time to bake pies and diaper babies.)

The Woman's Rights Movement has been fairly successful in helping women to laugh away Commandments #3, 4, 5, and 6. Number 1 is more difficult, and will take time. Perhaps retaining it will even be helpful. The Renaissance man of many interests no longer exists; the void may be filled by a new creature, the Renaissance woman. But the real ringer, of course, is #2. It is possible for a genius who has ample time, money, and materials to overcome lack of training, but it happens rarely. For a female genius, conditioned to self-doubt and self-sacrifice, it is still harder. Education enables one to leapfrog over the mistakes of the past, to sharpen one's palate by testing the art-wares of all nations and ages, to discover a yardstick by which one can measure one's own growth. Most important of all, specialized education provides a congenial setting and congenial companions. The free exchange of ideas, the brainstorming, the violent argument which hones perception can—and do—explode into new concepts and original methods. All this, under the present setup, women are denied.

Great art is the result of concentrated work and unfettered dreams. Can women create, and create greatly? Only when the manacles are torn from their dreams and the interruptions barred from their work will the answer be known.

DISCUSSION TOPICS

1. In the above chapter you met the phrase *"absurd dictum"* or *"dicta"* several times. What does it mean? Analyze the *"absurd dicta"* you have heard concerning women and art.

2. Imagine two male critics studying a one-man show. The subject of this particular one-"man" show is a woman artist. Write dialogue for these two men that will illustrate their general attitude toward women in art, and their specific attitude toward this woman artist and her paintings.

SUGGESTED ACTIVITIES

1. Choose an American woman who has been successful in one of the arts: literature, drama, art, music, or film. Do a thorough research job: What kind of education did she have? Was her home environment conducive to intensive study and practice? What obstacles did she meet at the beginning of her career? What did the critics say about her work? Was the judgment of her *as an artist* based on her sex or her work? After you have gathered as much material as possible, analyze the influence of custom and social mores on this particular woman artist.

2. From your family and the families of your friends, select half a dozen two-and three-year-olds, male and female, and watch them draw. Note use of color, kinds of lines, freedom or restriction of movement, purpose. Note any observable differences between boys and girls in their approach to drawing at this age. Next, obtain permission to observe a first-grade class during an art period. Note the same information for this age group. Finally, observe a high school art class. Note the same information. Study your notes and answer these questions: Do your observations suggest any real differences between boys and girls engaged in artistic creation? If the answer is yes, are these differences apparent at all ages, or do they begin at a certain age? Draw any conclusions you can, based on your observations.

3. Acute observation is a necessary ingredient in any artistic personality. Some say women do not observe as closely as men; others say women observe different things. To test this, choose a companion of the opposite sex and try this experiment. Equip yourselves with 35 mm. cameras and color film. Go to the same place at the same time—a small woods, a park, a country fair. Once there, separate. Each should use up the roll of film taking pictures of whatever appeals or seems worthy of record. After the film is developed, compare the two sets of pictures. Spend some time analyzing the subject matter, points of view, use of color and composition, moods. Then present the pictures, jumbled, to your colleagues. Ask them to determine which were taken by a female and which by a male. Then ask them on what basis they made their choices. Finally, rearrange the slides into the two original groups and show them again. Continue with analysis both of the slides and of your group's reactions.

The King's English

"Teach me your language, and I will explain you, even to yourself."

This statement is not arrogant; it is not even overly ambitious. It merely states a fact: that language is knitted to the values and traditions of a people so closely that they cannot be separated. Cut one and both ravel.

When ideas change, language must change. Newborn ideas need new words, demand new words. The surest way to stunt a civilization is to straitjacket its language. Bar word coinage, ban borrowing, "legalize" word order, and ideas, progress, growth die. Contrary to the views of pedants (and sometimes teachers), unsettled grammar and "instant" vocabulary are at once the reflectors and searchlights of a nation caught up in a quest for truth.

Because language is so closely tied to the development of new attitudes, women today are becoming increasingly aware of the sexist nature of English. This particular aspect of the battle has been little publicized, since many women, and men, too, consider it of little importance. What dif-

ference does it make if we use "he" as the generic pronoun to include "she"? What difference does it make if we use "she" when we refer to a ship? What difference does it make if we use "men" when we also mean "women"?

The answer is clearly, that it makes all the difference in the world!

We recognize this easily enough with non-human things: "As the twig is bent, so grows the tree"; and with males: "The child is father to the man." But if it is suggested that the "Girl is mother to the woman," people laugh and call it quibbling.

Consider the plight of a small girl who grows up in the United States of the twentieth century. When she is still a toddler, she gazes eagerly at the MAN in the moon. A few years later, she eagerly embraces BROTHERhood and accepts all MEN as her BROTHERS. She discovers she is part of MANkind and is told how wonderful it is that she is MAN, rather than a lower animal.

As a college student she puts in MAN-hours of study to earn a BACHELOR of Arts or a MASTER of Science degree. If she rebels, she can MAN the barricades or—if she prefers legal channels—she can become one of the "twelve good MEN and true" on a jury. As a "MAN in the street" her opinion may be asked by an inquiring photographer. If she paints MASTERpieces, she may be given a chance at a one-MAN show. If she writes poems, she may be complimented on her MASTERy of the English language. If she conducts an orchestra, she may be hailed as MAESTRO by the admiring audience.

And always and everywhere, she learns to respond when every citizen is asked to do HIS duty or submit HIS income tax return by April 15th. From books she learns to feed her baby when HE is hungry, to enroll HIM in school when HE is six, to save money for HIS college education. If she turns to the Bible for comfort, she is told to pray to God the FATHER and to Jesus, HIS SON, and is reminded to help her fellow MAN for HE is made in the image of God.

When—ill in body and in spirit—she seeks medical help, her doctor (probably a male) tells her she is suffering from a WOMAN's condition, and her psychiatrist (almost definitely a male) declares that she has a FATHER-complex.

Surveys indicate that while few men ever want to be women, many women at some time wish they were men. One wonders why....

Examples of Sexism in Language

The Alphabet: Few things seem as objective as the alphabet or alphabetical order, but even here sexism appears. Hurricanes, as everyone knows, are named after women (Alma, Barbara, Caroline, etc.), but the letters of the alphabet are defined by male names (Abel, Baker, Charlie, etc.). "He" *should* precede "she" alphabetically, but what about "hers" and "his"? "Husband" should precede "wife" and "man" should precede "woman" alphabetically, but "female" should precede "male." Does it?

Feminine Forms: A man who writes a novel is an author; a woman who writes a novel—until recently—was an author*ess*. Those three letters "-ess" signal the feminine form; they also, subtly, signal inferiority. An authoress, a poetess, a sculptress suggest a dabbler in the arts, while author, poet, sculptor suggest the professional artist. Women have won the first round, and these three terms are seldom used today—as indeed they shouldn't be. Sculpt*or* means, quite simply, one who sculpts; no gender is indicated and the term is equally appropriate for female or male. But the "-ess" lingers on in other words: adventuress, goddess, enchantress, hostess, stewardess. Still more sexist is the suffix "-ette," which means feminine *or* little: a drum major*ette*, a suffrag*ette*, an usher*ette*. The dual meaning may, of course, be coincidental.

Inanimate Objects: Surely, the male tendency to use "she" or "her" when referring to ships and cars and machinery is harmless. Women in the past have smiled approvingly at this tendency; only now are they beginning to analyze it. Men use the feminine pronoun for inanimate objects in two quite different ways: 1) to express love and possession—"She's my ship!" or (of his new car)—"Isn't she a beauty?" and 2) to express anger or disgust—(to a recalcitrant piece of machinery) "Give her a kick!"

It becomes suddenly clear that men think of some "things" as they think of women: as sex objects that they possess, or as sources of frustration. An exaggeration? Not when one studies children's books and discovers that in them engines, ships, and cars start out by being male. If the small boy is to identify with them and through them with the world of *doing*, they must be male; later, when the bigger boy wishes to possess and control them, they conveniently become female.

Descriptive Language: "Sue entered the restaurant with a blond. She smiled confidently, almost arrogantly as the other diners stared with frank interest at her companion. She was proud of his fair wavy hair, his shy blue eyes, and his well-shaped, graceful hands. As they sat down at a table, she watched, amused, as he crossed his legs self-consciously. It was that kind of small confiding gesture that had first appealed to her, underlining as it did his frail vulnerability. She frowned, forcing herself to concentrate on his problem rather than on his full lips or aquiline nose. Somehow, somehow she must find a way to protect this handsome but baffled boy!"

Paragraphs like the above appear constantly in fiction—with one small difference. The person described in purely physical terms is usually female. The fact that the person here described is male will throw most readers into confusion. If the reader is told, in addition, that it is an adult male, the confusion will change to contempt or fury.

Custom prescribes language, and language prescribes custom. In the past, custom has considered women as accessories—to be described superficially, i.e. physically. How degrading this custom is can be realized by reversing the roles in life or in literature.

This emphasis on the physical characteristics of a female results in irrelevant judgments. A woman who makes a speech or runs for office or manages a business is constantly described as "beautiful" or "ugly" or "fat" or "dowdy." Few men are ever subjected to this type of personal criticism. With males, brains and ideas and leadership count. With females, all too often, only appearances count.

Another kind of descriptive bias is seen in newspaper headlines and stories that attempt to re-define the new woman in old terms. Here is one such headline: "Grandmother Named Ambassador." Again the reversal of roles is illuminating. After Eisenhower's election in 1952, did any newspaper cry, "Grandfather Elected President." The insertion of family relationship into business and political situations is probably not deliberate, but it is indicative of society's narrow conception of a woman's role.

Sexist Language: A Grab Bag View

1. For women who nag, there are many names: fishwife, henpecker, virago, shrew, beldame. For men who nag there are none.

2. In poetry, a single syllable rhyme in which the final syllable is stressed is considered strong or *masculine*.

   A double or triple syllable rhyme in which the final syllable is not stressed is considered weak or *feminine*.

3. *Virago* once meant a strong courageous woman. Apparently strong courageous women are not admired, and the word has deteriorated to its present meaning: a noisy, domineering woman.

4. Surnames, which belong to the father not to the mother, are mostly masculine. Some are names of traditionally male occupations: miller, baker, carpenter. Others indicate a father-son relationship: Johnson = son of John. (Consider the following absurdity: Linda Johnson = Linda, son of John.)

5. Through custom, titles have become masculine. Note the surprise on someone's face when he discovers that *Dr.* Smith or *Judge* Brown is a woman.

6. The *American Heritage Dictionary* defines an "auxiliary" as "a group or organization that assists or is supplementary to a larger one: a *women's auxiliary*." Anyone ever hear of a *men's auxiliary*?

7. In journalism a woman who writes sentimental stories is called a *sob sister*. There is no equivalent term for a man who writes such stories.

   Mass TV entertainment for women are called *soap operas*; mass TV entertainment for men are called *sports events*. (The two terms have quite different connotations.)

   Stepmother and *stepfather* denote parallel relationships, but again, note the connotation of each term.

8. In music, the low masculine voice is considered superior to the high female voice. In musical instruments, however, the high-pitched instrument is considered more aggressive and therefore is called masculine; the low-pitched instrument, less aggressive, is called feminine.

9. Job titles are a linguistic device designed to raise the prestige (and salaries) of male employees and to lower the prestige (and salaries) of female employees. An especially acrid example of this type of bias occurs not infrequently on Wall Street in brokerage firms. Since orders may be taken only by registered representatives, some firms encourage secretaries to take the New York Stock Exchange examination. Successful secretaries can then function as brokers without title or commensurate salary. This technique saves money and keeps the male broker monopoly intact.

10. The most talked about language problem today involves the forms of address. All men are simply "Mr."—but, traditionally, married women are "Mrs." and single women "Miss." It was a convenient distinction for males who, upon being introduced to a woman, knew immediately whether she was "available." It was less convenient for the woman. Incidentally, it also provided instant input on job applications, credit forms, etc. As part of the thrust toward equality, many women have rejected "Miss" and "Mrs." and are now using "Ms.," a pleasantly neutral title that gives away no secrets.

Other suggested titles are all-embracing, intended for all men, women, and children: Person, or Pn., for short; Myself or Msf., for short; Citizen.

A living language is constantly changing. Now, in response to the Woman's Rights Movement, the English language is changing faster than ever. The "-ess" and "-ette" suffixes are rapidly disappearing.

Some newspapers, including the *Washington Post* and the *Washington Evening Star*, have already ordered reporters to avoid meaningless descriptions like "leggy blonde" and potentially biased words like "divorcee" and "housewife," unless, of course, they are germane. Reporters have also been reminded that a female celebrity need not be identified through her husband, and that it is possible to discuss a woman's achievements in a tone other than one of condescending amusement.

Inequities in job promotion and the granting of titles are being studied both by the EEOC and by women's groups. There is real possibility of improvement in this area during this decade.

One of the toughest aspects of language to change is the use of generic pronouns and nouns. Through the centuries, women have been conditioned to respond to "he, his, or him." They may wince, but they endure. Recently Dana Densome in a Boston periodical suggested that "she" should replace "he" since "he" is in "she"—that "women" replace "men" since "men" is in "women"—and that "herm" (a combination of "her" and "him") might be a useful objective case pronoun. Unquestionably men would wince, but would *they* be able to endure?

Suspecting that males might find such a reversal impossible, several women have suggested less emotion-laden replacements. Mary Orovan, a liberationist writer, proposes that "co" be used for "he" or "she"; "cos" for the possessive "his" or "hers"; "co" for the objective "him" or "her"; and "coself" for "himself" or "herself." Since "co" as in "coed" already implies both sexes, this proposal seems plausible.

Varda Murrell of California offers a system based on the "v" sound: "ve" for nominative, "vis" for possessive, and "ver" for objective. Ms. Murrell has written the following sentence to show how this system would work: "A teacher must learn to listen. Ve must respect vis students' opinions. They must be important to ver."

It is unlikely that the entire structure of English pronouns will change in a day or a year or even a decade. But it is likely that some modifica-

18

Women: They still have a long way to go.

tion will have to take place soon. The newly sensitized woman will no longer permit herself to be addressed as "he, his, or him." It is an insult to her as a person, and to her as a woman. It ignores —worse, it negates—her true self.

This chapter began with a statement: "Teach me your language, and I will explain you, even to yourself." Many women today are discontented, restless, angry without apparent reason. Is it not possible that the reason lies in their alienation from their native tongue? Born to English, they find themselves a blurred blot in the lexicon. Educated in English, they stumble over speech forms that are grotesquely inaccurate.

If language responds—as it must—to the needs of the people who speak it, then English (as well as other languages) must respond to the needs of the "new" woman—for the new woman refuses to be an accessory, refuses to be part of some male's paraphernalia, and insists on her separate identity as woman *and* as person. She no longer accepts the *King's* English.

DISCUSSION TOPICS

1. The case for (or against) the use of Ms. instead of Mrs. or Miss

2. Language, a tool of prejudice

SUGGESTED ACTIVITIES

1. Select from any short story or novel a three to four page scene describing an incident that involves a man and a woman. In one column, list the adjectives used to describe the man; in a second column, list the adjectives used to describe the woman. Compare the two lists. Do they have different patterns? Suggest a reason for the author's choices.

2. Using a number of generic pronouns, write a short speech on any topic. Tape it once, using the traditional "he, his, him." Tape it a second time using "she, hers, her." Tape it a third time using either Ms. Murrell's or Ms. Orovan's proposed new systems. Play all three to the people in your group and record their reactions.

3. For those who are familiar with a foreign language, choose 20 nouns and 20 adjectives in the language. Ascertain whether each of the 40 words is feminine, masculine, or neuter. Ask yourself *why* each is considered a particular gender. Is there any logical reason? any emotional reason? Present your lists and analysis to the other members of the group.

PART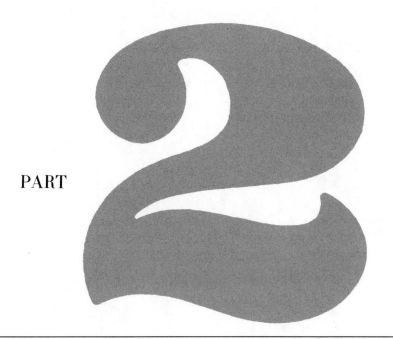

From Then To Now:

A BRIEF DOCUMENTARY HISTORY OF THE WOMAN'S RIGHTS MOVEMENT

Abigail Adams: A Forerunner

Abigail Adams (1744-1818), wife of the second President of the United States and mother of the sixth, was a noted letter writer. Lively, direct, and witty, her descriptions of her experiences managing a family of four children during the American Revolution while her husband was in Philadelphia with the Continental Congress make fascinating reading. Though not a truly emancipated woman, even for her time, Abigail displayed courage, imagination, and perhaps most important of all, a sense of humor. Well traveled for a Puritan lady—eight months in Paris and then three years in England while John Adams was the first American Minister there—Mrs. Adams kept her eyes open and her wits sharpened. Some of her observations on English life, manners, and personalities were pungent. The next twelve years were equally challenging. During George Washington's administration, John, who was the Vice President, and Abigail lived in New York. She was the first President's wife to live in the President's palace, as the White House was then called. She did not hesitate to record its shortcomings. Albert Gallatin called Abigail, unkindly, "Her Majesty." It was commonly reported that she had great political influence over her husband.

The selection below was written in a semi-serious vein. But truth often masquerades under the guise of humor. "Remember the Ladies" would have given the new country, which had just declared its independence, a breadth of liberty it was not to achieve for almost one hundred and fifty years. Abigail Adams's warning had an ominous ring: "Remember all men would be tyrants if they could."

Excerpt from Abigail Adams to John Adams, March 31, 1776

"... I long to hear that you have declared an independency—and by the way, in the new Code of Laws which I suppose it will be necessary for you to make I desire you would Remember the Ladies, and be more generous and favourable to them than your ancestors. Do not put such unlimited power into the hands of the Husbands. Remember all Men would be tyrants if they could.

19

Abigail Adams

If perticuliar [sic] care and attention is not paid to the Ladies we are determined to foment a Rebellion, and will not hold ourselves bound by any Laws in which we have no voice or Representation.

That your Sex are Naturally Tyrannical is a Truth so thoroughly established as to admit of no dispute, but such of you as wish to be happy willingly give us the harsh title of Master for the more tender and endearing one of Friend. Why then, not put it out of the power of the vicious and the Lawless to use us with cruelty and indignity with impunity. Men of Sense in all Ages abhor those customs which treat us only as the vassals of your Sex. Regard us then as Beings placed by providence under your protection and in immitation of the Supreme Being make use of that power only for our happiness."

DISCUSSION TOPICS

1. A study of the Puritan woman in Puritan society

2. The role of the southern plantation owner's wife in the slave society of the antebellum South

3. A study of the contribution that women made to the Revolutionary War effort

4. What education was available for girls at this time?

SUGGESTED ACTIVITIES

1. Read a biography of Abigail Adams and try to find evidence of her position on woman's rights.

2. Collect data on women in colonial and federal America. Find out their occupations, their place in the arts, their social life, their position in society.

3. Gather material from sources in order to reconstruct a typical day in the life of a twenty-five-year-old married colonial woman in middle class circumstances.

The Seneca Falls
Declaration

"We hold these truths to be self-evident: that all men and women are created equal"

In the summer of 1840, Lucretia Coffin Mott, Quaker, abolitionist, and founder of the first Female Anti-Slavery Society and Elizabeth Cady Stanton, a young New York housewife married to an abolitionist leader, came to London as part of the American delegation to the World Anti-Slavery Convention. To their disappointment and anger, the convention, after a bitter debate, decided that only male delegates would be seated. The women were banished to the galleries with the rest of the spectators. During the ten days of frustration that followed the two women became friends and allies discussing at length the need for some way of activating women in the anti-slavery cause. Eight years later, Lucretia Mott and Elizabeth Cady Stanton were the instigators of the Woman's Rights Convention that took place at Seneca Falls, New York.

Uncertain how to present the principles upon which the convention would be based, Mrs. Stanton had the idea that the American Declaration of Independence could be paraphrased into a declaration of woman's rights. Lucretia Mott was given the task of preparing the final version. The finished document had lasting influence on many generations of women as a guide and a goal. It still has things to say to modern women.

The Seneca Falls Declaration of Sentiments and Resolutions
July 19, 1848

1. Declaration of Sentiments

When in the course of human events, it becomes necessary for one portion of the family of man to assume among the people of the earth a position different from that which they have hitherto occupied, but one to which the laws of nature and of nature's God entitle them, a decent respect to the opinions of mankind requires that they should declare the causes that impel them to such a course.

We hold these truths to be self-evident; that all men and women are created equal; that

INTERNATIONAL CONVENTION OF WOMEN
Washington, D.C., 1888

20

When this grimly determined group of famous feminists gathered for its portrait in Washington in 1888, only one member so far forgot herself as to smile faintly at the camera. For these were serious women, some of them assembled from other countries for the first International Convention of Women, whose initial success came only five years later when New Zealand women won the vote. Third from the left in the front row is Susan B. Anthony, feminism's great organizer, and fourth from the right in the same row is Elizabeth Cady Stanton, her lifelong friend. At Mrs. Stanton's left is Matilda J. Gage, a tireless researcher who proved that Anna Ella Carroll, a secret agent of Lincoln, had helped General Grant plan the victorious Tennessee campaign of 1862. Third from the left in the second row is Frances Willard, leader of the W.C.T.U., and on her left is Lillie Devereux Blake who, under the nom de plume of "Tiger Lily," wrote books with such titles as *Fettered for Life*.

they are endowed by their Creator with certain inalienable rights; that among these are life, liberty, and the pursuit of happiness; that to secure these rights governments are instituted, deriving their just powers from the consent of the governed. Whenever any form of government becomes destructive of these ends, it is the right of those who suffer from it to refuse allegiance to it, and to insist upon the institution of a new government, laying its foundation on such principles, and organizing its powers in such form, as to them shall seem most likely to effect their safety and happiness. Prudence, indeed, will dictate that governments long established should not be changed for light and transient causes; and, accordingly all experience hath shown that mankind are more disposed to suffer while evils are sufferable, than to right themselves by abolishing the forms to which they are accustomed. But when a long train of abuses and usurpations, pursuing invariably the same object, evinces a design to reduce them under absolute despotism, it is their duty to throw off such a government, and to provide new guards for their future security. Such has been the patient sufferance of the women under this government, and such is now the necessity which constrains them to demand the equal station to which they are entitled.

The history of mankind is a history of repeated injuries and usurpations on the part of man toward woman, having in direct object the establishment of an absolute tyranny over her. To prove this, let facts be submitted to a candid world.

He has never permitted her to exercise her inalienable right to the elective franchise.

He has compelled her to submit to laws in the formation of which she had no voice.

He has withheld from her rights which are given to the most ignorant and degraded men—both natives and foreigners.

Having deprived her of this first right of a citizen, the elected franchise, thereby leaving her without representation in the halls of legislation, he has oppressed her on all sides.

He has made her, if married, in the eye of the law, civilly dead.

He has taken from her all right in property, even to the wages she earns.

He has made her, morally, an irresponsible being, as she can commit many crimes with impunity, provided they be done in the presence of her husband. In the covenant of marriage, she is compelled to promise obedience to her husband, he becoming, to all intents and purposes, her master—the law giving him power to deprive her of her liberty, and to administer chastisement.

He has so framed the laws of divorce, as to what shall be the proper causes, and in case of separation, to whom the guardianship of the children shall be given, as to be wholly regardless of the happiness of women—the law, in all cases, going upon a false supposition of the supremacy of man, and giving all power into his hands.

After depriving her of all rights as a married woman, if single, and the owner of property, he has taxed her to support a government which recognizes her only when her property can be made profitable to it.

He has monopolized nearly all the profitable employments and from those she is permitted to follow, she receives but a scanty remuneration. He closes against her all the avenues to wealth and distinction which he considers most honorable to himself. As a teacher of theology, medicine, or law, she is not known.

He has denied her the facilities for obtaining a thorough education, all colleges being closed against her.

He allows her in Church, as well as State, but a subordinate position, claiming Apostolic authority for her exclusion from the ministry, and, with some exceptions from any public participation in the affairs of the Church.

He has created a false public sentiment by giving to the world a different code of morals for men and women, by which moral delinquencies which exclude women from society, are not only tolerated, but deemed of little account in man.

He has usurped the prerogative of Jehovah

himself, claiming it as his right to assign to her a sphere of action, when that belongs to her conscience and to her God.

He has endeavored, in every way that he could, to destroy her confidence in her own powers, lessen her self-respect, and make her willing to lead a dependent and abject life.

Now, in view of this entire disenfranchisement of one-half the people of this country, in view of their social and religious degradation, in view of the unjust laws above mentioned, and because women do feel themselves aggrieved, oppressed, and fraudulently deprived of their most sacred rights, we insist that they have immediate admission to all the rights and privileges which belong to them as citizens of the United States.

In entering upon the great work before us, we anticipate no small amount of misconception, misrepresentation, and ridicule; but we shall use every instrumentality within our power to effect our object. We shall employ agents, circulate tracts, petition the State and National legislatures, and endeavor to enlist the pulpit and the press in our behalf. We hope this Convention will be followed by a series of Conventions embracing every part of the country.

2. Resolutions

Whereas, The great precept of nature is conceded to be that "man shall pursue his own true and substantial happiness." Blackstone in his *Commentaries* remarks, that this law of Nature being coeval with mankind, and dictated by God himself, is of course superior in obligation to any other. It is binding over all the globe, in all countries and at all times; no human laws are of any validity if contrary to this, and such of them as are valid, derive all their force, and all their validity, and all their authority, mediately and immediately, from this original; therefore,

Resolved, That all laws which prevent woman from occupying such a station in society as her conscience shall dictate, or which place her in a position inferior to that of man, are contrary to the great precept of nature, and therefore of no force or authority.

Resolved, That woman is man's equal—was intended to be so by the Creator, and the highest good of the race demands that she should be recognized as such.

Resolved, That the women of this country ought to be enlightened in regard to the laws under which they live, that they may no longer publish their degradation by declaring themselves satisfied with their present position, nor their ignorance, by asserting that they have all the rights they want.

Resolved, That inasmuch as man, while claiming for himself intellectual superiority, does accord to woman moral superiority, it is preeminently his duty to encourage her to speak and teach, as she has an opportunity, in all religious assemblies.

Resolved, That the same amount of virtue, delicacy, and refinement of behavior that is required of woman in the social state, should also be required of man, and the same transgressions should be visited with equal severity on both man and woman.

Resolved, That the objection of indelicacy and impropriety, which is so often brought against woman when she addresses a public audience, comes with a very ill-grace from those who encourage, by their attendance, her appearance on the stage, in the concert, or in feats of the circus.

Resolved, That woman has too long rested satisfied in the circumscribed limits which corrupt customs and a perverted application of the Scriptures have marked out for her, and that it is time she should move in the enlarged sphere which her great Creator has assigned her.

Resolved, That it is the duty of the women of this country to secure to themselves their sacred right to the elective franchise.

Resolved, That the equality of human rights results necessarily from the fact of the identity of the race in capabilities and responsibilities.

Resolved, That the speedy success of our cause depends upon the zealous and untiring efforts of both men and women, for the overthrow of the monopoly of the pulpit, and for the securing to women an equal participation with men in the various trades, professions, and commerce.

Resolved, therefore That, being invested by the Creator with the same capabilities, and the same consciousness of responsibility for their exercise, it is demonstrably the right and duty of woman, equally with man, to promote every righteous cause by every righteous means; and especially in regard to the great subjects of morals and religion, it is self-evidently her right to participate with her brother in teaching them, both in private and public, by writing and by speaking, by any instrumentalities proper to be used, and in any assemblies proper to be held; and this being a self-evident truth growing out of the divinely implanted principles of human nature, any custom or authority adverse to it, whether modern or wearing the hoary sanction of antiquity, is to be regarded as a self-evident falsehood, and at war with mankind.

DISCUSSION TOPICS

1. The Seneca Falls Conference—its inception, its delegates, its accomplishments, its influence

2. What role should men play in the implementation of the demands that women are making? Should they be excluded from membership in women's rights organizations?

SUGGESTED ACTIVITIES

1. Write an up-to-date version of the Seneca Falls Declaration using the form of the Declaration of Independence. This could be a group or individual activity.

2. Plan a mock Woman's Rights convention. Decide on the seating of delegates and then develop a program of action. This activity could involve the entire group. If you need help, consult guides on political conventions.

12
Ernestine Rose:
On Legal Discrimination
Against Women

"As long as woman shall be oppressed by unequal laws, so long will she be degraded by men."

Ernestine Louise Siismondi Potowski Rose (1810-1892), born in Russian Poland of Jewish parentage, became one of America's most eloquent and keen-minded advocates of Woman's Rights. At the age of sixteen, she left the oppressive and rigid atmosphere of her father's strictly orthodox home. After involving herself in the cause of the oppressed in Prussia and France, she went to England in 1832 where she met such kindred spirits as Elizabeth Fry and Robert Owen. There she married William E. Rose, a wealthy, well-educated Christian who shared her ideals. They settled in New York City in 1836.

Ms. Rose traveled throughout the eastern states and as far west as Michigan lecturing on such diverse causes as religion, free schools, abolition, and Woman's Rights. But her most outstanding triumph was her eleven-year crusade for the Married Woman's Property Bill, which was finally passed in New York in 1848. The law recognized the right of married women to hold property.

"The Queen of the Platform," as Ms. Rose was called, described her frustrating experiences in obtaining the signatures on the petitions she submitted to the New York State legislature in favor of the law. Some of the ladies she asked refused to sign because they were afraid that the gentlemen would laugh at them. Others protested that they had rights enough. The men, on the other hand, were almost unanimous in their belief that women had too many rights already.

Ernestine Rose On Legal Discrimination Against Women

. . . even here, (the United States) in this far-famed land of freedom, under a Republic that has inscribed on its banner the great truth that "all men are created free and equal, and endowed with inalienable rights to life, liberty, and the pursuit of happiness"—a declaration borne, like the vision of hope, on wings of light to the remotest parts of the earth, an omen of freedom to the oppressed and downtrodden children of man—when, even here, in the very face of this eternal truth, woman, the mockingly so-called "better half" of man, has yet to plead for her rights, nay, for her life. For what is life without liberty, and what is liberty without equality of rights? And, as for the pursuit of happiness, she is not allowed to choose any line of action that might promote it; she has only thankfully to accept what man in his magnanimity decides is best for her to do, and this is what he does not choose to do himself.

Is she then not included in that declaration? Answer, ye wise men of the nation, and answer truly; add not hypocrisy to oppression! Say that she is not created free and equal, and therefore (for the sequence follows on the premise) that she is not entitled to life, liberty and the pursuit of happiness. But with all the audacity arising from an assumed superiority, you dare not so libel and insult humanity as to say that she is not included in that declaration; and if she is, then what right has man, except that of might, to deprive woman of the rights and privileges he claims for himself? And why, in the name of reason and justice, why should she not have the same rights? Because she is a woman? Humanity recognizes no sex; virtue recognizes no sex; mind recognizes no sex. Like man, woman comes involuntarily into existence; like him she possesses physical and mental and moral powers, on the proper cultivation of which depends her happiness; like him she is subject to all the vicissitudes of life; like him she has to pay the penalty for disobeying nature's laws, and far greater penalties has she to suffer from ignorance of her more complicated nature; like him she enjoys or suffers with her country. Yet she is not recognized as his equal!

In the laws of the land she has no rights; in government she has no voice. And in spite of another principle, recognized in this Republic, namely, that "taxation without representation is tyranny," she is taxed to defray the expenses of that unholy, unrighteous custom called war, yet she has no power to give her vote against it. From the cradle to the grave she is subject to the power and control of man. Father, guardian, or husband, one conveys her like some piece of merchandise over to the other.

At marriage she loses her entire identity, and her being is said to have become merged in her husband. Has nature thus merged it? Has she ceased to exist and feel pleasure and pain? When she violates the laws of her being, does her husband pay the penalty? When she breaks the moral laws, does he suffer the punishment? When he supplies his wants, is it enough to satisfy her nature? And when at his nightly orgies, in the grog shop and the oyster cellar, or at the gaming table, he squanders the means she helped, by her co-operation and economy, to accumulate, and she awakens to penury and destitution, will it supply the wants of her children to tell them that, owing to the superiority of man she had no redress by law, and that as her being was merged in his, so also ought theirs to be? What an inconsistency, that from the moment she enters that compact, in which she assumes the high responsibility of wife and mother, she ceases legally to exist, and becomes a purely submissive being. Blind submission in women is considered a virtue, while submission to wrong is itself wrong, and resistance to wrong is virtue, alike in woman as in man.

But it will be said that the husband provides for the wife, or in other words, he feeds, clothes, and shelters her! I wish I had the power to make everyone before me fully realize the degradation contained in that ides. Yes! he *keeps* her, and so he does a favorite horse; by law they are both considered his property. Both may, when the cruelty of the owner compels them to run away, be brought back by the strong arm of the law, and according to a still extant law of England, both may be led by the halter to the marketplace and sold. This is humiliating indeed, but nevertheless true; and the sooner these things are known and understood, the better for humanity. It is no fancy sketch. I know that some endeavor to throw the mantle of romance over the subject, and treat woman like some ideal existence, not liable to the ills of life. Let those deal in fancy, that have nothing better to deal in; we have to do with sober, sad realities, with stubborn facts.

Again, I shall be told that the law presumes the husband to be kind, affectionate, and ready to provide for and protect his wife. But what right, I ask, has the law to presume at all on the subject? What right has the law to entrust the interest and happiness of one being into the hands of another? And if the merging of the interest of one being into the other is a necessary consequence of marriage, why should the woman always remain on the losing side? Turn the tables. Let the identity and interest of the husband be merged in the wife. Think you she is not capable of as much justice, disinterested devotion, and abiding affection as he is? Oh, how grossly you misunderstand and wrong her nature! But we desire no such undue power over man; it would be as wrong in her to exercise it as it now is in him. All we claim is an equal legal and social position. We have nothing to do with individual man, be he good or bad, but with the laws that oppress woman. We know that bad and unjust laws must in the nature of things make man so too. If he is kind, affectionate, and consistent, it is because the kindlier feelings, instilled by a mother, kept warm by a sister, and cherished by a wife, will not allow him to carry out these barbarous laws against woman.

But the estimation she is generally held in, is as degrading as it is foolish. Man forgets that woman cannot be degraded without its reacting on himself. The impress of her mind is stamped on him by nature, and the early education of the mother, which no aftertraining can entirely efface; and, therefore, the estimation she is held in falls back with double force upon him. Yet, from the force of prejudice against her, he knows it not. Not long ago, I saw an account of two offenders, brought before a Justice of New York. One was charged with stealing a pair of boots, for which offense he was sentenced to six months' imprisonment, the other's crime was assault and battery upon his wife; he was let off with a reprimand

from the judge! With my principles, I am entirely opposed to punishment, and hold that to reform the erring and remove the causes of evil is much more efficient, as well as just, than to punish. But the judge showed us the comparative value which he set on these two kinds of *property*. But then you must remember that the boots were taken by a stranger, while the wife was insulted by her legal owner! Here it will be said, that such degrading cases are but few. For the sake of humanity, I hope they are. But as long as woman shall be oppressed by unequal laws, so long will she be degraded by man.

. . . Give woman the elective franchise. Let married women have the same right to property that their husbands have, for whatever the difference in their respective occupations, the duties of the wife are as indispensable and far more arduous than the husband's. Why then should the wife, at the death of her husband, not be his heir to the same extent that he is heir to her? In this inequality there is involved another wrong. When the wife dies, the husband is left in the undisturbed possession of all there is; and the children are left with him; no change is made; no stranger intrudes on his home and his affliction. But when the husband dies, the widow at best receives but a mere pittance, while strangers assume authority denied to the wife. The sanctuary of affliction must be desecrated by executors; everything must be ransacked and assessed lest she should steal something out of her own house; and to cap the climax, the children must be placed under guardians. When the husband dies poor, to be sure, no guardian is required, and the children are left for the mother to care and toil for as best she may. But when anything is left for their maintenance, then it must be placed in the hands of strangers for safekeeping! . . .

According to a late act, the wife has a right to the property she brings at marriage or receives in any way after marriage. Here is some provision for the favored few; but for the laboring many, there is none. The mass of the people commence life with no other capital than the union of heads, hearts, and hands. To the benefit of the best of this capital, the wife has no right. If they are unsuccessful in married life, who suffers more the bitter consequences of poverty than the wife? But if successful, she cannot call a dollar for her own. The husband may will away every dollar of the personal property, and leave her destitute and penniless, and she has no redress by law. And even where real estate is left, she receives but a life interest in a third part of it, and at her death, she cannot leave it to anyone belonging to her; it falls back even to the remotest of his relatives. This is law, but where is the justice of it? . . .

DISCUSSION TOPICS

1. A study of the life of Ernestine Rose emphasizing her role in the Woman's Rights Movement

2. The legal status of women in colonial America

3. The legal status of women in the United States up to the Civil War

SUGGESTED ACTIVITIES

1. Search out the laws in your state that have governed a husband's treatment of his wife. Are there still objectionable laws on the books?

2. Write a law that provides for what you consider the just disposition of both the husband's and the wife's property after death.

13
Lucy Stone:
On Woman's Rights

Lucy Stone (1816-1893) was called the morning star of the woman's movement because of the many years that she spent lecturing for the movement from Massachusetts to Wisconsin. Her rebellion against woman's lot came early. Upon reading that male domination was supported in her Bible, she decided that the Scriptures must have been incorrectly translated and determined to study Hebrew and Greek to find out the truth. Denied financial aid for college from her father, who was outraged that a girl should make such a demand, Lucy worked as a teacher until she had enough money to enter Oberlin College in Ohio. At college she was regarded as a radical because she supported both abolition and Woman's Rights. A few weeks after graduation, Lucy Stone gave her first public address on Woman's Rights from the pulpit of her brother's church.

In the speech below, Lucy Stone said to men: "When woman can enter the lists with you and make money herself, she will marry you only for deep and earnest affection." Hence Lucy's decision to marry Henry Blackwell was arrived at only after much soul searching. The terms upon which she agreed to marry appear below. Following one of her deepest convictions, Lucy Stone kept her own name after she married. This was not only as a protest against loss of identity but was connected with the legal base of marriage in those days. When a woman married at that time, she ceased to have a legal existence and her husband became the master of her property and of all the areas of her life. Since Lucy Stone chose to call herself "Mrs. Stone," women who, upon marrying, retain their maiden name are called "Lucy Stoners."

A typical Lucy Stone anecdote concerned her personal appearance. When news reached a town that the formidable Mrs. Stone was coming, the propaganda was circulated that a big, cigar smoking, booted, masculine-looking woman who bellowed and swore like a trooper was arriving to harangue the crowd. Ladies who went to see the female Gargantua were amazed when a small, graceful lady wearing a black satin gown frilled with white lace at the throat addressed them in a gentle, firm voice.

21

Marriage Document between Henry B. Blackwell and Lucy Stone (1855)

Protest.

While acknowledging our mutual affection by publicly assuming the relationship of husband and wife, yet in justice to ourselves and a great principle, we deem it a duty to declare that this act on our part implies no sanction of, nor promise of voluntary obedience to such of the present laws of marriage, as refuse to recognize the wife as an independent, rational being, while they confer upon the husband an injurious and unnatural superiority, investing him with legal powers which no honorable man would exercise, and which no man should possess. We protest especially against the laws which give to the husband

1. The custody of the wife's person.

2. The exclusive control and guardianship of the children.

3. The sole ownership of her personal, and use of her real estate, unless previously settled upon her, or placed in the hands of trustees, as in the case of minors, lunatics, and idiots.

4. The absolute right to the product of her industry.

5. Also against laws which give to the widower so much larger and more permanent an interest in the property of his deceased wife than they give to the widow in that of the deceased husband.

6. Finally, against the whole system by which "the legal existence of the wife is suspended during marriage," so that in most States she neither has a legal part in the choice of her residence, nor can she make a will, nor sue or be sued in her own name, nor inherit property.

We believe that personal independence and equal human rights can never be forfeited, except for crime; that marriage should be an equal and permanent partnership, and so recognized by law; that until it is so recognized, married partners

Lucy Stone

should provide against the radical injustice of present laws by every means in their power.

We believe that where domestic difficulties arise, no appeal should be made to legal tribunals under existing laws, but that all difficulties should be submitted to the equitable adjustment of arbitrators mutually chosen.

Thus reverencing law, we enter our protest against rules and customs which are unworthy of the name, since they violate justice, the essence of law.

(Signed), Henry B. Blackwell
Lucy Stone

Speech by Lucy Stone (delivered at a national Woman's Rights convention in Cincinnati)

The last speaker alluded to the movement as being that of a few disappointed women. From the first years to which my memory stretches, I have been a disappointed woman. When, with my brothers, I reached forth after the source of knowledge, I was reproved with "It isn't fit for you; it doesn't belong to women." Then there was but one college in the world where women were admitted, and that was in Brazil. I would have found my way there, but by the time I was prepared to go, one was opened in the young state of Ohio—the first in the United States where women and Negroes could enjoy opportunities with white men. I was disappointed when I came to seek a profession worthy an immortal being—every employment was closed to me except those of the teacher, the seamstress, and the housekeeper. In education, in marriage, in religion, in everything, disappointment is the lot of woman. It shall be the business of my life to deepen this disappointment in every woman's heart until she bows down to it no longer. I wish that women, instead of being walking showcases, instead of begging of their fathers and brothers the latest and gayest new bonnet, would ask of them their rights.

The question of Woman's Rights is a practical one. The notion has prevailed that it was only an ephemeral idea; that it was but women claiming the right to smoke cigars in the streets, and to frequent barrooms. Others have supposed it a question of comparative intellect, others still, of sphere. Too much has already been said and written about woman's sphere. Trace all the doctrines to their source and they will be found to have no basis except in the usages and prejudices of the age. This is seen in the fact that what is tolerated in woman in one country is not tolerated in another. In this country women may hold prayer meetings etc., but in Mohammedan countries it is written upon their mosques, "Women and dogs, and other impure animals, are not permitted to enter." . . . Leave women, then, to find their sphere. And do not tell us before we are born even, that our province is to cook dinners, darn stockings, and sew on buttons. We are told woman has all the rights she wants; and even women, I am ashamed to say, tell us so. They mistake the politeness of men for rights—seats while men stand in this hall tonight, and their adulations; but these are mere courtesies. We want rights. The flour merchant, the house builder, and the postman charge us no less on account of our sex; but when we endeavor to earn money to pay all these, then, indeed, we find the difference. Man,

22

if he have energy, may hew out for himself a path where no mortal has ever trod, held back by nothing but what is in himself; the world is all before him, where to choose; and we are glad for you, brothers, men, that it is so. But the same society that drives forth the young man, keeps women at home—a dependent—working little cats on worsted and little dogs on punctured paper; but if she goes heartily and bravely to give herself to some worthy purpose, she is out of her sphere and she loses caste. Women working in tailor shops are paid one-third as much as men. Someone in Philadelphia has stated that women make fine shirts for twelve and a half cents apiece; that no woman can make more than nine a week, and the sum thus earned, after deducting rent, fuel, etc., leaves her just three and a half cents a day for bread. Is it a wonder that women are driven to prostitution? Female teachers in New York are paid fifty dollars a year, and for every such situation, there are five hundred applicants . . . The present condition of woman causes a horrible perversion of the marriage relation. It is asked of a lady, "Has she married well?" "Oh, yes, her husband is rich. Woman must marry for a home, and you men are the sufferers by this; for a woman who loathes you may marry you because you have the means to get money which she cannot have. But when a woman can enter the lists with you and make money for herself, she will marry you only for deep and earnest affection. . . .

DISCUSSION TOPICS

1. A study of early woman's colleges and co-ed colleges

2. An analysis of marriage and divorce laws in the nineteenth-century America

3. Draw up an ideal marriage contract explaining its terms. (Suggestion: A male and a female work together on this)

SUGGESTED ACTIVITIES

1. Tape an interview with a woman in a field other than one commonly considered "a woman's field." Ask her what made her choose her career, the attitude of her male colleagues toward her, and other problems that she has encountered.

2. Poll fifty women on their reaction to keeping their maiden names. Compose suitable questions which can be answered yes or no. This activity might be done by a team.

Susan B. Anthony: The Constitutional Argument

"I stand before you under indictment"

"I stand before you under indictment for the alleged crime of having voted at the last Presidential election without having a lawful right to vote!" Susan Anthony told her audiences. She and 15 other women had voted for President in 1872, in Rochester, to test the legality of woman suffrage. Two weeks later, Miss Anthony was arrested but was able to have the trial postponed in order to launch an intensive lecture campaign to try to win support for her cause. Though the case of the United States v. Susan B. Anthony was ably argued by the defendant's lawyers, she was convicted and fined one hundred dollars, which she refused to pay. The penalty was never collected.

Susan B. Anthony's life spanned almost a century (1820-1906) of relentless activity for such causes as temperance, the abolition of slavery, and woman's suffrage. Her stormy career was made possible by an excellent constitution and an amazing singlemindedness. Undeterred by hisses, obscenities, rotten eggs and vegetables, or threats of bodily harm, the angular, austere Quaker lady met her opposition with militant aggressiveness. She had the understandable shortcoming of most reformers, an inability to listen to anyone else, particularly those with whom she disagreed. Although she did not live long enough to see the ultimate success of her movement, she did see equal suffrage achieved in four states.

Susan B. Anthony Defends Her Right to Vote (1873)

Friends and Fellow Citizens:—I stand before you under indictment for the alleged crime of having voted at the last Presidential election without having a lawful right to vote. It shall be my work this evening to prove to you that in thus doing, I not only committed no crime, but instead simply

23

Susan B. Anthony

exercised my citizens right, guaranteed to me and all United States citizens by the National Constitution beyond the power of any state to deny.

Our democratic-republican government is based on the idea of the natural right of every individual member thereof to a voice and a vote in making and executing the laws. We assert the province of government to be to secure the people in the enjoyment of their inalienable rights. We throw to the winds the old dogma that government can give rights. No one denies that before governments were organized each individual possessed the right to protect his own life, liberty, and property. When 100 or 1,000,000 people enter into a free government, they do not barter away their natural rights; they simply pledge themselves to protect each other in the enjoyment of them through prescribed judicial and legislative tribunals. They agree to abandon the methods of brute force in the adjustment of their differences and adopt those of civilization. Nor can you find a word in any of the grand documents left us by the fathers which assumes for government the power to create or to confer rights. The Declaration of Independence, the United States Constitution, the constitutions of the several states, and the organic laws of the territories, all alike propose to *protect* the people in the exercise of their God-given rights. Not one of them pretends to bestow rights.

> All men are created equal, and endowed by their Creator with certain inalienable rights. Among these are life, liberty, and the pursuit of happiness. To secure these, governments are instituted among men, deriving their just powers from the consent of the governed.

Here is no shadow of government authority over rights, or exclusion of any class from their full and equal enjoyment. Here is the right of all men and "consequently", as the Quaker preacher said, "of all women," to a voice in the government. And here, in this first paragraph of the Declaration, is the assertion of the natural right of all to the ballot, for how can "the consent of the governed" be given if the right to vote be denied? Again:

> Whenever any form of government becomes destructive of these ends, it is the right of the people to alter and abolish it, and to institute a new government, laying its foundation on such principles, and organizing its powers in such form, as to them shall seem most likely to effect their safety and happiness.

Surely the right of the whole people to vote is here clearly implied, for however destructive to their happiness this government might become, a disenfranchised class could neither alter nor abolish it, nor institute a new one, except by the old brute force method of insurrection and rebellion. One-half of the people of this nation today are utterly powerless to blot from the statute books an unjust law, or to write there a new and just one. The women, dissatisfied as they are with this form of government—that enforces taxation without representation, that compels them to obey laws to which they have never given their consent, that imprisons and hangs them without a trial by a jury of their peers, that robs them, in marriage, of the custody of their own persons, wages, and children—are this half of the people who are wholly at the mercy of the other half, in direct violation of the spirit and letter of the declarations of the framers of this government, every one of which was based on the immutable principle of equal rights to all. By these declarations, kings, popes, priests, aristocrats, all were alike dethroned and placed on a common level, politically, with the lowliest born subject or serf. By them, too, men, as such, were deprived of their divine right to rule, and placed on a political level with women. By the practice of these declarations all class and caste distinctions would be abolished, and slave, serf, plebian, wife, woman, all alike rise from their subject position to the broader platform of equality.

The preamble of the Federal Constitution says:

> We, the people of the United States, in order to form a more perfect union, establish justice, insure domestic tranquillity, provide for the common defense, promote the general welfare and secure the blessings of liberty to ourselves and our posterity, do ordain and establish this Constitution for the United States of America.

It was we, the people, not we, the white male citizens, nor we, the male citizens; but we, the whole people, who formed this Union. We formed it not to give the blessings of liberty but to secure them; not to the half of ourselves and the half of our posterity, but to the whole people—women as well as men. It is downright mockery to talk to women of their enjoyment of the blessings of liberty while they are denied the only means of securing them provided by this democratic-republican government—the ballot. . . .

But, friends, when . . . I went to the ballot-box last November and exercised my citizen's right to vote, the courts did not wait for me to appeal to them—they appealed to me, and indicted me on the charge of having voted illegally. . . .

24

For any state to make sex a qualification, which must ever result in the disenfranchisement of one entire half of the people, is to pass a bill of attainder, an *ex post facto* law, and is therefore a violation of the supreme law of the land. By it the blessings of liberty are forever withheld from women and their female posterity.... this oligarchy of sex which makes fathers, brothers, husbands, sons, the oligarchs over the mothers and sisters, the wife and daughters of every household; which ordains all men sovereigns, all women subjects carries discord and rebellion into every home of the nation.

The moment you deprive a person of his right to a voice in the government, you degrade him from the status of a citizen of the republic to that of a subject. It matters very little to him whether his monarch be an individual tyrant, as is the Czar of Russia, or a 15 million-headed monster, as here in the United States; he is a powerless subject, serf or slave; not in any sense a free and independent citizen....

If once we establish the false principle that United States citizenship does not carry with it the right to vote in every state in this Union, there is no end to the petty tricks and cunning devices which will be attempted to exclude one and another class of citizens from the right of suffrage. It will not always be the men combining to disenfranchise all women; native born men combining to abridge the rights of all naturalized citizens, as in Rhode Island. It will not always be the rich and educated who may combine to cut off the poor and ignorant; but we may live to see the hardworking, uncultivated day laborers, foreign and native born, learning the power of the ballot and their vast majority of numbers, combine and amend the state constitutions so as to disenfranchise the Vanderbilts, the Stewarts, the Conklings, and the Fentons. It is a poor rule that won't work more ways than one. Establish this precedent, admit the state's right to deny suffrage, and there is no limit to the confusion, discord, and disruption that may await us. There is and can be but one safe principle of government— equal rights to all. Discrimination against any class on account of color, race, nativity, sex, property, culture, can but embitter and disaffect that class, and thereby endanger the safety of the whole people. . . .

DISCUSSION TOPICS

1. At the first International Congress of Women held in London in 1900, Queen Victoria was asked if she would meet any of the delegates. She answered: "Only one of them, Susan B. Anthony." Speculate on the reasons the Queen had for wanting to meet her?

2. It has been said that effective leaders of causes must be single-minded, aggressive, and unyielding. Discuss the career of Susan B. Anthony in these terms.

3. Study the childhood and young womanhood of Susan B. Anthony. What was the influence of her home, background, and parents, particularly her father, on her later development?

SUGGESTED ACTIVITIES

1. Dramatize the trial of Susan B. Anthony for presentation to the group, using the case as source material.

CHAPTER 15

Charlotte Perkins Gilman: The Economic Basis

One of the most gifted and forthright champions of Woman's Rights, Charlotte Perkins Gilman had an unhappy childhood and a disturbed life. Her father deserted his family soon after Charlotte's birth leaving her stern, rigid mother to struggle with poverty and debt. Equipped with little formal schooling, Charlotte made up for the deficiencies in her education with voracious reading.

At eighteen, Charlotte Perkins attended the Rhode Island School of Design where she met Charles Walter Stetson, a painter. They were married in 1884. In the interim, Charlotte supported herself teaching art and painting advertising cards. The marriage was a disaster despite "an exquisite baby, healthy, intelligent, and good."* A nervous breakdown, apparently due to Charlotte's inability to accept marriage and motherhood, persuaded Stetson to agree to a separation and then a divorce. In a short time, Charlotte sent her daughter to live with Stetson.

Free from domestic responsibilities, Charlotte traveled to England to attend the International Socialist and Labor Congress. Her socialism had been inspired by Edward Bellamy's Looking Backward. Writing, lecturing, and organization work occupied Charlotte's time. Her most influential book was Women and Economics, which she wrote in 58 days. It was published in 1898 and translated into six languages, including Hungarian and Japanese. Its theme was the one set forth in the following selection. In order for a woman to develop as an individual, she must have economic independence.

In 1900, Charlotte married her cousin, George Houghton Gilman of New York City. She founded a magazine of social reform, the Forerunner, which was a one-woman venture. It ran for seven years with its founder serving as editor, publisher, and only contributor. When her husband died in 1934, Charlotte joined her daughter in California. A year later, a victim of cancer, she committed suicide, stating: "I have preferred chloroform to cancer."

* Quoted from: *The Living of Charlotte Perkins Gilman: An Autobiography* (New York, 1935).

Charlotte Perkins Gilman

Economic Basis of the Woman Question (1898)

A peculiar condition of women is that their environment has been almost wholly that of the home; and the home is the most ancient of human institutions; the most unalterably settled in its ideals and convictions; the slowest and last to move. . . .

This movement among women, so characteristic of this century, has many faces, many voices, and many aims. It has been upheld and defended, it has been vilified and opposed by many honest persons of both sexes, and has made wonderful progress withal; yet it is still possible that the true basis and purpose of the great change are unknown to many of the supporters and opponents alike. Without attempting an exhaustive study of this enormous social change, one most important factor is here put forward, the economic conditions which underlie the previous condition of woman, and the changes in economic conditions which must accompany her change. . . .

The economic position of women in the world heretofore has been that of the domestic servant. . . . Human beings are animals. Animals must eat. Food is produced by labor. Those who do not labor for their food must have it given to them

—or steal it. So far as women, taken the world over, throughout history, have labored, it has been mainly in domestic service.

Domestic service is the lowest grade of labor remaining extant. . . . When he (a man) makes a servant of his wife, or she of herself by choice, whatever her social, civil, mental, or moral status may be, her economic status is that of domestic service. What she is entitled to receive from society for her labor is the wages of the housemaid. What she gets more than that is given her by her husband without any economic equivalent. She is supported by him on account of her sex. It is a low position in this mighty world so complex and stirring, so full of noble activities, to earn no higher place than was open to the slave of countless centuries ago, but it is a far lower position to be fed and clothed as a sex-dependent, a creature without economic usefulness. . . .

Husband, father, or brother, may give wealth to wife, daughter, or sister, but that does not make her economically independent in the true sense. As well pile your canary's cage with seed and sugar and say he is independent of your care. . . .

Only in a large, well-managed business combination can these matters of heating, lighting, feeding, clothing, and cleaning be rightly carried out; and only in the ample scope of such orderly industry, in its regular hours of labor and free time of rest, and in its well earned liberal payment for each grade of service, can women fulfill their duties in this line and be free human creatures too. We shall have far cleaner, stiller, healthier, happier homes, when their long outgrown industries are at last cut loose and sent where they belong; and women will enjoy their homes, places of pure rest and loving companionship, far more than is pos-sible to the overworked housewife or idle house-mistress of today.

Against all this so visible trend of change rises the great cry of frightened motherhood; the protest that women must stay alone at home and do their housework because only so can they do their duty by their children.

How do we know this? How do we know that the care of children by one individual mother in the personally conducted home is the best thing for the world?

There is nothing to reply except that it is "natural"—that it always was so and always will be —the same old dead weight of blank feeling without one glimmering flash of thought. Without trying to argue—it is useless to reason against feeling—let it be flatly asserted, first that the vast majority of children are very ill cared for and ill trained by their most loving mothers; that they die in vast propor-tions; that they are most unnecessarily sick; that they are not conspicuously happy; that they grow up—such of them as survive—to be the kind of tired, timid, selfish, unprogressive people of whom the world is all too full. . . . Only an independent motherhood, working wisely in well organized busi-nesses, will grow to see that the care of children is a profession in itself . . . not to be lightly under-taken and bunglingly struggled through by every female who can bear young. . . . Only as we learn to work and care for each other in the largest sense shall we grow towards better living for ourselves and those dearest to us. And with all the negative moral superiority of women, there is nothing more absolutely in the way of social progress today than the huge, blind, sluggish mass and primitive preju-dice embodied in the economically dependent woman.

DISCUSSION TOPICS

1. Elaborate on the following quote: "Husband, father, or brother may give wealth to wife, daughter, or sister—but that does not make her economically independent in the true sense. As well pile your canary's cage with seed and sugar and say that he is independent of your care."

2. Charlotte Perkins Gilman was less single-minded than the first wave of woman's righters active in the early nineteenth century. Compare her with Elizabeth Cady Stanton or one of the other "greats."

SUGGESTED ACTIVITIES

1. Read Virginia Woolf's *A Room of One's Own* and compare her ideas with those of Charlotte Gilman.

2. Survey a group of housewives. Ask them what they consider a fair wage for their work. Also ask them the number of hours that they work and get a breakdown of their chores. A committee could then develop statistical charts.

3. Visit a child-care center. Evaluate it and then work on a plan for a better center. This could be done individually or by a group.

16

Women And The Labor Movement: Muller v. Oregon

The pathetic condition of working women in the nineteenth and early twentieth centuries became a national scandal after the publication, in 1907, of a nineteen-volume report that revealed their plight. Twenty states had laws limiting the number of hours that women were allowed to work, but adverse decisions in the courts had canceled out the intent of the laws. Muller v. Oregon was a test case that dealt with the Oregon statute limiting the number of hours a woman was permitted to work in laundries.

Louis D. Brandeis, who later became a United States Supreme Court Justice, argued the case. He was provided with extensive material by Florence Kelley and Josephine Goldmark, his sister-in-law, both members of the Consumers League. This "Oregon brief," as it was called, introduced a new concept into the American legal system. Instead of basing a case wholly on legal points, Brandeis offered voluminous evidence to the court that overlong hours are harmful to women. The human element replaced reliance on constitutional questions alone. The case became a model for the handling of other problems of social welfare. Though some of Brandeis's arguments might be unacceptable to the current Woman's Rights movement, the work of Florence Kelley and the Goldmarks must be regarded as an important contribution.

Muller v. Oregon (1908)

. . . . It may not be amiss, in the present case, before examining the constitutional question, to notice the course of legislation, as well as expressions of opinion from other than judicial sources. In the brief filed by Mr. Louis D. Brandeis for the defendant in error is a very copious collection of all these matters. . . .

The legislation and opinions referred to . . . may not be, technically speaking, authorities, and

in them is little or no discussion of the constitutional question presented to us for determination, yet they are significant of a widespread belief that woman's physical structure, and the functions she performs in consequence thereof, justify special legislation restricting or qualifying the conditions under which she should be permitted to toil. Constitutional questions, it is true, are not settled by even a consensus of present public opinion, for it is the peculiar value of a written constitution that it places in unchanging form limitations upon legislative action, and thus gives a permanence and stability to popular government which otherwise would be lacking. At the same time, when a question of fact is debated and debatable, and the extent to which a special constitutional limitation goes is affected by the truth in respect to that fact, a widespread and long-continued belief concerning it is worthy of consideration. We take judicial cognizance of all matters of general knowledge . . .

That woman's physical structure and the performance of maternal functions place her at a disadvantage in the struggle for subsistence is obvious. This is especially true when the burdens of motherhood are upon her. Even when they are not, by abundant testimony of the medical fraternity continuance for a long time on her feet at work, repeating this from day to day, tends to injurious effects upon the body, and, as healthy mothers are essential to vigorous offspring, the physical well-being of woman becomes an object of public interest and care in order to preserve the strength and vigor of the race. . . .

Differentiated by these matters from the other sex, she is properly placed in a class by herself, and legislation designed for her protection may

The working woman always had the least desirable, lowest-paying jobs—they could hardly be called careers.

be sustained even when like legislation is not necessary for men, and could not be sustained. It is impossible to close one's eyes to the fact that she still looks to her brother and depends upon him. Even though all restrictions on political, personal, and contractual rights were taken away, and she stood, so far as statutes are concerned, upon an absolutely equal plane with him, it would still be true that she is so constituted that she will rest upon and look to him for protection; that her physical structure and a proper discharge of her maternal functions—having in view not merely her own health, but the well-being of the race—justify legislation to protect her from the greed as well as the passion of man. The limitations which this statute places upon her contractual powers, upon her right to agree with her employer as to the time she shall labor, are not imposed solely for her benefit, but also largely for the benefit of all. Many words cannot make this plainer. The two sexes differ in structure of body, in the functions to be performed by each, in the amount of physical strength, in the capacity for long continued labor, particularly when done standing, the influence of health upon the future well-being of the race, the self reliance which enables one to assert full rights, and in the capacity to maintain the struggle for subsistence. This difference justifies a difference in legislation, and upholds that which is designed to compensate for some of the burdens which rest upon her. . . . For these reasons, . . . we are of the opinion that it cannot be adjudged that the act in question is in conflict with the federal Constitution, so far as it respects the work of a female in a laundry, and the judgment of the supreme court of Oregon is Affirmed.

DISCUSSION TOPICS

1. Develop the thesis that the courts could do more to implement the existing laws on equality of the sexes.

2. Make an analysis of the areas in which women could establish their rights by taking their grievances to court. Include such matters as fair employment, discrimination in the professions, discrimination in professional schools and the academic world, discrimination in athletics, etc.

SUGGESTED ACTIVITIES

1. Investigate the latest medical and biological evidence on women's physical strength and endurance, discuss your findings.

2. Observe a housewife with two pre-school children for a day, keeping an accurate record of the physical work done and then compare it with a man who has a desk job. Report your findings.

3. A debate: Resolved that men and women should be treated equally on the job in every way.

The Nineteenth Amendment

> "The Vote, at last!"
> "Vote Yes on Women Suffrage"
> "How long Must Women Wait for Liberty"

The "Silent Sentinels" stood motionless outside the White House gates, their banners carrying the message to the crowds that gathered to see them. Starting in January 1917, the Suffragettes maintained their watch no matter what the weather. When the President drove through the gates of his home passing the silent women, he raised his hat politely.

The peaceful picketing stage lasted until World War I began. Then violence and hostility assailed the Suffragettes because they did not become active in support of the war. Instead they changed their signs to read: "Democracy Should Begin At Home." Retribution from angry crowds, often aided by the police, followed. Arrests were made and the still passively resistant women were led off to jail.

At first, the judges let off the suffragettes without a sentence. Gradually, when they persisted, angry judges ordered them to jail for several days, then for six weeks, then finally for as long as six months. In Washington, the jails that received the women were dirty, loathsome, and corrupt. In protest, some of the Suffragettes went on hunger strikes. They were forcibly fed and brutally treated. Eventually, President Wilson could no longer pretend that he was ignorant of what was going on. The pickets were released. The impact of their heroic demonstration of courage and determination can never be measured. There were, of course, many other factors—political, economic, and social—that resulted in the final reluctant acceptance of the Nineteenth Amendment. But the actions of the martyrs to the cause cannot be ignored.

The Nineteenth Amendment (1920)

The right of citizens of the United States to vote shall not be denied or abridged by the United States or by any State on account of sex.

Congress shall have power to enforce this article by appropriate legislation.

DISCUSSION TOPICS

1. Who opposed woman suffrage in 1917–1919?

2. What factors caused the woman's suffrage movement to be accepted at that particular time?

SUGGESTED ACTIVITIES

1. Trace the activities of the Woman's Party that led to the Nineteenth Amendment.

2. Study and then analyze the history of the passage and the ratification of the Nineteenth Amendment.

3. Have one person or a committee report on the struggle for woman suffrage in England and its effect on the United States effort.

18

Beyond The Suffrage: The Equal Rights Amendment

After the achievement of the suffrage, the woman's movement divided on support for an Equal Rights Amendment to the Constitution. To Quaker militant Alice Paul, such an amendment seemed to be the next logical step. But to others, particularly those concerned with the needs of working class women, the proposed amendment was a threat to the gains made as a result of the decision in Muller v. Oregon.

The Equal Rights Amendment was presented in Congress many times before its passage in the Senate by a vote of 84-8 on March 22, 1972. Earlier the House of Representatives had accepted it. Final victory was due to the heroic efforts of Women United, a coordinating group that pooled the resources of some 92 national organizations. Among them were such diverse groups as the women's conference of the AFL-CIO and women libbers. The modus operandi was to deluge congressmen with letters and telegrams. Senator Jacob Javits (Republican, New York) received about 10,000 letters while the total number mailed was estimated at over 5 million. A proposal for a similar campaign directed at the White House brought an early endorsement from President Nixon.

Immediately after congressional passage of the amendment, Hawaii, Delaware, Nebraska, New Hampshire, Iowa, and Idaho ratified it. Other states have followed, but endorsement by the required 38 has not yet been achieved.

The Equal Rights Amendment

"Men and Women shall have equal rights throughout the United States and every place subject to its jurisdiction. Congress shall have power to enforce this article by appropriate legislation."

Emma Willard (1787–1870) was a leader in the fight to open the doors of academia to women. She did not live to see her dream fulfilled.

These women have carved out a place in contemporary America—as well as its history. They are, and have been, leaders in politics, education, science, and social work.

Jane Addams (1860–1935) social reformer and founder of Hull House was a recipient of the Nobel Peace Prize in 1931.

Margaret Mead is a world-renowned
anthropologist and academician.

Sen. Margaret Chase Smith

Rep. Shirley Chisolm

Rep. Patsy Mink

DISCUSSION TOPICS

1. Support or refute the thesis that feminists are superb agitators but disastrously poor politicians. Use some contemporary examples to prove your point of view.

SUGGESTED ACTIVITIES

1. Write biographical sketches of Alice Paul, who favored the Equal Rights Amendment, and Florence Kelley, who opposed it. Analyze their personalities and try to understand why they took different positions.

2. Interview women workers in a local factory. Ask such questions as: Do you feel capable of working the same hours as a man? Can you work under the same conditions as a man? Do you feel that certain allowances should be made for the female worker? What are they?

PART  **3**

The Looking Glass:
THE WOMAN
IN AMERICAN LITERATURE

CHAPTER

Some Have Eyes...

Our self-image is what and how we feel about ourselves. It determines how we feel about our physical appearance, how we feel about the people around us, and finally how we judge our personal worth.

The simplest reflection of our self-image is our personal appearance. Our dress, our hair styles, and our personal hygiene make a statement about ourselves to the people that we meet.

The quality and quantity of our friendships say something about ourselves. The amount of loyalty, support, trust, and respect we give to our friends and that we expect in return contributes to our self-image.

If we are happy in our relationships with the people around us and with our physical appearance, then our judgment of our personal worth will be high. If, on the other hand, we are actively unhappy or apathetic, our self-image will be low.

Each of the two works in this chapter comments on the self-images of two women in very different ways. The poem by Sylvia Plath describes a woman fighting an impossible battle against age. In "Sex Education," a woman reveals a constantly changing self-image by reliving an event in her past.

Sylvia Plath's brief literary career began at age eight when one of her poems was published in the Boston Traveler. Ariel, her best known volume of poetry, has had a tremendous impact on modern readers and young authors. In addition to her poetry she wrote a novel, The Bell Jar. *Sylvia Plath, fascinated by death in her writing, committed suicide at age thirty-one.*

Mirror

Sylvia Path

I am silver and exact. I have no preconceptions.
Whatever I see I swallow immediately
Just as it is, unmisted by love or dislike.
I am not cruel, only truthful—
The eye of a little god, four-cornered.
Most of the time I meditate on the opposite wall.
It is pink, with speckles. I have looked at it so long
I think it is a part of my heart. But it flickers.
Faces and darkness separate us over and over.

Now I am a lake. A woman bends over me,
Searching my reaches for what she really is.
Then she turns to those liars, the candles
　　or the moon.
I see her back, and reflect it faithfully.
She rewards me with tears and an agitation
　　of hands.
I am important to her. She comes and goes.
Each morning it is her face that replaces
　　the darkness.
In me she has drowned a young girl, and in me
　　an old woman
Rises toward her day after day, like a terrible fish.

*A highly educated woman for her time,
Dorothy Canfield received her Bachelor's degree
from Ohio State where her father was president.
She earned her Ph.D. in French from Columbia
University in 1905. During World War I, she and
her husband, James Redwood Fisher, spent time
in France where she worked with soldiers and later
established a home for refugee French children.*

*Although Ms. Canfield's plan to be a col-
lege teacher of languages never materialized, she
maintained a lifetime interest in education, especially in the educational work of Dr. Maria Mon-
tessori.*

*Aunt Minnie in "Sex Education" disproves
the theory that people who repeat themselves are
boring. She tells three different versions of the
same story at three different stages of her life.
Each version reveals more of her character.*

Sex Education

Dorothy Canfield

It was three times—but at intervals of
many years—that I heard my Aunt Minnie tell
about an experience of her girlhood that had made
a never-to-be-forgotten impression on her. The
first time she was in her thirties, still young. But
she had then been married for ten years, so that
to my group of friends, all in the early teens, she
seemed quite of another generation.

The day she told us the story, we had
been idling on one end of her porch as we made
casual plans for a picnic supper in the woods.
Darning stockings at the other end, she paid no
attention to us until one of the girls said, "Let's
take blankets and sleep out there. It'd be fun."

"No," Aunt Minnie broke in sharply, "you
mustn't do that."

"Oh, for goodness' sakes, why not!" said
one of the younger girls, rebelliously, "the boys
are always doing it. Why can't we, just once?"

Aunt Minnie laid down her sewing. "Come
here, girls," she said, "I want you should hear
something that happened to me when I was your
age."

Her voice had a special quality which, perhaps, young people of today would not recognize.
But we did. We knew from experience that it was
the dark voice grownups used when they were
going to say something about sex.

Yet at first what she had to say was like
any dull family anecdote; she had been ill when
she was fifteen; and afterwards she was run down,
thin, with no appetite. Her folks thought a change
of air would do her good, and sent her from Vermont out to Ohio—or was it Illinois? I don't remember. Anyway, one of those places where the
corn grows high. Her mother's Cousin Ella lived
there, keeping house for her son-in-law.

The son-in-law was the minister of the village church. His wife had died some years before,
leaving him a young widower with two little girls
and a baby boy. He had been a normally persona-
ble man then, but the next summer, on the Fourth

of July when he was trying to set off some fire-works to amuse his children, an imperfectly manu-factured rocket had burst in his face. The explosion had left one side of his face badly scarred. Aunt Minnie made us see it, as she still saw it, in horrid detail: the stiffened, scarlet scar tissue distorting one check, the lower lip turned so far out at one corner that the moist red mucous membrane lining always showed, one lower eyelid hanging loose, and watering.

After the accident, his face had been a long time healing. It was then that his wife's elderly mother had gone to keep house and take care of the children. When he was well enough to be about again, he found his position as pastor of the little church waiting for him. The farmers and vil-lage people in his congregation, moved by his misfortune, by his faithful service and by his un-blemished character, said they would rather have Mr. Fairchild, even with his scarred face, than any other minister. He was a good preacher, Aunt Minnie told us, "and the way he prayed was kind of exciting. I'd never known a preacher, not to live in the same house with him, before. And when he was in the pulpit, with everybody looking up at him, I felt the way his children did, kind of proud to think we had just eaten breakfast at the same table. I liked to call him 'Cousin Malcolm' before folks. One side of his face was all right, anyhow. You could see from that he *had* been a good-looking man. In fact, probably one of those min-isters that all the women . . ." Aunt Minnie paused, drew her lips together, and looked at us uncertainly.

Then she went back to the story as it hap-pened—as it happened that first time I heard her tell it. "I thought he was a saint. Everybody out there did. That was all *they* knew. Of course, it made a person sick to look at that awful scar—the drooling corner of his mouth was the worst. He tried to keep that side of his face turned away from folks. But you always knew it was there. That was what kept him from marrying again, so Cousin Ella said. I heard her say lots of times that he knew no woman would touch any man who looked the way he did, not with a ten-foot pole.

"Well, the change of air did do me good. I got my appetite back, and ate a lot and played outdoors a lot with my cousins. They were younger than I (I had my sixteenth birthday there) but I still liked to play games. I got taller and laid on some weight. Cousin Ella used to say I grew as fast as the corn did. Their house stood at the edge of the village. Beyond it was one of those big corn-fields they have out West. At the time when I first got there, the stalks were only up to a person's knee. You could see over their tops. But it grew like lightning, and before long, it was the way thick woods are here, way over your head, the stalks growing so close together it was dark under them.

"Cousin Ella told us youngsters that it was lots worse for getting lost in than woods, because there weren't any landmarks in it. One spot in a cornfield looked just like any other. 'You children keep out of it,' she used to tell us almost every day, '*especially you girls*. It's no place for a decent girl. You could easy get so far from the house no-body could hear you if you hollered. There are plenty of men in this town that wouldn't like any-thing better than ——' she never said what.

"In spite of what she said, my little cous-ins and I had figured out that if we went across one corner of the field, it would be a short cut to the village, and sometimes, without letting on to Cousin Ella, we'd go that way. After the corn got really tall, the farmer stopped cultivating, and we soon beat down a path in the loose dirt. The min-ute you were inside the field it was dark. You felt as if you were miles from anywhere. It sort of scared you. But in no time the path turned and brought you out on the far end of Main Street. Your breath was coming fast, maybe, but that was what made you like to do it.

"One day I missed the turn. Maybe I didn't keep my mind on it. Maybe it had rained and blurred the tramped-down look of the path. I don't know what. All of a sudden, I knew I was lost. And the minute I knew that, I began to run, just as hard as I could run. I couldn't help it, any more than you can help snatching your hand off a hot stove. I didn't know what I was scared of, I didn't even know I *was* running, till my heart was pounding so hard I had to stop.

"The minute I stood still, I could hear Cousin Ella saying, 'There are plenty of men in this town that wouldn't like anything better than ——' I didn't know, not really, what she meant. But I knew she meant something horrible. I opened my mouth to scream. But I put both hands over my mouth to keep the scream in. If I made any noise, one of those men would hear me. I thought I heard one just behind me, and whirled around. And then I thought another one had tiptoed up behind me, the other way, and I spun around so fast I almost fell over. I stuffed my hands hard up against my mouth. And then—I couldn't help it—I ran again— but my legs were shaking so I soon had to stop. There I stood, scared to move for fear of rustling the corn and letting the men know where I was. My hair had come down, all over my face. I kept pushing it back and looking around, quick, to make sure one of the men hadn't found out where I was. Then I thought I saw a man coming towards me, and I ran away from him and fell down, and burst some of the buttons off my dress, and was sick to my stomach—and thought I heard a man close to me and got up and staggered around, knocking into the corn because I couldn't even see where I was going.

"And then, off to one side, I saw Cousin Malcolm. Not a man. The minister. He was standing still, one hand up to his face, thinking. He hadn't heard me.

"I was so *terrible* glad to see him, instead of one of those men, I ran as fast as I could and just flung myself on him, to make myself feel how safe I was."

Aunt Minnie had become strangely agitated. Her hands were shaking, her face was crimson. She frightened us. We could not look away from her. As we waited for her to go on, I felt little spasms twitch at the muscles inside my body. "And what do you think that *saint*, that holy minister of the Gospel, did to an innocent child who clung to him for safety? The most terrible look came into his eyes—you girls are too young to know what he looked like. But once you're married, you'll find out. He grabbed hold of me—that dreadful face of his was *right on mine*—and began clawing the clothes off my back."

She stopped for a moment, panting. We were too frightened to speak. She went on, "He had torn my dress right down to the waist before I—then I *did* scream—all I could—and pulled away from him so hard I almost fell down, and ran and all of a sudden I came out of the corn, right in the back yard of the Fairchild house. The children were staring at the corn, and Cousin Ella ran out of the kitchen door. They had heard me screaming. Cousin Ella shrieked out, 'What is it? What happened? Did a man scare you?' And I said, 'Yes, yes, yes, a man—I ran——!' And then I fainted away. I must have. The next thing I knew I was on the sofa in the living room and Cousin Ella was slapping my face with a wet towel."

She had to wet her lips with her tongue before she could go on. Her face was gray now. "There! that's the kind of thing girls' folks ought to tell them about—so they'll know what men are like."

She finished her story as if she were dismissing us. We wanted to go away, but we were too horrified to stir. Finally one of the youngest girls asked in a low trembling voice, "Aunt Minnie, did you tell on him?"

"No, I was ashamed to," she said briefly. "They sent me home the next day anyhow. Nobody ever said a word to me about it. And I never did either. Till now."

By what gets printed in some of the modern child-psychology books, you would think that girls to whom such a story had been told would never develop normally. Yet, as far as I can remember what happened to the girls in that group, we all grew up about like anybody. Most of us married, some happily, some not so well. We kept house. We learned—more or less—how to live with our husbands, we had children and struggled to bring them up right—we went forward into life, just as if we had never been warned not to.

Perhaps, young as we were that day, we had already had enough experience of life so that we were not quite blank paper for Aunt Minnie's frightening story. Whether we thought of it then or not, we couldn't have failed to see that at this very time, Aunt Minnie had been married for ten years or more, comfortably and well married, too. Against what she tried by that story to brand into our minds stood the cheerful home life in that house, the good-natured, kind, hard-working husband, and the children—the three rough-and-tumble, nice little boys, so adored by their parents, and the sweet girl baby who died, of whom they could never speak without tears. It was such actual contact with adult life that probably kept generation after generation of girls from being scared by tales like Aunt Minnie's into a neurotic horror of living.

Of course, since Aunt Minnie was so much older than we, her boys grew up to be adolescents and young men, while our children were still little enough so that our worries over them were nothing more serious than whooping cough and trying to get them to make their own beds. Two of our aunt's three boys followed, without losing their footing, the narrow path which leads across adolescence into normal adult life. But the middle one, Jake, repeatedly fell off into the morass. "Girl trouble," as the succinct family phrase put it. He was one of those boys who have "charm," whatever we mean by that, and was always being snatched at by girls who would be "all wrong" for him to marry. And once, at nineteen, he ran away from home, whether with one of these girls or not we never heard, for through all her ups and downs with this son, Aunt Minnie tried fiercely to protect him from scandal that might cloud his later life.

Her husband had to stay on his job to earn the family living. She was the one who went to find Jake. When it was gossiped around that Jake was in "bad company" his mother drew some money from the family savings-bank account, and silent, white-cheeked, took the train to the city where rumor said he had gone.

Some weeks later he came back with her. With no girl. She had cleared him of that entangle-ment. As of others, which followed, later. Her troubles seemed over when, at a "suitable" age, he fell in love with a "suitable" girl, married her and took her to live in our shire town, sixteen miles away, where he had a good position. Jake was always bright enough.

Sometimes, idly, people speculated as to what Aunt Minnie had seen that time she went after her runaway son, wondering where her search for him had taken her—very queer places for Aunt Minnie to be in, we imagined. And how could such an ignorant, homekeeping woman ever have known what to say to an errant willful boy to set him straight?

Well, of course, we reflected, watching her later struggles with Jake's erratic ways, she certainly could not have remained ignorant, after seeing over and over what she probably had; after talking with Jake about the things which, a good many times, must have come up with desperate openness between them.

She kept her own counsel. We never knew anything definite about the facts of those experiences of hers. But one day she told a group of us—all then married women—something which gave us a notion about what she had learned from them.

We were hastily making a layette for a not-especially welcome baby in a poor family. In those days, our town had no such thing as a district-nursing service. Aunt Minnie, a vigorous woman of fifty-five, had come in to help. As we sewed, we talked, of course; and because our daughters were near or in their teens, we were comparing notes about the bewildering responsibility of bringing up girls.

After a while, Aunt Minnie remarked, "Well, I hope you teach your girls some *sense*. From what I read, I know you're great on telling them 'the facts,' facts we never heard of when we were girls. Like as not, some facts I don't know, now. But knowing the facts isn't going to do them any more good than *not* knowing the facts ever did, unless they have some sense taught them, too."

"What do you mean, Aunt Minnie?" one of us asked her uncertainly.

She reflected, threading a needle, "Well, I don't know but what the best way to tell you what I mean is to tell you about something that happened to me, forty years ago. I've never said anything about it before. But I've thought about it a good deal. Maybe——"

She had hardly begun when I recognized the story—her visit to her Cousin Ella's Midwestern home, the widower with his scarred face and saintly reputation and, very vividly, her getting lost in the great cornfield. I knew every word she was going to say—to the very end, I thought.

But no, I did not. Not at all.

She broke off, suddenly, to exclaim with impatience, "Wasn't I the big ninny? But not so big a ninny as that old cousin of mine. I could wring her neck for getting me in such a state. Only she didn't know any better, herself. That was the way they brought young people up in those days, scaring them out of their wits about the awfulness of getting lost, but not telling them a thing about how *not* to get lost. Or how to act, if they did.

"If I had had the sense I was born with, I'd have known that running my legs off in a zig-zag was the worst thing I could do. I couldn't have been more than a few feet from the path when I noticed I wasn't on it. My tracks in the loose plow dirt must have been perfectly plain. If I'd h' stood still, and collected my wits, I could have looked down to see which way my footsteps went and just walked back over them to the path and gone on about my business.

"Now I ask you, if I'd been told how to do that, wouldn't it have been a lot better protection for me—if protection was what my aunt thought she wanted to give me—than to scare me so at the idea of being lost that I turned deef-dumb-and-blind when I thought I was?

"And anyhow that patch of corn wasn't as big as she let on. And she knew it wasn't. It was no more than a big field in a farming country. I was a well-grown girl of sixteen, as tall as I am

now. If I couldn't have found the path, I could have just walked along one line of cornstalks—*straight*—and I'd have come out somewhere in ten minutes. Fifteen at the most. Maybe not just where I wanted to go. But all right, safe, where decent folks were living."

She paused, as if she had finished. But at the inquiring blankness in our faces, she went on, "Well, now, why isn't teaching girls—and boys, too, for the Lord's sake don't forget they need it as much as the girls—about this man-and-woman business, something like that? If you give them the idea—no matter whether it's *as* you tell them the facts, or as you *don't* tell them the facts, that it is such a terribly scary thing that if they take a step into it, something's likely to happen to them so awful that you're ashamed to tell them what—well, they'll lose their heads and run around like crazy things, first time they take one step away from the path.

"For they'll be trying out the paths, all right. You can't keep them from it. And a good thing too. How else are they going to find out what it's like? Boys' and girls' going together is a path across one corner of growing up. And when they go together, they're likely to get off the path some. Seems to me, it's up to their folks to bring them up so when they do, they don't start screaming and running in circles, but stand still, right where they are, and get their breath and figure out how to get back.

"And anyhow, you don't tell 'em the truth about sex" (I was astonished to hear her use the actual word, taboo to women of her generation) "if they get the idea from you that it's all there is to living. It's not. If you don't get to where you want to go in it, well, there's a lot of landscape all around it a person can have a good time in.

"D'you know, I believe one thing that gives girls and boys the wrong idea is the way folks *look*! My old cousin's face, I can see her now, it was as red as a rooster's comb when she was telling me about men in that cornfield. I believe now she kind of *liked* to talk about it."

(Oh, Aunt Minnie—and yours! I thought.)

Someone asked, "But how *did* you get out, Aunt Minnie?"

She shook her head, laid down her sewing. "More foolishness. That minister my mother's cousin was keeping house for—her son-in-law—I caught sight of him, down along one of the aisles of cornstalks, looking down at the ground, thinking, the way he often did. And I was so glad to see him I rushed right up to him, and flung my arms around his neck and hugged him. He hadn't heard me coming. He gave a great start, put one arm around me and turned his face full towards me—I suppose for just a second he had forgotten how awful one side of it was. His expression, his eyes—well, you're all married women, you know how he looked, the way any able-bodied man thirty-six or -seven, who'd been married and begotten children, would look—for a minute anyhow, if a full-blooded girl of sixteen, who ought to have known better, flung herself at him without any warning, her hair tumbling down, her dress half unbuttoned, and hugged him with all her might.

"I was what they called innocent in those days. That is, I knew just as little about what men are like as my folks could manage I should. But I was old enough to know all right what that look meant. And it gave me a start. But of course the real thing of it was that dreadful scar of his, so close to my face—that wet corner of his mouth, his eye drawn down with the red inside of the lower eyelid showing——

"It turned me so sick, I pulled away with all my might, so fast that I ripped one sleeve nearly loose, and let out a screech like a wildcat. And ran. Did I run? And in a minute, I was through the corn and had come out in the back yard of the house. I hadn't been more than a few feet from it, probably, any of the time. And then I fainted away. Girls were always fainting away; it was the way our corset strings were pulled tight, I suppose, and then—oh, a lot of fuss.

"But anyhow," she finished, picking up her work and going on, setting neat, firm stitches with steady hands, "there's one thing, I never told any-body it was Cousin Malcolm I had met in the cornfield. I told my old cousin that 'a man had scared me.' And nobody said anything more about it to me, not ever. That was the way they did in those days. They thought if they didn't let on about something, maybe it wouldn't have happened. I was sent back to Vermont right away and Cousin Malcolm went on being minister of the church. I've always been," said Aunt Minnie moderately, "kind of proud that I didn't go and ruin a man's life for just one second's slip-up. If you could have called it that. For it *would* have ruined him. You know how hard as stone people are about other folks' let-downs. If I'd have told, not one person in that town would have had any charity. Not one would have tried to understand. One slip, *once*, and they'd have pushed him down in the mud. If I had told, I'd have felt pretty bad about it, later—when I came to have more sense. But I declare, I can't see how I came to have the decency, dumb as I was then, to know that it wouldn't be fair."

It was not long after this talk that Aunt Minnie's elderly husband died, mourned by her, by all of us. She lived alone then. It was peaceful October weather for her, in which she kept a firm roundness of face and figure, as quiet-living countrywomen often do, on into her late sixties.

But then Jake, the boy who had had girl trouble, had wife trouble. We heard he had taken to running after a young girl, or was it that she was running after him? It was something serious. For his nice wife left him and came back with the children to live with her mother in our town. Poor Aunt Minnie used to go to see her for long talks which made them both cry. And she went to keep house for Jake, for months at a time.

She grew old, during those years. When finally she (or something) managed to get the marriage mended so that Jake's wife relented and went back to live with him, there was no trace left of her pleasant brisk freshness. She was stooped and slow-footed and shrunken. We, her kinspeople, although we would have given our lives for any one of our own children, wondered whether Jake was worth what it had cost his mother to—well, steady him, or reform him. Or perhaps just understand him. Whatever it took.

She came of a long-lived family and was able to go on keeping house for herself well into her eighties. Of course we and the other neighbors stepped in often to make sure she was all right. Mostly, during those brief calls, the talk turned on nothing more vital than her geraniums. But one midwinter afternoon, sitting with her in front of her cozy stove, I chanced to speak in rather hasty blame of someone who had, I thought, acted badly. To my surprise this brought from her the story about the cornfield which she had evidently quite forgotten telling me, twice before.

This time she told it almost dreamily, swaying to and fro in her rocking chair, her eyes fixed on the long slope of snow outside her window. When she came to the encounter with the minister she said, looking away from the distance and back into my eyes, "I know now that I had been, all along, kind of *interested* in him, the way any girl as old as I was would be, in any youngish man living in the same house with her. And a minister, too. They have to have the gift of gab so much more than most men, women get to thinking they are more alive than men who can't talk so well. I *thought* the reason I threw my arms around him was because I had been so scared. And I certainly had been scared, by my old cousin's horrible talk about the cornfield being full of men waiting to grab girls. But that wasn't all the reason I flung myself at Malcolm Fairchild and hugged him. I know that now. Why in the world shouldn't I have been taught *some* notion of it then? 'Twould do girls good to know that they are just like everybody else—human nature *and* sex, all mixed up together. I didn't have to hug him. I wouldn't have, if he'd been dirty or fat and old, or chewed tobacco."

I stirred in my chair, ready to say, "But it's not so simple as all that to tell girls——" and she hastily answered my unspoken protest. "I know, I know, most of it can't be put into words. There just aren't any words to say something that's so both-ways-at-once all the time as this man-and-woman business. But look here, you know as well as I do that there are lots more ways than in words to teach young folks what you want 'em to know."

The old woman stopped her swaying rocker to peer far back into the past with honest eyes. "What was in my mind back there in the cornfield —partly anyhow—was what had been there all the time I was living in the same house with Cousin Malcolm—that he had long straight legs, and broad shoulders, and lots of curly brown hair, and was nice and flat in front, and that one side of his face was good-looking. But most of all, that he and I were really alone, for the first time, without anybody to see us.

"I suppose, if it hadn't been for that dreadful scar, he'd have drawn me up, tight, and—most any man would—kissed me. I know how I must have looked, all red and hot and my hair down and my dress torn open. And, used as he was to big cornfields, he probably never dreamed that the reason I looked that way was because I was scared to be by myself in one. He may have thought—you know what he may have thought.

"Well—if his face had been like anybody's —when he looked at me the way he did, the way a man does look at a woman he wants to have, it would have scared me—some. But I'd have cried, maybe. And probably he'd have kissed me again. You know how such things go. I might have come out of the cornfield halfway engaged to marry him. Why not? I was old enough, as people thought then. That would have been nature. That was probably what he thought of, in that first instant.

"But what did I do? I had one look at his poor, horrible face, and started back as though I'd stepped on a snake. And screamed and ran.

"What do you suppose *he* felt, left there in the corn? He must have been sure that I would tell everybody he had attacked me. He probably thought that when he came out and went back to the village he'd already be in disgrace and put out of the pulpit.

"But the worst must have been to find out, so rough, so plain from the way I acted—as if somebody had hit him with an ax—the way he would look at any woman he might try to get close to. That must have been——" she drew a long breath, "well, pretty hard on him."

After a silence, she murmured pityingly, "Poor man!"

DISCUSSION TOPICS

1. Aunt Minnie says, " 'Twould do girls good to know that they are just like everybody else—human nature and sex, all mixed together." Imagine that you're a parent—how you would educate your daughter on human nature and sex.

2. Assume you are a mirror and three different women look into you. Describe them.

SUGGESTED ACTIVITIES

1. Assign a team to listen to conversations in order to quote comments made about women. The selection of quotes should be from adult men and women and teen-agers. When the team has recorded twenty comments, it should analyze them and report to the group.

2. Anyone who holds a job can do this activity. Keep a notebook detailing your observations of various women. Be sure to include the situations in which you found these women and report on your conclusions about human nature.

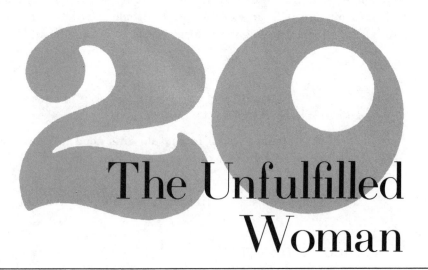

The Unfulfilled Woman

Many American housewives have a chronic disease. Some of the symptoms are listlessness, boredom, restlessness, and a sense of futility. The question is—what causes this disease? For a long time nobody admitted, much less identified, this illness. Perhaps the first writer to examine the problem openly was Betty Friedan in her book <u>The Feminine Mystique</u>. "The Problem That Has No Name," one of the chapters in her book that closely inspects this almost-universal problem, is included in Part IV of <u>The Women, Yes</u>.

In two of the three selections that follow, the women depicted are suffering from this nameless malaise. The third work, a poem, shows us a woman who has escaped the problem thanks to the sensitivity of her husband.

Sally Benson, whose early New Yorker *short stories were known for their satire, and urbane wit, was also a successful playwright and screenwriter. One of her screenplays,* Meet Me in St. Louis, *honored her birthplace. Her best known book,* Junior Miss, *was produced as a play and then as a movie.*

In "Profession: Housewife," written over thirty years ago, Sally Benson depicts a married woman suffering from "The Problem That Has No Name."

Profession: Housewife

Sally Benson

Although the window by the breakfast nook was open, it was very warm. The yellow-and-white gingham curtains hung still and the blue oilcloth tiebacks showed beads of moisture. Even the painted table top felt damp and sticky, and Joe Grannis was conscious of the discomfort of the hard bench on which he sat. He heard Dorothy tear open the letter and, leaning back as far as he could, he shook out his paper and held it before his face.

In a few minutes, she slapped the letter down on the table so hard that the coffee in her cup spilled over into the saucer. "I might have known," she said. "They can't come. At least, she *says* they can't come."

Although it was what he had expected, Joe Grannis lowered his paper and managed to look surprised. "That's funny," he answered. "Maybe some other time."

"Some other time," his wife repeated. "Don't be dumb. The point is they don't want to come, now or any other time."

"I wouldn't say that," he said. "There's no reason why they shouldn't want to come."

Dorothy Grannis lifted her saucer and poured the coffee that had spilled back into the cup. Her face, normally a solid pink, had turned a bright cerise and her hair lay against her forehead with the metallic fixity of a doll's wig. "I'm sorry I asked them in the first place," she told him.

Joe Grannis made a mistake. "Well, you can't say I didn't warn you," he said. "You can't expect to make friends with people who were friends of Louise's. Those things never work out. People feel funny, sort of."

She pushed the sleeves of her chintz house coat further up on her arms with a hard, deliberate gesture and rested her elbows on the table. "Why?" she asked. "From the way you used to talk, I got the impression they were friends of yours. I got the impression that they didn't think so much of *Louise*, that you were the fair-haired boy with them. I got the impression that they couldn't wait until the divorce and everything was over so they could come here again."

She look around the bright, shiny kitchen and laughed. "My God!" she went on. "If they saw this place now it might be too much for them. They might drop dead. Digging this place out was like excavating. It might be too much for them to see it clean for a change."

Joe Grannis took his watch from his pocket and looked at it. He edged from behind the table and stood up. "Time to go," he said.

"I suppose so," she told him. "You never know the answers to anything. Well, what are we going to do tonight? Sit here and listen to the radio?"

"Now, don't be sarcastic," he answered. "You've got friends of your own. Why don't you call Ruth and Van up and ask them out?"

"And have them wondering why nobody else ever drops in?" she asked indignantly. "That was all right at first. They didn't think anything of it the first few times. But the last time she acted plenty funny about it. Wanting to know if I didn't get lonesome here all day and everything. I'd rather rot."

He looked at her and his face grew set. "Suit yourself," he said. "And since you're speaking of impressions, I got some myself. I got the impression that all you needed to make you happy was a home of your own and to be able to quit work. God knows you sang that tune long enough. Three years, wasn't it? Well, you got what you wanted. You've spent money like a drunken sailor on this place and if you can't make friends for yourself, I can't help you."

"Well, really!" she exclaimed, her voice politely formal. "Really!"

She remained seated at the table until she heard the front door slam behind him, and then she got up and with brisk, efficient movements carried the breakfast dishes to the sink. The sink was of glaring yellow porcelain and the faucets were shiny and new. The hot water on her hands made her feel warmer and she pulled down the zipper of her house coat. Her grasp on the dishes was rough, but she arranged them almost gently in the wire rack to drain.

Pretty soon now the girls would come straggling into the office where she used to work, cool and neat in their new summer dresses. Because the day was warm, the atmosphere about the place would relax and Mannie, the office boy, would be sent to the drugstore for double cokes.

There would be gossip and cigarettes in the washroom and speculation as to whether Mr. Ackerman would leave early for a round of golf.

She opened the drawer of the kitchen cabinet and took out a towel, yellow, with blue featherstitching, and dried the dishes hurriedly. Glancing at the clock and seeing that it was not yet nine, she tried to slow her movements. She wiped the breakfast table with a damp cloth and put away the oilcloth doilies.

The dining room was cool and bare. In the center of the shiny mahogany table was placed an etched silver bowl around which huddled four thin silver candlesticks. Going to the sideboard, she opened the drawers one by one, looking with satisfaction at the rows of silver-plated knives, forks, and spoons lying on their squares of felt. In each drawer was a lump of camphor to prevent tarnishing.

The stairs led out of the dining room and she walked up them to the upstairs hall. Four doors opened out into the hall, but only two of them stood ajar—the door to the bathroom and the one to their bedroom. She liked to keep the extra bedrooms shut off until she felt she could do them over decently. There was little disorder in their own room. Joe's striped silk pajamas lay folded on his bed and her pale-green satin nightgown lay on a chair by the window. She hung these in the closet and then spread the beds, fitting their lavender taffeta covers smoothly.

As she finished, the front-door bell rang briefly, and looking out the window, she saw a man standing there, a leather briefcase under his arm. She loosened her hair slightly about her face and pulled the zipper up on her house coat.

The man who stood at the door was very young and very thin. His light-gray suit was shabby and the coat hung limply from his shoulders. He wore no hat and his fine, light hair was too long and fell untidily over his forehead. He had been looking down when she opened the door, his whole figure drooping, but hearing the sound of the latch, he straightened up to face her, jerking his head up alertly, smiling pleasantly.

"Good morning, Madam," he said.

She stood looking at him for so long without speaking that he shifted his feet in embarrassment, the smile growing fixed on his face.

"Yes?" she asked finally. "Yes?"

He took the briefcase from under his arm, and after struggling with the catch, opened it and drew forth a book, which he held toward her. Its bright, flowered cover looked worn and dirty, as though it had been often handled. She made no motion to take it from him, but he stood bravely facing her, the book in his hand.

"I'm not interested in buying any books," she told him. "Nor anything else."

The young man laughed brightly. "This book, Madam," he said, "is not for sale. It is a gift to you from the company I represent."

"Yes, I know," she answered. "A gift if I subscribe to what?"

The young man lowered his arm, slightly abashed.

"Well?" she asked, raising her eyebrows and putting her head to one side. "Am I right?"

The young man gave another slight laugh. "I can see that you've learned, Madam, that we don't get anything in this world for nothing. A lot of people haven't learned that, and I guess you must be cleverer than average." For a minute he combed his mind to gather up the first rules of salesmanship, which lay scattered there. Then he went on with more assurance. "No, this book is not exactly free, and yet it is free in the sense that you will not actually be paying for this book. What you will be paying for is a three-year subscription to *Good Homes Magazine*. And you will be paying the exact price you would pay if you went to your local dealer. But by taking a subscription now from me, you also will receive this book of five hundred tested recipes, how to set your table for any occasion, and other helpful household hints. So, you see, in a manner of speaking, this book *is* absolutely free. And what is more, Madam, you are permitted to take it now, look it over, and return it to me if you decide you do not care to take a subscription to *Good Homes*."

He smiled triumphantly at her. "Could anything be fairer than that?"

Mrs. Grannis had heard his speech coldly, but now suddenly she opened the door wider and extended her hand for the book. "How long can I keep it before I decide?" she asked.

"For five days, Madam," he told her. Then he dropped his professional manner, and his voice changed. "To tell you the truth, we are supposed to leave them five days. And that's all right for guys that have a car and can come back for them. But I got to figure differently. It's like this—I go to one of these suburbs and spend a day there. I leave a book, if that's what the lady of the house wants, and then I stop by later in the day and pick it up. You see, we're responsible for the books we hand out, and if you don't take a subscription you can't keep the book. The company couldn't afford it. Why, those books cost three dollars to buy."

She stepped back and laid the book on the hall table. "I see," she said. "Well, I'll let you know."

There was something in her gesture that caused the young man to clear his throat anxiously before he spoke again. "May I ask what time will be most convenient for you?"

"Oh, any time," she answered. "I'll be in, all right."

His face cleared. "Well, let's see," he said. "It isn't ten yet and I'll come back about three. That'll give me plenty of time to cover this neighborhood, come back and write out your subscription, and grab a train back to New York. Now, don't think I am too confident, Madam, but I can safely say it will be worth your while to retain the book *plus* receiving *Good Homes* for three entire years."

He refastened the catch of his briefcase and tucked it under his arm. There was a dark spot where the moisture from his hand had stained the leather. He felt very thirsty and wondered if he dared ask for a drink of water. But the lady acted strange. To be sure, she had taken the book, but you never could tell how people were going to act if you asked for a favor. She might think he was trying to get fresh.

So with the sun beating on his head, he stepped back from the door, smiling. "Good day, Madam," he said. "I will be back later."

Halfway down the path, he turned and called to her. "You're the first lady that's taken a book today. It must be good luck or something."

Mrs. Grannis closed the door and walked into the living room. The glare of the sun hurt her eyes and she lowered the shades. Even then, because of the newness of the light, shiny maple furniture, the room had a sort of glint. She lay down on the couch and closed her eyes, trying to decide whether or not to put on her things and run in to see the girls at the office. She could tell them about the house, she thought, and might even ask them out to see it sometime, although she had almost decided to drop them gradually. Still, you had to see somebody, and with Joe's friends acting the way they did, there didn't seem to be much to look forward to in that direction. The dimness of the room soothed her and she fell asleep.

It was after twelve when she woke up, and her head felt stuffy. She made herself a glass of iced tea, heavily sugared, and toasted a cheese sandwich on the electric grill. Then she dressed leisurely and started for the center of the village. It was almost three when she arrived back home, her hair freshly washed and waved, her face flushed from sitting under the drier. Remembering the young man, she glanced anxiously up and down the street, but he was not in sight. Upstairs, she took off her street things and slipped once more into her housecoat. Then, carefully turning back the taffeta spread from her bed, she lay down and lit a cigarette. She heard the bell ring in the kitchen and, propping herself up on one elbow, she peered cautiously out the window. On the steps below stood the young man, who had come for his book. His clothes were even limper than they had been in the morning and he leaned against the side of the door ready to spring into alert attention at the sound of footsteps. She let the curtain drop and lay back on the bed, smoking and staring at the ceiling. The bell rang again, and then, after a few minutes, more urgently.

For a long while she lay there listening to the bell and then she got up and walked silently down the stairs. She picked up the book from the hall table and carried it back to her room. In a few minutes she heard steps once more on the outside walk and the bell began, persistently now. She sat up on the edge of the bed and, taking the book, deliberately and slowly ripped the pages out. When they all lay scattered on the bed beside her, she began tearing them across. With some difficulty she bent the cover. Then, gathering the pieces together, she went to the window and opened it.

The young man looked up at her and the expression on his face changed. He began to smile. "Wake you up?" he asked pleasantly.

She fumbled with the screen and slowly let the torn pages of the book fall to the grass below.

For a minute the young man stared at them, dazed. Without a word he stooped to pick them up, but realizing the hopelessness of his task, he straightened and stood staring up at the window. For a dreadful moment they looked at one another. Then he turned and walked away.

She fastened the screen, lit a cigarette, and lay down again on the bed, smoking and staring at the ceiling.

Shirley Jackson, who died in 1965, first achieved fame with her short story, "The Lottery." She was fascinated with the eerie and the bizarre as illustrated in her novel, We Have Always Lived in the Castle.

In "The Beautiful Stranger," one of her early short stories, she develops a cryptic tale about a dissatisfied suburban housewife.

The Beautiful Stranger

Shirley Jackson

What might be called the first intimation of strangeness occurred at the railroad station. She had come with her children, Smalljohn and her baby girl, to meet her husband when he returned from a business trip to Boston. Because she had been oddly afraid of being late, and perhaps even seeming uneager to encounter her husband after a week's separation, she dressed the children and put them into the car at home a long half hour before the train was due. As a result, of course, they had to wait interminably at the station, and what was to have been a charmingly staged reunion, family embracing husband and father, became at last an ill-timed and awkward performance. Smalljohn's hair was mussed, and he was sticky. The baby was cross, pulling at her pink bonnet and her dainty lace-edged dress, whining. The final arrival of the train caught them in mid-movement, as it were; Margaret was tying the ribbons on the baby's bonnet, Smalljohn was half over the back of the car seat. They scrambled out of the car, cringing from the sound of the train, hopelessly out of sorts.

John Senior waved from the high steps of the train. Unlike his wife and children, he looked utterly prepared for his return, as though he had taken some pains to secure a meeting at least painless, and had, in fact, stood just so, waving cordially from the steps of the train, for perhaps as long as half an hour ensuring that he should not be caught half-ready, his hand not lifted so far as to overemphasize the extent of his delight in seeing them again.

His wife had an odd sense of lost time. Standing now on the platform with the baby in her arms and Smalljohn beside her, she could not for a minute remember clearly whether he was coming home, or whether they were yet standing here to say good-by to him. They had been quarreling when he left, and she had spent the week of his absence determining to forget that in his presence she had been frightened and hurt. This will be a good time to get things straight, she had been telling herself; while John is gone I can try to get hold of myself again. Now, unsure at last whether this was an arrival or a departure, she felt afraid again, straining to meet an unendurable tension.

This will not do, she thought, believing that she was being honest with herself, and as he came down the train steps and walked toward them she smiled, holding the baby tightly against her so that the touch of its small warmth might bring some genuine tenderness into her smile.

This will not do, she thought, and smiled more cordially and told him "hello" as he came to her. Wondering, she kissed him and then when he held his arm around her and the baby for a minute the baby pulled back and struggled, screaming. Everyone moved in anger, and the baby kicked and screamed, "No, no, no."

"What a way to say hello to Daddy," Margaret said, and she shook the baby, half-amused, and yet grateful for the baby's sympathetic support. John turned to Smalljohn and lifted him, Smalljohn kicking and laughing helplessly. "Daddy, Daddy," Smalljohn shouted, and the baby screamed, "No, no."

Helplessly because no one could talk with the baby screaming so, they turned and went to the car. When the baby was back in her pink basket in the car, and Smalljohn was settled with another lollipop beside her, there was an appalling quiet which would have to be filled as quickly as possible with meaningful words. John had taken the driver's seat in the car while Margaret was quieting the baby, and when Margaret got in beside him she felt a little chill of animosity at the sight of his hands on the wheel; I can't bear to relinquish even this much, she thought; for a week no one has driven the car except me. Because she could see so clearly that this was unreasonable—John owned half the car, after all—she said to him with bright interest, "And how was your trip? The weather?"

"Wonderful," he said, and again she was angered at the warmth in his tone; if she was unreasonable about the car, he was surely unreasonable to have enjoyed himself quite so much. "Everything went very well. Im pretty sure I got the contract, everyone was very pleasant about it, and I go back in two weeks to settle everything."

The stinger is in the tail, she thought. He wouldn't tell it all so hastily if he didn't want me to miss half of it; I am supposed to be pleased that he got the contract and that everyone was so pleasant, and the part about going back is supposed to slip past me painlessly.

"Maybe I can go with you, then," she said. "Your mother will take the children."

"Fine," he said, but it was much too late; he had hesitated noticeably before he spoke.

"I want to go too," said Smalljohn. "Can I go with Daddy?"

They came into their house, Margaret carrying the baby, and John carrying his suitcase and arguing delightedly with Smalljohn over which of them was carrying the heavier weight of it. The house was ready for them; Margaret had made sure that it was cleaned and emptied of the qualities which attached so surely to her position of wife alone with small children; the toys which Smalljohn had thrown around with unusual freedom were picked up, the baby's clothes (no one, after all, came to call when John was gone) were taken from the kitchen radiator where they had been drying. Aside from the fact that the house gave no impression of waiting for any particular people, but only for anyone well-bred and clean enough to fit within its small trim walls, it could have passed for a home, Margaret thought, even for a home where a happy family lived in domestic peace. She set the baby down in the playpen and turned with the baby's bonnet and jacket in her hand and saw her husband, head bent gravely as he listened to Smalljohn. Who? she wondered suddenly; is he taller? That is not my husband.

She laughed, and they turned to her, Smalljohn curious, and her husband with a quick bright recognition; she thought, why, it is *not* my husband, and he knows that I have seen it. There was no astonishment in her; she would have thought perhaps thirty seconds before that such a thing was impossible, but since it was now clearly possible, surprise would have been meaningless. Some other emotion was necessary, but she found at first only peripheral manifestations of one. Her heart was beating violently, her hands were shaking, and her fingers were cold. Her legs felt weak and she took hold of the back of a chair to steady herself. She found that she was still laughing, and then her emotion caught up with her and she knew what it was: it was relief.

"I'm glad you came," she said. She went over and put her head against his shoulder. "It was hard to say hello in the station," she said.

Smalljohn looked on for a minute and then wandered off to his toybox. Margaret was thinking this is not the man who enjoyed seeing me cry; I need not be afraid. She caught her breath and was quiet; there was nothing that needed saying.

For the rest of the day she was happy. There was a constant delight in the relief from her weight of fear and unhappiness, it was pure joy to know that there was no longer any residue of suspicion and hatred; when she called him "John" she did so demurely, knowing that he participated in her secret amusement; when he answered her civilly there was, she thought, an edge of laughter behind his words. They seemed to have agreed soberly that mention of the subject would be in bad taste, might even, in fact, endanger their pleasure.

They were hilarious at dinner. John would not have made her a cocktail, but when she came downstairs from putting the children to bed the stranger met her at the foot of the stairs, smiling up at her, and took her arm to lead her into the living room where the cocktail shaker and glasses stood on the low table before the fire.

"How nice," she said, happy that she had taken a moment to brush her hair and put on fresh lipstick, happy that the coffee table which she had chosen with John and the fireplace which had seen many fires built by John and the low sofa where John had slept sometimes, had all seen fit to welcome the stranger with grace. She sat on the sofa and smiled at him when he handed her a glass; there was an odd illicit excitement in all of it; she was "entertaining" a man. The scene was a little marred by the fact that he had given her a martini with neither olive nor onion; it was the way she preferred her martini, and yet he should not have, strictly, known this, but she reassured herself with the thought that naturally he would have taken some pains to inform himself before coming.

He lifted his glass to her with a smile; he is here only because I am here, she thought.

"It's nice to be here," he said. He had, then, made one attempt to sound like John, in the car coming home. After he knew that she had recognized him for a stranger, he had never made any attempt to say words like "coming home" or "getting back," and of course she could not, not without pointing her lie. She put her hand in his and lay back against the sofa, looking into the fire.

"Being lonely is worse than anything in the world," she said.

"You're not lonely now?"

"Are you going away?"

"Not unless you come too." They laughed at his parody of John.

They sat next to each other at dinner; she and John had always sat at formal opposite ends of the table, asking one another politely to pass the salt and the butter.

"I'm going to put in a little set of shelves over there," he said, nodding toward the corner of the dining room. "It looks empty here, and it needs things. Symbols."

"Like?" She liked to look at him; his hair, she thought, was a little darker than John's, and his hands were stronger; this man would build whatever he decided he wanted built.

"We need things together. Things we like, both of us. Small delicate pretty things. Ivory."

With John she would have felt is necessary to remark at once that they could not afford such delicate pretty things, and put a cold finish to the idea, but with the stranger she said, "We'd have to look for them; not everything would be right."

"I saw a little creature once," he said. "Like a tiny little man, only colored all purple and blue and gold."

She remembered this conversation; it contained the truth like a jewel set in the evening. Much later, she was to tell herself that it was true; John could not have said these things.

She was happy, she was radiant, she had no conscience. He went obediently to his office the next morning, saying good-by at the door with a rueful smile that seemed to mock the present necessity for doing the things that John always did, and as she watched him go down the walk she reflected that this was surely not going to be permanent; she could not endure having him gone for so long every day, although she had felt little about parting from John; moreover, if he kept doing John's things he might grow imperceptibly more like John. We will simply have to go away, she thought. She was pleased, seeing him get into the car; she would gladly share with him—indeed, give him outright—all that had been John's, so long as he stayed her stranger.

She laughed while she did her housework and dressed the baby. She took satisfaction in unpacking his suitcase, which he had abandoned and forgotten in a corner of the bedroom, as though prepared to take it up and leave again if she had not been as he thought her, had not wanted him to stay. She put away his clothes, so disarmingly like John's and wondered for a minute at the closet; would there be a kind of delicacy in him about John's things? Then she told herself no, not so long as he began with John's wife, and laughed again.

The baby was cross all day, but when Smalljohn came home from nursery school his first question was—looking up eagerly—"Where is Daddy?"

"Daddy has gone to the office," and again she laughed, at the moment's quick sly picture of the insult to John.

Half a dozen times during the day she went upstairs, to look at his suitcase and touch the leather softly. She glanced constantly as she passed through the dining room into the corner where the small shelves would be someday, and told herself that they would find a tiny little man, all purple and blue and gold, to stand on the shelves and guard them from intrusion.

When the children awakened from their naps she took them for a walk and then, away from the house and returned violently to her former lonely pattern (walk with the children, talk meaninglessly of Daddy, long for someone to talk to in the evening ahead, restrain herself from hurrying home: he might have telephoned), she began to feel frightened again; suppose she had been wrong? It would not be possible that she was mistaken; it would be unutterably cruel for John to come home tonight.

Then, she heard the car stop and when she opened the door and looked up she thought, no, it is not my husband, with a return of gladness. She was aware from his smile that he had perceived her doubts, and yet he was so clearly a stranger that, seeing him, she had no need of speaking.

She asked him, instead, almost meaningless questions during that evening, and his answers were important only because she was storing them away to reassure herself while he was away. She asked him what was the name of their Shakespeare professor in college, and who was that girl he liked so before he met Margaret. When he smiled and said that he had no idea, that he would not recognize the name if she told him, she was in delight. He had not bothered to master all of the past, then; he had learned enough (the names of the children, the location of the house, how she liked her cocktails) to get to her, and after that, it was not important, because either she would want him to stay, or she would, calling upon John, send him away again.

"What is your favorite food?" she asked him. "Are you fond of fishing? Did you ever have a dog?"

"Someone told me today," he said once, "that he had heard I was back from Boston, and I distinctly thought he said that he heard I was dead in Boston."

He was lonely, too, she thought with sadness, and that is why he came, bringing a destiny with him: now I will see him come every evening through the door and think, this is not my husband, and wait for him remembering that I am waiting for a stranger.

"At any rate," she said, "*you* were not dead in Boston, and nothing else matters."

She saw him leave in the morning with a warm pride, and she did her housework and dressed the baby; when Smalljohn came home from nursery school he did not ask, but looked with quick searching eyes and then sighed. While the children were taking their naps she thought that she might take them to the park this afternoon, and then the thought of another such afternoon, another long afternoon with no one but the children, another afternoon of widowhood, was more than she could submit to; I have done this too much, she thought, I must see something today beyond the faces of my children. No one should be so much alone.

Moving quickly, she dressed and set the house to rights. She called a high-school girl and asked if she would take the children to the park; without guilt, she neglected the thousand small orders regarding the proper jacket for the baby, whether Smalljohn might have popcorn, when to bring them home. She fled, thinking, I must be with people.

She took a taxi into town, because it seemed to her that the only possible thing to do was to seek out a gift for him, her first gift to him, and she thought she would find him, perhaps, a little creature all blue and purple and gold.

She wandered through the strange shops in the town, choosing small lovely things to stand on the new shelves, looking long and critically at ivories, at small statues, at brightly colored meaningless expensive toys, suitable for giving to a stranger.

It was almost dark when she started home, carrying her packages. She looked from the window of the taxi into the dark streets, and thought with pleasure that the stranger would be home before her, and look from the window to see her hurrying to him; he would think, this is a stranger, I am waiting for a stranger, as he saw her coming. "Here," she said, tapping on the glass, "right here, driver." She got out of the taxi and paid the driver, and smiled as he drove away. I must look well, she thought, the driver smiled back at me.

She turned and started for the house, and then hesitated; surely she had come too far? This is not possible, she thought, this cannot be; surely our house was white?

The evening was very dark, and she could see only the houses going in rows, with more rows beyond them and more rows beyond that, and somewhere a house which was hers, with the beautiful stranger inside, and she lost out here.

The solitary poet, Emily Dickinson (1830–1886), lived and died in Amherst, Massachusetts. A shy woman, Emily Dickinson was a recluse who never went farther than her garden gate. In her lifetime, only two of her poems were published and those without her consent. In fact, she was such a private person that she requested her manuscripts be burned after her death. Fortunately for us this request was denied. She is one of the great American poets.

In the poem, "She rose to his requirement," Emily Dickinson depicts the joys of a woman whose husband appreciates what she has given up to marry him.

She rose to his requirement, dropped
The playthings of her life
To take the honorable work
Of woman and of wife.

If aught she missed in her new day
Of amplitude, or awe,
Or first prospective, or the gold
In using wore away,

It lay unmentioned, as the sea
Develops pearl and weed,
But only to himself is known
The fathoms they abide.

DISCUSSION TOPICS

1. Housewives like Dorothy Grannis spend a great deal of their time waiting for something to happen. Support or refute this statement.

2. Describe what happens to Margaret after she steps out of the cab at the end of "The Beautiful Stranger."

3. Read several of Emily Dickinson's poems and from the poems alone describe the kind of woman you think she was.

SUGGESTED ACTIVITIES

1. Do a time study of the daily activities of a housewife following her regular routine. Prepare a chart indicating the amount of time spent on particular activities such as cleaning, ironing, shopping, tending to children, pursuing individual interests, etc.

2. Examine the lyrics of songs that have been popular over the last forty years. From these lyrics, deduce the image of the woman that was favored in each decade and report the findings to the group.

21

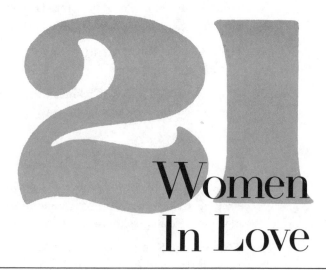

Women In Love

When men and women fall in love there is often a complete reversal of self. They feel exquisite joy and pain, sometimes simultaneously. For the sake of a beloved they will even reject institutions and ideas and morals that they have always cherished. Few of us can love so purely that we do not need a return for our feelings. We hope that the one we love will show a concern for us that equals our concern for them. In the past the idea of love being life or death to a woman has been almost universally accepted. Too often a woman springs to mind when we picture the unrequited lover who pines away until death grants relief, the jilted lover who is embittered and becomes a recluse, the abandoned lover who spends a lifetime saying <u>mea culpa</u>, or the unfaithful lover who takes religious vows as means of atonement.

While it has been thought that love is less important to a man than it is to a woman, love was not all that important to a woman either. Getting and keeping a man and having children were the ultimate goals of womanhood.

In contrast, the woman who did not marry was pitied and sometimes resented. Frequently her attempts to create an identity for herself as a free and independent human being were smothered. The woman who made her own choices and accepted the consequences of her action was regarded, when she could be found, as something of a "freak."

The sardonic, scathing wit of Dorothy Parker was enjoyed by all except those at whom it was aimed. Her long and varied writing career began in 1916 when she joined the staff of Vanity Fair, *a popular magazine of the time. In addition to her writing, she worked actively for many political causes. In fact, she was arrested in Boston while protesting against the execution of Sacco and Van-* zetti.* *Besides short stories, Ms. Parker wrote poems, screen plays, and served as a critic for the* New Yorker. *Among her principal works are* Enough Rope, Death and Taxes *and* Here Lies.

* Nicola Sacco and Bartolomeo Vanzetti were two immigrant anarchists who were indicted, tried, and found guilty of murder in South Braintree, Massachusetts.

"A Telephone Call" is a typical Dorothy Parker short story. At first glance, it may seem funny, however, the careful reader will soon see that underneath the humor lies an essentially tragic picture.

A Telephone Call

Dorothy Parker

Please, God, let him telephone me now. Dear God, let him call me now. I won't ask anything else of You, truly I won't. It isn't very much to ask. It would be so little to You, God, such a little, little thing. Only let him telephone now. Please, God. Please, please, please.

If I didn't think about it, maybe the telephone might ring. Sometimes it does that. If I could think of something else. If I could think of something else. Maybe if I counted five hundred by fives, it might ring by that time. I'll count slowly. I won't cheat. And if it rings when I get to three hundred, I won't stop; I won't answer it until I get to five hundred. Five, ten, fifteen, twenty, twenty-five, thirty, thirty-five, forty, forty-five, fifty. . . . Oh, please ring. Please.

This is the last time I'll look at the clock. I will not look at it again. It's ten minutes past seven. He said he would telephone at five o'clock. "I'll call you at five, darling." I think that's where he said "darling." I'm almost sure he said it there. I know he called me "darling" twice, and the other time was when he said good-by. "Good-by, darling." He was busy, and he can't say much in the office, but he called me "darling" twice. He couldn't have minded my calling him up. I know you shouldn't keep telephoning them—I know they don't like that. When you do that, they know you are thinking about them and wanting them, and that makes them hate you. But I hadn't talked to him in three days—not in three days. And all I did was ask him how he was; it was just the way anybody might have called him up. He couldn't have minded that. He couldn't have thought I was bothering him. "No, of course you're not," he said. And he said he'd telephone me. He didn't have to say that. I didn't ask him to, truly I didn't. I'm sure I didn't. I don't think he would say he'd telephone me, and then just never do it. Please don't let him do that, God. Please don't.

"I'll call you at five, darling." "Good-by, darling." He was busy, and he was in a hurry, and there were people around him, but he called me "darling" twice. That's mine, that's mine. I have that, even if I never see him again. Oh, that's so little. That isn't enough. Nothing's enough, if I never see him again. Please let me see him again, God. Please, I want him so much. I want him so much. I'll be good, God. I will try to be better, I will, if You will let me see him again. If You will let him telephone me. Oh, let him telephone me now.

Ah, don't let my prayer seem too little to You, God. You sit up there, so white and old, with all the angels about You and the stars slipping by. And I come to You with a prayer about a telephone call. Ah, don't laugh, God. You see, You don't know how it feels. You're so safe, there on Your throne, with the blue swirling under You. Nothing can touch You; no one can twist Your heart in his hands. This is suffering, God, this is bad, bad suffering. Won't You help me? For Your Son's sake, help me. You said You would do whatever was asked of You in His name. Oh, God, in the name of Thine only beloved Son, Jesus Christ, our Lord, let him telephone me now.

I must stop this. I mustn't be this way. Look. Suppose a young man says he'll call a girl up, and then something happens, and he doesn't. That isn't so terrible, is it? Why, it's going on all over the world, right this minute. Oh what do I care what's going on all over the world? Why can't that telephone ring? Why can't it, why can't it? Couldn't you ring? Ah, please, couldn't you? You damned, ugly, shiny thing. It would hurt you to ring, wouldn't it? Oh, that would hurt you. Damn you, I'll pull your filthy roots out of the wall, I'll smash your smug black face in little bits. Damn you to hell.

No, no, no. I must stop. I must think about something else. This is what I'll do. I'll put the clock in the other room. Then I can't look at it. If I do have to look at it, then I'll have to walk into the bedroom, and that will be something to do. Maybe, before I look at it again, he will call me. I'll be so sweet to him, if he calls me. If he says he can't see me tonight, I'll say, "Why, that's all right, dear. Why, of course it's all right." I'll be the way I was when I first met him. Then maybe he'll like me again. I was always sweet, at first. Oh, it's so easy to be sweet to people before you love them.

I think he must still like me a little. He couldn't have called me "darling" twice today, if he didn't still like me a little. It isn't all gone, if he still likes me a little; even if it's only a little, little bit. You see, God, if You would just let him telephone me, I wouldn't have to ask You anything more. I would be sweet to him, I would be gay, I would be just the way I used to be, and then he would love me again. And then I would never have to ask You for anything more. Don't You see, God? So won't You please let him telephone me? Won't You please, please, please?

Are You punishing me, God, because I've been bad? Are You angry with me because I did that? Oh, but, God, there are so many bad people —You could not be hard only to me. And it wasn't very bad; it couldn't have been bad. We didn't hurt anybody, God. Things are only bad when they hurt people. We didn't hurt one single soul; You know that. You know it wasn't bad, don't You, God? So won't You let him telephone me now?

If he doesn't telephone me, I'll know God is angry with me. I'll count five hundred by fives, and if he hasn't called me then, I will know God isn't going to help me, ever again. That will be the sign. Five, ten, fifteen, twenty, twenty-five, thirty, thirty-five, forty, forty-five, fifty, fifty-five. . . . It was bad. I knew it was bad. All right, God, send me to hell. You think You're frightening me with Your hell, don't You? You think Your hell is worse than mine.

I mustn't. I mustn't do this. Suppose he's a little late calling me up—that's nothing to get hysterical about. Maybe he isn't going to call—maybe he's coming straight up here without telephoning. He'll be cross if he sees I have been crying. They

don't like you to cry. He doesn't cry. I wish to God I could make him cry. I wish I could make him cry and tread the floor and feel his heart heavy and big and festering in him. I wish I could hurt him like hell.

He doesn't wish that about me. I don't think he even knows how he makes me feel. I wish he could know, without my telling him. They don't like you to tell them they've made you cry. They don't like you to tell them you're unhappy because of them. If you do, they think you're possessive and exacting. And then they hate you. They hate you whenever you say anything you really think. You always have to keep playing little games. Oh, I thought we didn't have to; I thought this was so big I could say whatever I meant. I guess you can't, ever. I guess there isn't ever anything big enough for that. Oh, if he would just telephone, I wouldn't tell him I had been sad about him. They hate sad people. I would be so sweet and so gay, he couldn't help but like me. If he would only telephone. If he would only telephone.

Maybe that's what he is doing. Maybe he is coming on here without calling me up. Maybe he's on his way now. Something might have happened to him. No, nothing could ever happen to him. I can't picture anything happening to him. I never picture him run over. I never see him lying still and long and dead. I wish he were dead. That's a terrible wish. That's a lovely wish. If he were dead, he would be mine. If he were dead, I would never think of now and the last few weeks. I would remember only the lovely times. It would be all beautiful. I wish he were dead. I wish he were dead, dead, dead.

This is silly. It's silly to go wishing people were dead just because they don't call you up the very minute they said they would. Maybe the clock's fast; I don't know whether it's right. Maybe he's hardly late at all. Anything could have made him a little late. Maybe he had to stay at his office Maybe he went home, to call me up from there, and somebody came in. He doesn't like to telephone me in front of people. Maybe he's worried, just a little, little bit, about keeping me waiting. He might even hope that I would call him up. I could do that. I could telephone him.

I mustn't. I mustn't, I mustn't. Oh, God, please don't let me telephone him. Please keep me from doing that. I know, God, just as well as You do, that if he were worried about me, he'd telephone no matter where he was or how many people there were around him. Please make me know that. God. I don't ask You to make it easy for me—You can't do that, for all that You could make a world. Only let me know it, God. Don't let me go on hoping. Don't let me say comforting things to myself. Please don't let me hope, dear God. Please don't.

I won't telephone him. I'll never telephone him again as long as I live. He'll rot in hell, before I'll call him up. You don't have to give me strength, God; I have it myself. If he wanted me, he could get me. He knows where I am. He knows I'm waiting here. He's so sure of me, so sure. I wonder why they hate you, as soon as they are sure of you. I should think it would be so sweet to be sure.

It would be so easy to telephone him. Then I'd know. Maybe it wouldn't be a foolish thing to do. Maybe he wouldn't mind. Maybe he'd like it. Maybe he has been trying to get me. Sometimes people try and try to get you on the telephone, and they say the number doesn't answer. I'm not just saying that to help myself; that really happens. You know that really happens, God. Oh, God, keep me away from that telephone. Keep me away. Let me still have just a little bit of pride. I think I'm going to need it, God. I think it will be all I'll have.

Oh, what does pride matter, when I can't stand it if I don't talk to him? Pride like that is such a silly, shabby little thing. The real pride, the big pride, is in having no pride. I'm not saying that just because I want to call him. That's true, I know that's true. I will be big. I will be beyond little prides.

Please, God, keep me from telephoning him. Please, God.

I don't see what pride has to do with it. This is such a little thing, for me to be bringing in pride, for me to be making such a fuss about. I may have misunderstood him. Maybe he said for me to call him up, at five. "Call me at five, darling." He could have said that, perfectly well. It's so possible that I didn't hear him right. "Call me at five, darling." I'm almost sure that's what he said. God, don't let me talk this way to myself. Make me know, please make me know.

I'll think about something else. I'll just sit quietly. If I could sit still. If I could sit still. Maybe I could read. Oh, all the books are about people who love each other, truly and sweetly. What do they want to write about that for? Don't they know it isn't true? Don't they know it's a lie, it's a God damned lie? What do they have to tell about that for, when they know how it hurts? Damn them, damn them, damn them.

I won't. I'll be quiet. This is nothing to get excited about. Look. Suppose he were someone I didn't know very well. Suppose he were another girl. Then I'd just telephone and say, "Well, for goodness' sake, what happened to you" That's what I'd do, and I'd never even think about it. Why can't I be casual and natural, just because I love him? I can be. Honestly, I can be. I'll call him up, and be so easy and pleasant. You see if I won't, God. Oh, don't let me call him. Don't, don't, don't.

God, aren't You really going to let him call me? Are You sure, God? Couldn't You please relent? Couldn't You? I don't even ask You to let him telephone me this minute, God; only let him do it in a little while. I'll count five hundred by fives. I'll do it so slowly and so fairly. If he hasn't telephoned then, I'll call him. I will. Oh, please, dear God, dear kind God, my blessed Father in Heaven, let him call before then. Please, God. Please.

Five, ten, fifteen, twenty, twenty-five, thirty, thirty-five. . . .

Edna St. Vincent Millay was still a student at Vassar when her first major poem, "Renascence," was published in 1912. Like many artists of that period, she spent her early writing years in Greenwich Village where, according to her, all the artists and writers were "very, very poor and very, very merry." In 1923 she was awarded the Pulitzer Prize for poetry for The Harp Weaver. Other Millay works include A Few Figs From Thistles, Wine From These Grapes, and Make Bright The Arrows.

"The Merry Maid" presents a picture of one who has adopted an air of sophistication and nonchalance to cover up a heart broken by an unhappy love affair.

The Merry Maid

Edna St. Vincent Millay

Oh, I am grown so free from care
　　Since my heart broke!
I set my throat against the air,
　　I laugh at simple folk!

There's little kind and little fair
　　Is worth its weight in smoke
To me, that's grown so free from care
　　Since my heart broke!
Lass, if to sleep you would repair

　　As peaceful as you woke,
Best not besiege your lover there
　　For just the words he spoke
To me, that's grown so free from care
　　Since my heart broke!

In the few short years of her creative period, 1921 to 1928, Elinor Wylie produced prose and verse which received high critical acclaim. After her death in 1928, critic Louis Untermeyer wrote "She lived in her work with a vehement exclusiveness; she was a fever of creation." Among her principal poetry works are Trivial Breath and Angels and Earthly Creatures. Outstanding among her prose works are The Venetian Glass Nephew and Mr. Hodge and Mr. Hazard.

Ms. Wylie's "Fair Annet" is the new woman. She is sure enough of herself to accept things as they come, appreciate them while they are there, and intelligent enough not to rage against things that cannot be changed.

Fair Annet's Song

Elinor Wylie

One thing comes and another thing goes:
Frosts in November drive away the rose;
Like a blowing ember the windflower blows
And drives away the snows.

It is sad to remember and sorrowful to pray:
Let us laugh and be merry, who have seen today
The last of the cherry and the first of the may;
And neither one will stay.

DISCUSSION TOPICS

1. Describe what He is doing while She is waiting for the call in Dorothy Parker's short story, "A Telephone Call."

2. "The Merry Maid," "Fair Annet," and our nameless heroine in "A Telephone Call" have each been told by their lovers that their relationship has ended. What kind of written reply would each of them send?

SUGGESTED ACTIVITIES

1. Arrange to have four adult women on a panel discussing the IDEAL and REAL relationship between men and women in love. Be sure to include single as well as married women of varied ages.

2. Acting as "inquiring reporters," ask a cross section of the community, young people and adults alike, to choose the first word or group of words that comes to mind as descriptive of a single adult male and single adult female. Break down the replies for each sex from most to least pejorative.

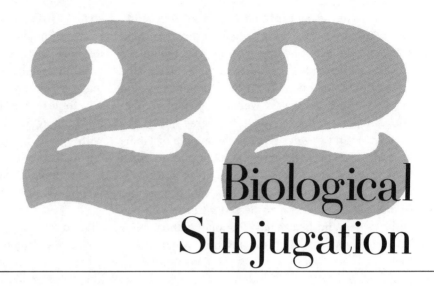

22
Biological Subjugation

Some opponents of the movement for the liberation of women argue, in part, that certain functions of women limit their freedom. Women give birth to and raise children, and in today's society, motherhood is an almost sacred institution.

It is true that at this time, only women can bear children. But sometimes a woman, for her own reasons, is unwilling or unable to accept the "duties and obligations" of propagating the human race. Others accept these "duties and obligations," but fail at them. The pressure of family, friends, and society on such a woman can make her feel incomplete and aggravate her already strong sense of failure.

One of the outstanding woman writers about contemporary America is Mary McCarthy, known for her satirical view of life. In 1933 she received her A.B. from Vassar, the college which the girls in The Group *attended. Some of Ms. McCarthy's other well-known works are* Memories of A Catholic Girlhood, A Charmed Life, *and her most recent book,* Birds of America.

There were eight girls in "the group" that graduated from Vassar in the 1930s. The selection presented here concentrates on Priss Hartshorn Crockett, who has just given birth to her first child.

The Group
Mary McCarthy

Priss Hartshorn Crockett was nursing her baby. That was the big news. "I never expected a breast-fed grandson," said Priss's mother, laughing and accepting a martini from her son-in-law, Dr. Sloan Crockett, the budding pediatrician. It was the cocktail hour in Priss's room at New York Hospital —terribly gay. Over the weekend, Sloan stopped in every afternoon and shook up martinis for visitors. He had done his residency at the hospital, so that he could get ice from the diet kitchen and generally break the rules.

"You never expected a *g-grandson*, Mother," pointed out Priss with her slight nervous stammer from the bed. She was wearing a pale-blue bed jacket, and her thin ashy hair was set in waves; the student nurse had done it for her that morning. On her lips, which were dry, was a new shade of lipstick, by Tussy; her doctor had ordered her to put on lipstick and powder right in the middle of labor; he and Sloan both thought it was important for a maternity patient to keep herself up to the mark. Priss, whose personality was confessed to be rather colorless, looked unreal to herself sitting up in bed all bedecked and bedizened—like one of those New York children dressed in furs and trailing satins and their mothers' slippers to beg in the streets at Halloween. Little Ella Cinders, Sloan called her, after that funny in the paper. She would have been more comfortable in the short cotton hospital nightshirt that tied in back, but the floor nurses every morning made her struggle into a satin-and-lace "nightie" from her trousseau. Doctor's orders, they said.

The nurses treated Priss as a special pet because she had been in Obstetrics and Gynecology three times with miscarriages before she had made the grade. To be sure of coming to term this time, she had quit her job with the League of Women Shoppers and stayed in bed or on the sofa for the first five months of pregnancy—her uterus was retroverted. Even so, in the last month she had had a kidney complication; they had rushed her to the hospital and fed her intravenously till the inflammation went down. But now, as Mrs. Hartshorn said, the nativity had been accomplished. Glory be, on the Feast of St. Stephen, the day after Christmas, Priss had been brought to bed with a seven-and-a-half-pound son; delivery had been normal, though labor had been protracted—twenty-two hours. Her room was full of holly, mistletoe, azaleas, and cyclamen, and there was a little Christmas tree by her bedside. The child was to be called Stephen, after the first martyr.

He was in the nursery now, behind the plate-glass window at the end of the corridor—roaring his head off; his feeding time was six o'clock. Priss was drinking an eggnog, to help her lactate; liquids were very important, but she had lost her taste for milk during pregnancy, doing nothing and having to force herself to drink that quart a day that the doctors insisted on if she were not to lose her teeth building the baby's bones. Now, to tempt her, the nurses flavored her milk with egg and sugar and vanilla and gave her fruit juices on the hour and ginger ale and Coke—every kind of liquid but alcohol, for if she drank a martini, Stephen would have gin for his dinner.

Sloan rattled the ice in the silver shaker and chatted with Priss's brother, Allen, who was down for the holidays from Harvard Law. Those two were great friends, both being staunch Republicans, unlike Priss and Mrs. Hartshorn. Liberalism seemed to run in the female line: Mrs. Hartshorn and her dead husband had had a running battle over Wilson and the League, and now Priss and Sloan were at swords' points over Roosevelt and socialized medicine. It had been a red-letter day for Sloan and Allen when the Supreme Court killed the Blue Eagle and put Priss out of a job. Working for the League of Women Shoppers had never seemed as exciting to her; it was more like a volunteer thing, which had made it easier for her to resign to have Stephen.

Priss had been good about that, though she missed her work and fretted about finances, since Sloan was just getting established in practice (with an older pediatrician), and they had depended on her salary for cigarettes and concerts and theatres and contributions to charity and their library membership—Priss was a great reader. Her mother could not help very much, because she still had her two youngest in college (Linda was at Bennington), which was quite a bit for a poor widow woman, as Mrs. Hartshorn gaily called herself, to swing. She had been sending Priss her maid, the faithful Irene, to do the housework mornings, and most evenings Lily, the cook, would nip over with a casserole for Priss to heat, so that Sloan would have one good hot meal, at least, in his daily round. When Priss came home from the hospital, Irene, who had had children of her own, was to move in for two weeks and sleep on an army cot in the baby's room (the dining room as *was*) to save the cost of a practical nurse.

This was Mrs. Hartshorn's present to the young parents; to the newborn himself she was giving an English pram, a mad extravagance, and, come the spring, she was going to send them Linda's old crib, which was shut up in the attic in Oyster Bay, and her high chair and odds and ends, though high chairs, they said, were out now. For the time being, Stephen would sleep in a laundry basket on the baby-carriage mattress—quite a clever idea that Priss had got from a pamphlet on child care issued by the Department of Labor.

"Yes, my dear, no pun intended," said Mrs. Hartshorn to Polly Andrews, who had dropped in to see Priss. Allen guffawed. "Why not the Department of the Interior?" Priss winced at her brother's witticism. "The pamphlet's an excellent home manual," she said earnestly. "Sloan thinks so too, believe it or not, Allen." "Some of your friend Madam Perkins' work?" retorted Allen. In the bed, Priss grew tense, preparing an answer; her lips moved voicelessly, in spasms, "No politics today," said Mrs. Hartshorn firmly. "We've declared a moratorium. Priss has to think of her milk."

Lakey, she went on to Polly, had sent the most exquisite christening robe from Paris, fit for a dauphin—a great surprise, because she had not written for ages; she was doing her doctorate at the Sorbonne. And Pokey Prothero Beauchamp, who had had twins herself the year before, had sent a baby scale, a most thoughtful gift. Everyone had been frightfully kind. Dottie Renfrew Latham had arranged, from way out in Arizona, for Bloomingdale's to deliver a sterilizer, all complete with bottles and racks, instead of the conventional baby cup or porringer. That would come in handy later on, when Priss's milk ran out.

Mrs. Hartshorn glanced at her daughter and lowered her voice. "Just fancy little Priss being the first of your set to do it, Polly. She's so flat there she's never had to wear a brassiere. But Sloan says it's not the size that counts. I do hope he's right. The miracle of the loaves and fishes, *I* call it.

All the other babies in the nursery are on bottles. The nurses prefer it that way. I'm inclined to agree with them. Doctors are all theory. Nurses see the facts." She swallowed her martini in a single draft, like medicine; this was the style among advanced society women of her age. She wiped her lips and refused a "dividend" from the silver shaker. "Which way progress, Polly?" she demanded, in a slightly louder voice, shaking her white bobbed locks. "The bottle was the war cry of my generation. Linda was bottle-fed. And you can't imagine the difference. For us, the bottle spelled the end of colic, and the frantic young husband walking the baby all night. We swore by the bottle, we of the avant-garde. My mother-in-law was horripilated. And now, I confess, Polly, I'm horripilated myself."

Her son-in-law pricked up his ears and gave a tolerant smile. He was a tall young man with glasses and an Arrow-collar profile who had worked his way through medical school; his father, an army surgeon, had died of influenza during the war, and his mother was a housemother at a girls' school in Virginia. Priss had met him at her cousin's coming-out party junior year, through another cousin, a medical student, who had been ordered to bring some extra men.

"Medicine seems to be all cycles," continued Mrs. Hartshorn. "That's the bone I pick with Sloan. Like what's his name's new theory of history. First we nursed our babies; then science told us not to. Now it tells us we were right in the first place. Or were we wrong then but would be right now? Reminds me of relativity, if I understand Mr. Einstein."

Sloan ignored this excursion. "By nursing Stephen," he said patiently, "Priss can give him her immunities for at least the first year. He won't be liable to chicken pox or measles or whooping cough. And he will have a certain protection from colds. Of course, in some cases the mother's milk disagrees with the child. You get a rash or stomach upsets. Then you have to weigh the advantages of breast feeding against the negative side effects."

"And psychologically," appended Polly, "isn't the breast-fed baby supposed to have a warmer relation with his mother than the bottle-fed baby?" Sloan frowned. "Psychology is still a long way from being a science," he declared. "Let's stick to measurable facts. Demonstrable facts. We can demonstrate that the breast-fed infant gets his mother's immunities. And we know from the scales that Stephen is gaining. An ounce a day, Cousin Louisa." This was his name for Mrs. Hartshorn. "You can't argue with the scales."

The sound of a baby's crying made itself heard in the silence that followed this speech. "That's Stephen again," said Mrs. Hartshorn. "I recognize his voice. He yells louder than any other baby in the nursery." "Shows he's a healthy young fellow," replied Sloan. "Time to worry if he didn't cry for his dinner. Eh, Priss?" Priss smiled wanly. "Sloan says it's good for his lungs," she said, grimacing. "Develops them," agreed Sloan. "Like a bellows." He drew air into his chest and released it.

Mrs. Hartshorn looked at her watch. "Can't the nurse bring him in now?" she wondered. "It's quarter to six." "The *schedule*, Mother!" cried Priss. "The reason babies in your time had colic wasn't because they were breast-fed, but because they were picked up at all sorts of irregular times and fed whenever they cried. The point is to have a schedule and stick to it absolutely!"

There was a knock on the half-open door. More visitors were arriving: Connie Storey and her husband and young Dr. Edris, who had been Sloan's roommate in medical school. The conversation grew louder, and the room was full of cigarette smoke. Mrs. Hartshorn opened a window and tried to produce a *courant d'air*. What was the point of keeping the infant behind glass if he were then brought in to nurse in a smoke-filled room? "Not to mention our germs," she added, exhaling with a certain complacency, as though her germs were especially vigorous and well-pedigreed. Sloan shook his head. "A baby needs to build up some immunities before going home from the hospital. If he's never been exposed to germs, he gets sick the minute he gets home. I think we overdo the sterility business, don't you, Bill? Just a bit?" "Depends," said Dr. Edris. "You can't impress it too much on the average

mother." Sloan smiled faintly. " 'Boil baby's rattle every time he drops it,' " he quoted. "Don't you believe in boiling everything, Sloan?" anxiously demanded Priss. "That's what the child-care pamphlet says to do." "You goop," said her brother. "That pamphlet was written for slum women; by a Vassar graduate, I bet." "Rattles are out anyway," Priss replied stoutly. "Everyone knows they're unsanitary and likely to break." "A dangerous toy," agreed Sloan. There was a silence. "Sometimes Sloan likes to play the heretic," smiled Priss. "You should hear him *épater* the floor nurses." Mrs. Hartshorn nodded. "A promising sign in a doctor. Inspires confidence," she observed. "Though goodness knows why. We all trust a doctor who doesn't believe in medicine."

In the middle of the general laugh, a nurse tapped at the door. "Excuse us, ladies and gentlemen. Feeding time." When the room was cleared of guests, she closed the window Mrs. Hartshorn had opened and then brought the baby in on her shoulder. He was wearing a long white nightgown and his face was red and swollen; she placed him next to Priss in the bed. It was exactly six o'clock. "Which one is it tonight, dear?" she demanded. Priss, who had managed to lower one shoulder of her nightgown, indicated her right breast. The nurse swabbed it with cotton and alcohol and laid the baby to suck; as usual, he made a face at the alcohol and pushed the nipple away. The nurse settled it firmly in his mouth again; then she went about the room emptying ashtrays and collecting glasses to take back to the diet kitchen. "You had quite a party tonight."

To Priss, this sounded like a criticism, and she did not reply. Instead, she gritted her teeth. The baby's mouth always hurt her nipple at the beginning, like a bite. Her breasts were very sensitive, and she hated to have Sloan touch them in love-making; she had hoped that nursing the baby would get her over that. People said that nursing was very satisfying, sensually, to the mother, and she had thought that if she got in the habit with a baby, she would not mind so much with a grown man. Though she had not told Sloan, this was one of her principal reasons for agreeing to breast-feed Stephen: so that she could give Sloan, who was entitled to it, more fun in bed. But so far nursing, like most of sex, was an ordeal she had to steel herself for each time it happened by using all her will power and thinking about love and self-sacrifice. The nurse was watching her now, to make sure that the baby was drawing at the nipple properly. "Relax, Mrs. Crockett," she said kindly. "Baby can sense it if you're tense." Priss sighed and tried to let go. But naturally the more she concentrated on relaxing, the more tense she got. "Bless braces, damn relaxes," she joked feebly. "You're tired this evening," said the nurse. Priss nodded, feeling grateful that someone knew and disloyal, at the same time, to Sloan, who did not know that it wore her out to have company, especially mixed company that sat there discussing her milk.

But as the baby (she wished the nurse would call him "Stephen," not "Baby") commenced to suck rhythmically, making a little noise like a snore, Priss grew somewhat easier. She did not *enjoy* the sucking, but she liked his fresh, milky smell, which made her think of churns and dairies, and his pale fuzz of hair and his warmth. Soon she was unaware of his sucking, except as a hypnotic rhythm; the nurse put the bell in her hand and tiptoed out. Priss was almost asleep when she came to, with a start; Stephen was asleep himself. His little mouth had ceased to tug, and the noise he was making *was* a light snore. She joggled him a little, as she had been taught to do, but her nipple slipped out of his mouth. He turned his round soft head away and lay sleeping with his cheek flat on her chest. Priss was terrified; she tried to turn his head and thrust her breast into his mouth. He resisted; his little hands rose and beat feebly at her breast to push it away. She shifted her position and looked at her watch. He had only been nursing seven minutes, and he was supposed to nurse fifteen to get the milk he needed to carry him through till the next feeding, which would be at ten o'clock. She had been cautioned before not to let him fall asleep. She rang the bell, which turned the light on outside her door.

No one came; she listened; there was complete silence in the corridor. Not even the sound of a baby crying came from the far end at the nursery. They were all being fed, obviously—all but poor Stephen—and the nurses were all busy, giving them their bottles. She was always fearful of being left alone with Stephen and usually she contrived to keep a nurse with her, making conversation. But since yesterday there were two new babies in the nursery and two new mothers to care for, so that Priss had become an "old" mother, who ought to be able to look after herself. But this was the first time she had been left entirely alone; normally the nurse popped her head in the door from time to time, to see how things were going. Priss was afraid the nurses knew that she was afraid of Stephen—her own flesh and blood.

Still no one came; another three minutes had passed. She thought of Sloan, who would be in the Visitors' Lounge with her mother and Bill Edris, talking and enjoying himself; it was against the hospital rules for the husband to watch the mother nurse, and this was one rule that Sloan did not care to break. Perhaps a passing interne would notice her light. She raised her arm to look at her watch again; two more minutes gone. She felt as though she and Stephen were marooned together in eternity or tied together like prisoners in some gruesome form of punishment. It was useless to remind herself that this frightening bundle was her own child and Sloan's. Rather, she felt, to her shame, that he was a piece of hospital property that had been dumped on her and abandoned—they would never come to take him away.

Just then Stephen woke. He gave a long sigh and turned his head, burying it in her breast, and at once went back to sleep again. Priss could feel his nose pressing against her shrinking skin, and the idea that he might suffocate made her suddenly cold with fear. That was always happening to babies in their cribs. Maybe he had already suffocated; she listened and could not hear his breathing —only the loud noise of her own. Her heart was pounding with a sort of stutter. She tried to move his head gently, but again he resisted, and she was afraid of accidentally touching the soft part of his skull. But at least he was still alive. Gratefully, she tried to collect herself and make an intelligent decision. She could telephone down to the switchboard and get them to send help. But two things deterred her: first, her shyness and dislike of being a nuisance; second, the fact that the telephone was on the right side of the bed and she would have to move Stephen to reach it, but moving Stephen was just the problem. She was scared to. Scared of what, she asked herself. Scared that he might cry, she answered.

"Priss Hartshorn Crockett!" she said sternly to herself. "Are you ready to let your newborn baby die of suffocation because you're shy and/or because you can't bear to hear him cry? What would your mother think?" Determined, she half sat up, and this abrupt movement dislodged the baby, who slipped to her side in a little heap, woke up and began to cry furiously. At that moment, the door opened.

"Well, what's going on here?" exclaimed the student nurse, who was Priss's favorite; she was glad it was not the other one, at any rate. The girl, in her blue-striped uniform, picked up Stephen and cuddled him in her arms. "Have you two been having a fight?" Priss replied with a weak chime of laughter; humor was not her strong point, but now that she saw the baby safe in the nurse's strong bare arms, she laughed with relief. "Is he all right? I'm afraid I lost my head." "Stephen's just plain mad, isn't he?" the girl said, addressing the baby. "Does he want to go back to bed?" She picked up his blanket and wrapped him in it; she patted his back to "bubble" him. "No, no!" cried Priss. "Give him back, please. He hasn't finished nursing. I let him go to sleep in the middle."

"Oh, my!" said the girl. "You must have been scared, all right. I'll stay with you this time till he finishes." The baby belched, and the girl unwrapped him and laid him, under the covers, on Priss's breast. "Somebody should have come in to bubble him," she said. "He swallowed a lot of air." She gently slid the nipple into his mouth. The baby pushed it away and began to cry again. He was evidently angry. The two girls—Priss was the older —gazed at each other sadly. "Does that happen often?" said Priss. "I don't know," said the girl. "Most of our babies are bottle babies. But they do that sometimes with the bottle if the holes in the nipple aren't big enough; they get mad and push the bottle away." "Because the milk doesn't come fast enough," said Priss. "That's my trouble. But I wouldn't mind if he pushed a *b-bottle* away." Her thin little face looked rueful. "He's tired," said the student nurse. "Did you hear him this afternoon?" Priss nodded, looking down at the baby. "It's a vicious circle," she said gloomily. "He wears himself out crying because he's famished and then he's too exhausted to nurse."

The door opened again. "You left Mrs. Crockett's light on," the older nurse chided the student. "You should remember to snap it off when you come in. What was the trouble here, anyway?" "He won't nurse," said Priss. The three women looked at each other and sighed jointly. "Let's see if you have any milk left," said the older nurse finally, in a practical tone. She moved the baby's head slightly to one side and squeezed Priss's breast; a drop of watery liquid appeared. "You can try it," she conceded. "But he'll have to learn to work for his supper. The harder he works, of course, the more milk you produce. The breast should be well drained." She squeezed Priss's breast again, then clapped "Baby's" head to the moist nipple. While both nurses watched he sucked for another minute, for two minutes, and stopped. "Shall we prime the pump again?" said Priss with a feeble smile. The older nurse bent down. "The breast is empty. No sense in wearing him out for nothing. I'll take him now and weigh him."

In a moment the student nurse was back, breathless. "Two ounces!" she reported. "Shall I tell your company they can come back?" Priss was overjoyed; her supper tray appeared while she was waiting for her family to return, and she felt almost hungry. "We've heard your vital statistic," announced Mrs. Hartshorn. "Is two ounces a lot?" asked Allen dubiously. An excellent average feeding, declared Sloan: Priss's milk was highly concentrated, though the volume was not large; that was why the baby was gaining steadily, despite the little fuss he made before meals. Then they all trooped out for the evening, to let Priss have her supper in peace. Sloan was carrying the cocktail shaker; they would not need it any more in the hospital, for next weekend Priss would be home. . . .

John Ciardi has written several volumes of poetry including I Marry You *and* The Stone Works. *He is equally noted for his lively translation of Dante's* Divine Comedy. *The poem included in this selection deals with the intimacy of married life.*

Men Marry What They Need. I Marry You

John Ciardi

Men marry what they need. I marry you,
morning by morning, day by day, night by night,
and every marriage makes this marriage new.

In the broken name of heaven, in the light
that shatters granite, by the spitting shore,
in air that leaps and wobbles like a kite,

I marry you from time and a great door
is shut and stays shut against wind, sea, stone,
sunburst, and heavenfall. And home once more

inside our walls of skin and struts of bone,
man-woman, woman-man, and each the other,
I marry you by all dark and all dawn

and learn to let time spend. Why should I bother
the flies about me? Let them buzz and do.
Men marry their queen, their daughter, or their
    mother

by names they prove, but that thin buzz whines
    through:
when reason falls to reasons, cause is true.
Men marry what they need. I marry you.

DISCUSSION TOPICS

1. Read *The Group* and discuss the relationships that Priss and her classmates had with men.

2. Compose a poem from a female point of view in answer to John Ciardi's poem.

SUGGESTED ACTIVITIES

1. Prepare an anthology of poems by American men and women authors that reflect views on love and marriage. If possible, Xerox and distribute the anthology to the other members of your group.

2. Practices of childbirth and child rearing have styles and fashions just like everything else. In this century there have been many theories that have gained popularity and have later been discredited. Trace the rise and fall of some of the major trends in childbirth and child rearing in the twentieth century and relate these trends to their times.

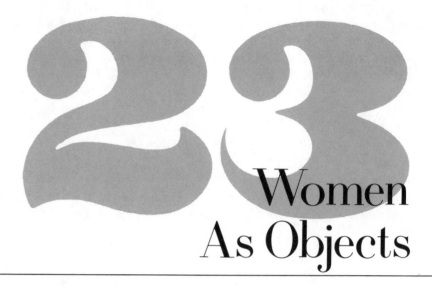

23 Women As Objects

Ideally, dignity and respect should be accorded to all human beings and, in a perfect world The Golden Rule would be honored by everyone. Each person would be sensitive to another's desires, feelings, and intelligence; someone else's ego would be as precious to us as our own. In this Utopia there would be no disparagement of ideas, no curt refusals of an overture of friendship, and no sneering at dreams. The put-down, obvious or subtle, would be dead.

The put-down is part of what the feminist movement is about. Those involved in the movement are crying for women to be treated with the dignity and respect that rightfully belong to all human beings. To many women, the automatic assumption that they are "The Weaker Sex" or "The Fair Sex" robs them of opportunities to participate fully in a modern society.

Assuming that women are weaker means that they cannot compete in the working world. The logical conclusion of this assumption is that the natural environment for a woman is the home, where she can tend the nest of her man and his young. Intelligence and sensitivity are not expected from this inferior being. Nor is she—as an inferior being—treated with intelligence and sensitivity, as is evident from remarks like: "She's smart for a woman," "Don't worry your pretty little head about it" or "Why do you want an education? You're going to get married."

One area where the "inferior" female is consciously and unconsciously insulted by the "superior" male is in the intimate relationship between one man and one woman. To prove his superiority as a present or prospective mate, the male seems compelled to boast of his past conquests as well as to be on the prowl for possible future ones. He is no more caring of his wife's or lover's feelings than he is of a chair's feeling when he sits on it. He treats the woman as an object. "The Girls in their Summer Dresses" by Irwin Shaw and "De Profundis" by Dorothy Parker reveal how the woman as object reacts to this situation.

Among the best known works of Irwin Shaw are the novels The Young Lions *and* Two Weeks in Another Town. *In addition, the New York-born author is an accomplished playwright and short story writer. Mr. Shaw's experiences as a truck driver, semi-professional ball player, and soldier in World War II have all provided him with material for his writings. "The Girls in their Summer Dresses" is considered one of the finest modern American short stories.*

"The Girls in their Summer Dresses" pictures a young married couple on a sunny Sunday in Manhattan. Although the tone at the beginning of the story is warm and optimistic, it soon changes to one of bitterness and resignation. Observe carefully how the husband treats his wife.

The Girls In Their Summer Dresses

Irwin Shaw

Fifth Avenue was shining in the sun when they left the Brevoort. The sun was warm, even though it was February, and everything looked like Sunday morning—the buses and the well-dressed people walking slowly in couples and the quiet buildings with the windows closed.

Michael held Frances' arm tightly as they walked toward Washington Square in the sunlight. They walked lightly, almost smiling, because they had slept late and had a good breakfast and it was Sunday. Michael unbuttoned his coat and let it flap around him in the mild wind.

"Look out," Frances said as they crossed Eighth Street. "You'll break your neck."

Michael laughed and Frances laughed with him.

"She's not so pretty," Frances said. "Anyway, not pretty enough to take a chance of breaking your neck."

Michael laughed again. "How did you know I was looking at her?"

Frances cocked her head to one side and smiled at her husband under the brim of her hat. "Mike, darling," she said.

"O.K.," he said. "Excuse me."

Frances patted his arm lightly and pulled him along a little faster toward Washington Square. "Let's not see anybody all day," she said. "Let's just hang around with each other. You and me. We're

always up to our neck in people, drinking their Scotch or drinking our Scotch; we only see each other in bed. I want to go out with my husband all day long. I want him to talk only to me and listen only to me."

"What's to stop us?" Michael asked.

"The Stevensons. They want us to drop by around one o'clock and they'll drive us into the country."

"The cunning Stevensons," Mike said. "Transparent. They can whistle. They can go driving in the country by themselves."

"Is it a date?"

"It's a date."

Frances leaned over and kissed him on the tip of the ear.

"Darling," Michael said, "this is Fifth Avenue."

"Let me arrange a program," Frances said. "A planned Sunday in New York for a young couple with money to throw away."

"Go easy."

"First let's go to the Metropolitan Museum of Art," Frances suggested, because Michael had said during the week he wanted to go. "I haven't been there in three years and there're at least ten pictures I want to see again. Then we can take the bus down to Radio City and watch them skate. And later we'll go down to Cavanagh's and get a steak as big as a blacksmith's apron, with a bottle of wine, and after that there's a French picture at the Filmarte that everybody says—say, are you listening to me?"

"Sure," he said. He took his eyes off the hatless girl with the dark hair, cut dancer-style like a helmet, who was walking past him.

"That's the program for the day," Frances said flatly. "Or maybe you'd just rather walk up and down Fifth Avenue."

"No," Michael said. "Not at all."

"You always look at other women," Frances said. "Everywhere. Every damned place we go."

"Now, darling," Michael said, "I look at everything. God gave me eyes and I look at women and men and subway excavations and moving pictures and the little flowers of the field. I casually inspect the universe."

"You ought to see the look in your eye," Frances said, "as you casually inspect the universe on Fifth Avenue."

"I'm a happily married man." Michael pressed her elbow tenderly. "Example for the whole twentieth century—Mr. and Mrs. Mike Loomis. Hey, let's have a drink," he said, stopping.

"We just had breakfast."

"Now listen, darling," Mike said, choosing his words with care, "it's a nice day and we both felt good and there's no reason why we have to break it up. Let's have a nice Sunday."

"All right. I don't know why I started this. Let's drop it. Let's have a good time."

They joined hands consciously and walked without talking among the baby carriages and the old Italian men in their Sunday clothes and the young women with Scotties in Washington Square Park.

"At least once a year everyone should go to the Metropolitan Museum of Art," Frances said after a while, her tone a good imitation of the tone she had used at breakfast and at the beginning of their walk. "And it's nice on Sunday. There's a lot of people looking at the pictures and you get the feeling maybe Art isn't on the decline in New York City, after all—"

"I want to tell you something," Michael said very seriously. "I have not touched another woman. Not once. In all the five years."

"All right," Frances said.

"You believe that, don't you?"

"All right."

They walked between the crowded benches, under the scrubby city-park trees.

"I try not to notice it," Frances said, "but I feel rotten inside, in my stomach, when we pass a woman and you look at her and I see that look in your eye and that's the way you looked at me the first time. In Alice Maxwell's house. Standing there in the living room, next to the radio, with a green hat on and all those people."

"I remember the hat," Michael said.

"The same look," Frances said. "And it makes me feel bad. It makes me feel terrible."

"Sh-h-h, please, darling, sh-h-h."

"I think I would like a drink now," Frances said.

They walked over to a bar on Eighth Street, not saying anything, Michael automatically helping her over curbstones and guiding her past automobiles. They sat near a window in the bar and the sun streamed in and there was a small cheerful fire in the fireplace. A little Japanese waiter came over and put down some pretzels and smiled happily at them.

"What do you order after breakfast?" Michael asked.

"Brandy, I suppose," Frances said.

"Courvoisier," Michael told the waiter. "Two Courvoisiers."

The waiter came with the glasses and they sat drinking the brandy in the sunlight. Michael finished half his and drank a little water.

"I look at women," he said. "Correct. I don't say it's wrong or right. I look at them. If I pass them on the street and don't look at them, I'm fooling you, I'm fooling myself."

"You look at them as though you want them," Frances said, playing with her brandy glass. "Every one of them."

"In a way," Michael said, speaking softly and not to his wife, "in a way that's true. I don't do anything about it, but it's true."

"I know it. That's why I feel bad."

"Another brandy," Michael called. "Waiter, two more brandies."

He sighed and closed his eyes and rubbed them gently with his fingertips. "I love the way women look. One of the things I like best about New York is the battalions of women. When I first came to New York from Ohio that was the first thing I noticed, the million wonderful women, all over the city. I walked around with my heart in my throat."

"A kid," Frances said. "That's a kid's feeling."

"Guess again," Michael said. "Guess again.

I'm older now, I'm a man getting near middle age, putting on a little fat and I still love to walk along Fifth Avenue at three o'clock on the east side of the street between Fiftieth and Fifty-seventh Streets. They're all out then, shopping, in their furs and their crazy hats, everything all concentrated from all over the world into seven blocks—the best furs, the best clothes, the handsomest women, out to spend money and feeling good about it."

The Japanese waiter put the two drinks down, smiling with great happiness.

"Everything is all right?" he asked.

"Everything is wonderful," Michael said.

"If it's just a couple of fur coats," Frances said, "and forty-five-dollar hats—"

"It's not the fur coats. Or the hats. That's just the scenery for that particular kind of woman. Understand," he said, "you don't have to listen to this."

"I want to listen."

"I like the girls in the offices. Neat, with their eyeglasses, smart, chipper, knowing what everything is about. I like the girls on Forty-fourth Street at lunchtime, the actresses, all dressed up on nothing a week. I like the salesgirls in the stores, paying attention to you first because you're a man, leaving lady customers waiting. I got all this stuff accumulated in me because I've been thinking about it for ten years and now you've asked for it and here it is."

"Go ahead," Frances said.

"When I think of New York City, I think of all the girls on parade in the city. I don't know whether every man in the city walks around with the same feeling inside him, but I feel as though I'm at a picnic in this city. I like to sit near the women in the theatres, the famous beauties who've taken six hours to get ready and look it. And the young girls at the football games, with the red cheeks, and when the warm weather comes, the girls in their summer dresses." He finished his drink. "That's the story."

Frances finished her drink and swallowed two or three times extra. "You say you love me?"

"I love you."

"I'm pretty, too," Frances said. "As pretty as any of them."

"You're beautiful," Michael said.

"I'm good for you," Frances said, pleading. "I've made a good wife, a good housekeeper, a good friend. I'd do any damn thing for you."

"I know," Michael said. He put his hand out and grasped hers.

"You'd like to be free to—" Frances said.

"Sh-h-h"

"Tell the truth." She took her hand away from under his.

Michael flicked the edge of his glass with his finger. "O.K.," he said gently. "Sometimes I feel I would like to be free."

"Well," Frances said, "any time you say."

"Don't be foolish." Michael swung his chair around to her side of the table and patted her thigh.

She began to cry silently into her handkerchief, bent over just enough so that nobody else in the bar would notice. "Someday," she said, crying, "you're going to make a move."

Michael didn't say anything. He sat watching the bartender slowly peel a lemon.

"Aren't you?" Frances asked harshly. "Come on, tell me. Talk. Aren't you?"

"Maybe," Michael said. He moved his chair back again. "How the hell do I know?"

"You know," Frances persisted. "Don't you know?"

"Yes," Michael said after a while, "I know."

Frances stopped crying them. Two or three snuffles into the handkerchief and she put it away and her face didn't tell anything to anybody. "At least do me one favor," she said.

"Sure."

"Stop talking about how pretty this woman is or that one. Nice eyes, nice breasts, a pretty figure, good voice." She mimicked his voice. "Keep it to yourself. I'm not interested."

Michael waved to the waiter. "I'll keep it to myself," he said.

Frances flicked the corners of her eyes. "Another brandy," she told the waiter.

"Two," Michael said.

"Yes, Ma'am, yes sir," said the waiter, backing away.

Frances regarded Michael cooly across the table. "Do you want me to call the Stevensons?" she asked. "It'll be nice in the country."

"Sure," Michael said. "Call them."

She got up from the table and walked across the room toward the telephone. Michael watched her walk, thinking what a pretty girl, what nice legs.

The poem, "De Profundis," by Dorothy Parker is short; however, the message is essentially the same as that in Shaw's short story. Ms. Parker's heroine is more aware of the way she is treated and hopes that she'll meet a different kind of man.

De Profundis

Dorothy Parker

Oh, is it, then, Utopian
To hope that I may meet a man
Who'll not relate, in accents suave,
The tales of girls he used to have?

DISCUSSION TOPICS

1. Imitating the style of Dorothy Parker's "De Profundis," write a poem about women that could be written by Michael Loomis.

2. Do you believe Michael Loomis when he tells Frances that he has not touched another woman in five years? In your answer you should include why you think it is that he is so compelled to talk about women.

SUGGESTED ACTIVITIES

1. Buy three different magazines aimed at a female audience and three aimed at a male audience. Analyze their content for attitudes toward the opposite sex. Pay special note to advertisements, advice columns, cartoons, and fiction. Your report should summarize the roles that these magazines think men and women should play.

2. Soap operas are tremendously addictive to a great number of people, especially women. Watch soap operas a minimum of three hours and take note of how the men treat the women. In other words, is the world of soap operas populated with Michael and Frances Loomis's?

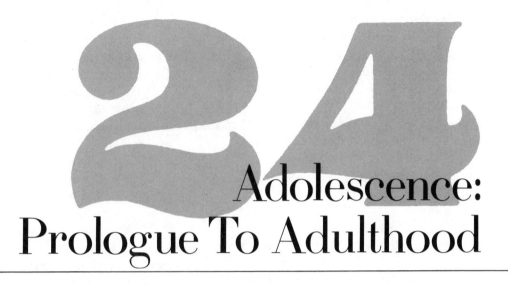

Adolescence: Prologue To Adulthood

Each of us can recollect a number of specific incidents in our childhood. Yet no one of us has total recall of our entire childhood. The reason that we remember certain episodes is that they have meaning for us. Sometimes the significance of these episodes is not clear to our young minds until much later. However, instinctively we do realize their importance and we retain forever the memory of them.

The sensitive adult can look back on childhood and recognize those moments that helped to define an adult personality. For example, adult attitudes towards our parents have been shaped by our remembrances of them from childhood.

In the poem that follows, a grown woman reflects on her childhood; in the other work, a child is undergoing a painful experience that she will understand only when she is much older.

Born in Knoxville, Tennessee, in 1943, Nikki Giovanni was raised in Cincinnati. While a student at Fisk University, she participated in a writer's workshop and founded a chapter of the Student Non-Violent Coordinating Committee (SNCC).

Ms. Giovanni describes herself as a revolutionary poet. Her works have been collected in a volume entitled Black Judgment. *In "Nikki Roasa" she looks back on her early family life.*

Nikki Roasa

Nikki Giovanni

childhood remembrances are always a drag
if you're Black
you always remember things like living in
   Woodlawn
with no inside toilet
and if you become famous or something
they never talk about how happy you were to have
   your mother
all to yourself and

how good the water felt when you got your bath
  from one of those
big tubs that folk in chicago barbecue in
and somehow when you talk about home
it never gets across how much you
understood their feelings
as the whole family attended meetings about
  Hollydale
and even though you remember
your biographers never understand
your father's pain as he sells his stock
and another dream goes
and though you're poor it isn't poverty that
concerns you
and though they fought a lot
it isn't your father's drinking that makes any
  difference
but only that everybody is together and you
and your sister have happy birthdays and very
  good christmases
and I really hope no white person ever has cause
  to write about me
because they never understand Black love is Black
  wealth and they'll
probably talk about my hard childhood and never
  understand that
all the while I was quite happy

The South is usually the setting for the works of Georgia-born Carson McCullers. She began writing in her early teens and continued until her death in 1967. Outstanding among her works are The Heart is a Lonely Hunter, Member of the Wedding *and* Reflections in a Golden Eye.

"Like That," an early story which was unpublished until 1971, captures the confusion and alienation felt by a young girl who cannot understand what has happened to the relationship between her and her sister.

Like That

Carson McCullers

Even if Sis is five years older than me and eighteen we used always to be closer and have more fun together than most sisters. It was about the same with us and our brother Dan, too. In the summer we'd all go swimming together. At nights in the wintertime maybe we'd sit around the fire in the living room and play three-handed bridge or Michigan, with everybody putting up a nickel or a dime to the winner. The three of us could have more fun by ourselves than any family I know. That's the way it always was before this.

Not that Sis was playing down to me, either. She's smart as she can be and has read more books than anybody I ever knew—even school teachers. But in High School she never did like to priss up flirty and ride around in cars with girls and pick up the boys and park at the drug store and all that sort of thing. When she wasn't reading she'd just like to play around with me and Dan. She wasn't too grown up to fuss over a chocolate bar in the refrigerator or to stay awake most of Christmas Eve night either, say, with excitement. In some ways it was like I was heaps older than her. Even when Tuck started coming around last summer I'd sometimes have to tell her she shouldn't wear ankle socks because they might go downtown or she ought to pluck out her eyebrows above her nose like the other girls do.

In one more year, next June, Tuck'll be graduated from college. He's a lanky boy with an eager look to his face. At college he's so smart he has a free scholarship. He started coming to see Sis the last summer before this one, riding in his family's car when he could get it, wearing crispy white linen suits. He came a lot last year but this summer he came even more often—before he left he was coming around for Sis every night. Tuck's O.K.

It began getting different between Sis and me a while back, I guess, although I didn't notice it at the time. It was only after a certain night this summer that I had the idea that things maybe were bound to end like they are now.

It was late when I woke up that night. When I opened my eyes I thought for a minute it must be about dawn and I was scared when I saw Sis wasn't on her side of the bed. But it was only the moonlight that shone cool looking and white outside the window and made the oak leaves hanging down over the front yard pitch black and separate seeming. It was around the first of September, but I didn't feel hot looking at the moonlight. I pulled the sheet over me and let my eyes roam around the black shapes of the furniture in our room.

I'd waked up lots of times in the night this summer. You see Sis and I have always had this room together, and when she would come in and turn on the light to find her nightgown or something it woke me. I liked it. In the summer when school was out I didn't have to get up early in the morning. We would lie and talk sometimes for a good while. I'd like to hear about the places she and Tuck had been or to laugh over different things. Lots of times before that night she had talked to me privately about Tuck just like I was her age—asking me if I thought she should have said this or that when he called and giving me a hug, maybe, after. Sis was really crazy about Tuck. Once she said to me: "He's so lovely—I never in the world thought I'd know anyone like him—"

We would talk about our brother too. Dan's seventeen years old and was planning to take the co-op course at Tech in the fall. Dan had gotten older by this summer. One night he came in at four o'clock and he'd been drinking. Dad sure had it in for him the next week. So he hiked out to the country and camped with some boys for a few days. He used to talk to me and Sis about Diesel motors and going away to South America and all that, but by this summer he was quiet and not saying much to anybody in the family. Dan's real tall and thin as a rail. He has bumps on his face now and is clumsy and not very good looking. At nights sometimes I know he wanders all around by himself, maybe going out beyond the city limits sign into the pine woods.

Thinking about such things I lay in bed wondering what time it was and when Sis would be in. That night after Sis and Dan had left, I had gone down to the corner with some of the kids in the neighborhood to chunk rocks at the street light and try to kill a bat up there. At first I had the shivers and imagined it was a smallish bat like the kind in Dracula. When I saw it looked just like a moth I didn't care if they killed it or not. I was just sitting there on the curb drawing with a stick on the dusty street when Sis and Tuck rode by slowly in his car. She was sitting over very close to him. They weren't talking or smiling—just riding slowly down the street, sitting close, looking ahead. When they passed and I saw who it was I hollered to them. "Hey, Sis!" I yelled.

The car just went on slowly and nobody hollered back. I just stood there in the middle of the street feeling sort of silly with all the other kids standing around.

That hateful little old Bubber from down on the other block came up to me. "That your sister?" he asked.

I said yes.

"She sure was sitting up close to her beau," he said.

I was mad all over like I get sometimes. I hauled off and chunked all the rocks in my hand right at him. He's three years younger than me and it wasn't nice, but I couldn't stand him in the first place and he thought he was being so cute about Sis. He started holding his neck and bellering and I walked off and left them and went home and got ready to go to bed.

When I woke up I finally began to think of that too and old Bubber Davis was still in my mind when I heard the sound of a car coming up the block. Our room faces the street with only a short front yard between. You can see and hear everything from the sidewalk and the street. The car was creeping down in front of our walk and the light went slow and white along the walls of the room. It stopped on Sis's writing desk, showed up the books there plainly and half a pack of chewing gum. Then the room was dark and there was only the moonlight outside.

The door of the car didn't open but I could hear them talking. Him, that is. His voice was low and I couldn't catch any words but it was like he was explaining something over and over again. I never heard Sis say a word.

I was still awake when I heard the car door open. I heard her say, "Don't come out." And then the door slammed and there was the sound of her heels clopping up the walk, fast and light like she was running.

Mama met Sis in the hall outside our room. She had heard the front door close. She always listens out for Sis and Dan and never goes to sleep when they're still out. I sometimes wonder how she can just lie there in the dark for hours without going to sleep.

"It's one-thirty, Marian," she said. "You ought to get in before this." Sis didn't say anything.

"Did you have a nice time?"

That's the way Mama is. I could imagine her standing there with her nightgown blowing out fat around her and her dead white legs and the blue veins showing, looking all messed up. Mama's nicer when she's dressed to go out.

"Yes, we had a grand time," Sis said. Her voice was funny—sort of like the piano in the gym at school, high and sharp on your ear. Funny.

Mama was asking more questions. Where did they go? Did they see anybody they knew? All that sort of stuff. That's the way she is.

"Goodnight," said Sis in that out-of-tune voice.

She opened the door of our room real quick and closed it. I started to let her know I was awake but changed my mind. Her breathing was quick and loud in the dark and she did not move at all. After a few minutes she felt in the closet for her nightgown and got in the bed. I could hear her crying.

"Did you and Tuck have a fuss?" I asked.

"No," she answered. Then she seemed to change her mind. "Yeah, it was a fuss."

There's one thing that gives me the creeps sure enough—and that's to hear somebody cry. "I wouldn't let it bother me. You'll be making up tomorrow."

The moon was coming in the window and I could see her moving her jaw from one side to the other and staring up at the ceiling. I watched her for a long time. The moonlight was cool looking and there was a wettish wind coming cool from the window. I moved over like I sometimes do to snug up with her, thinking maybe that would stop her from moving her jaw like that and crying.

She was trembling all over. When I got close to her she jumped like I'd pinched her and pushed me over quick and kicked my legs over. "Don't," she said. "Don't."

Maybe Sis had suddenly gone batty, I was thinking. She was crying in a slower and sharper way. I was a little scared and I got up to go to the bathroom a minute. While I was in there I looked out the window, down toward the corner where the street light is. I saw something then that I knew Sis would want to know about.

"You know what?" I asked when I was back in the bed.

She was lying over close to the edge as she could get, stiff. She didn't answer.

"Tuck's car is parked down by the street light. Just drawn up to the curb. I could tell because of the box and the two tires on the back. I could see it from the bathroom window."

She didn't even move.

"He must be just sitting out there. What ails you and him?"

She didn't say anything at all.

"I couldn't see him but he's probably just sitting there in the car under the street light. Just sitting there."

It was like she didn't care or had known it all along. She was as far over the edge of the bed as she could get, her legs stretched out stiff and her hands holding tight to the edge and her face on one arm.

She used always to sleep all sprawled over on my side so I'd have to push at her when it was hot and sometimes turn on the light and draw the line down the middle and show her how she really was on my side. I wouldn't have to draw any line that night, I was thinking. I felt bad. I looked out at the moonlight a long time before I could get to sleep again.

The next day was Sunday, and Mama and Dad went in the morning to church because it was the anniversary of the day my aunt died. Sis said she didn't feel well and stayed in bed. Dan was out and I was there by myself, so naturally I went into our room where Sis was. Her face was white as the pillow and there were circles under her eyes. There was a muscle jumping on one side of her jaw like she was chewing. She hadn't combed her hair and it flopped over the pillow, glinty red and messy and pretty. She was reading with a book held up close to her face. Her eyes didn't move when I came in. I don't think they even moved across the page.

It was roasting hot that morning. The sun made everything blazing outside so that it hurt your eyes to look. Our room was so hot that you could almost touch the air with young finger. But Sis had the sheet pulled up clear to her shoulders.

"Is Tuck coming today?" I asked. I was trying to say something that would make her look more cheerful.

"Gosh! Can't a person have *any* peace in this house?"

She never did used to say mean things like that out of a clear sky. Mean things, maybe, but not grouchy ones.

"Sure," I said. "Nobody's going to notice you."

I sat down and pretended to read. When footsteps passed on the street Sis would hold onto the book tighter and I knew she was listening hard as she could. I can tell between footsteps easy. I can even tell without looking if the person who passes is colored or not. Colored people mostly make a slurry sound between the steps. When the steps would pass Sis would loosen the hold on the

book and bite at her mouth. It was the same way with passing cars.

I felt sorry for Sis. I decided then and there that I never would let any fuss with any boy make me feel or look like that. But I wanted Sis and me to get back like we'd always been. Sunday mornings are bad enough without having any other trouble.

"We fuss a lots less than most sisters do," I said. "And when we do it's all over quick, isn't it?"

She mumbled and kept staring at the same spot on the book.

"That's one good thing," I said.

She was moving her head slightly from side to side—over and over again, with her face not changing. "We never do have any real long fusses like Bubber Davis's two sisters have—"

"No." She answered like she wasn't thinking about what I'd said.

"Not one real one like that since I can remember."

In a minute she looked up the first time. "I remember one," she said suddenly.

"When?"

Her eyes looked green in the blackness under them and like they were nailing themselves into what they saw. "You had to stay in every afternoon for a week. It was a long time ago."

All of a sudden I remembered. I'd forgotten it for a long time. I hadn't wanted to remember. When she said that it came back to me all complete.

It was really a long time ago—when Sis was about thirteen. If I remember right I was mean and even more hardboiled than I am now. My aunt who I'd liked better than all my other aunts put together had had a dead baby and she had died. After the funeral Mama had told Sis and me about it. Always the things I've learned new and didn't like have made me mad—mad clean through and scared.

That wasn't what Sis was talking about, though. It was a few mornings after that when Sis started with what every big girl has each month, and of course I found out and was scared to death. Mama then explained to me about it and what she had to wear. I felt then like I'd felt about my aunt, only ten times worse. I felt different toward Sis, too, and was so mad I wanted to pitch into people and hit.

I never will forget it. Sis was standing in our room before the dresser mirror. When I remembered her face it was white like Sis's there on the pillow and with the circles under her eyes and the glinty hair to her shoulders—it was only younger.

I was sitting on the bed, biting hard at my knee. "It shows," I said. "It does too!"

She had on a sweater and a blue pleated skirt and she was so skinny all over that it did show a little.

"Any body can tell. Right off the bat. Just to look at you anybody can tell."

Her face was white in the mirror and did not move.

"It looks terrible. I wouldn't ever ever be like that. It shows and everything."

She started crying then and told Mother and said she wasn't going back to school and such. She cried a long time. That's how ugly and hard-boiled I used to be and am still sometimes. That's why I had to stay in the house every afternoon for a week a long time ago . . .

Tuck came by in his car that Sunday morning before dinner time. Sis got up and dressed in a hurry and didn't even put on any lipstick. She said they were going out to dinner. Nearly every Sunday all of us in the family stay together all day, so that was a little funny. They didn't get home until almost dark. The rest of us were sitting on the front porch drinking ice tea because of the heat when the car drove up again. After they got out of the car Dad, who had been in a very good mood all day, insisted Tuck stay for a glass of tea.

Tuck sat on the swing with Sis and he didn't lean back and his heels didn't rest on the floor—as though he was all ready to get up again. He kept changing the glass from one hand to the other and starting new conversations. He and Sis

didn't look at each other except on the sly, and then it wasn't at all like they were crazy about each other. It was a funny look. Almost like they were afraid of something. Tuck left soon.

"Come sit by your Dad a minute, Puss," Dad said. Puss is a nickname he calls Sis when he feels in a specially good mood. He still likes to pet us.

She went and sat on the arm of his chair. She sat stiff like Tuck had, holding herself off a little so Dad's arm hardly went around her waist Dad smoked his cigar and looked out on the front yard and the trees that were beginning to melt into the early dark.

"How's my big girl getting along these days?" Dad still likes to hug us up when he feels good and treat us, even Sis, like kids.

"O.K.," she said. She twisted a little bit like she wanted to get up and didn't know how to without hurting his feelings.

"You and Tuck have had a nice time together this summer, haven't you, Puss?"

"Yeah," she said. She had begun to see-saw her lower jaw again. I wanted to say something but couldn't think of anything.

Dad said: "He ought to be getting back to Tech about now, oughtn't he? When's he leaving?"

"Less than a week," she said. She got up so quick that she knocked Dad's cigar out of his fingers. She didn't even pick it up but flounced on through the front door. I could hear her half running to our room and the sound the door made when she shut it. I knew she was going to cry.

It was hotter than ever. The lawn was beginning to grow dark and the locusts were droning out so shrill and steady that you wouldn't notice them unless you thought to. The sky was bluish grey and the trees in the vacant lot across the street were dark. I kept on sitting on the front porch with Mama and Papa and hearing their low talk without listening to the words. I wanted to go in our room with Sis but I was afraid to. I wanted to ask her what was really the matter. Was hers and Tuck's fuss so bad as that or was it that she was so crazy about him that she was sad because he was leaving? For a minute I didn't think it was either one of those things. I wanted to know but I was scared to ask. I just sat there with the grown people. I never have been so lonesome as I was that night. If ever I think about being sad I just remember how it was then—sitting there looking at the long bluish shadows across the lawn and feeling like I was the only child left in the family and that Sis and Dan were dead or gone for good.

It's October now and the sun shines bright and a little cool and the sky is the color of my turquoise ring. Dan's gone to Tech. So has Tuck gone. It's not at all like it was last fall, though. I come in from High School (I go there now) and Sis maybe is just sitting by the window reading or writing to Tuck or just looking out. Sis is thinner and sometimes to me she looks in the face like a grown person. Or like, in a way, something has suddenly hurt her hard. We don't do any of the things we used to. It's good weather for fudge or for doing so many things. But no, she just sits around or goes for long walks in the chilly late afternoon by herself. Sometimes she'll smile in a way that really gripes—like I was such a kid and all. Sometimes I want to cry or to hit her.

But I'm hardboiled as the next person. I can get along by myself if Sis or anybody else wants to. I'm glad I'm thirteen and still wear socks and can do what I please. I don't want to be any older if I'd get like Sis has. But I wouldn't. I wouldn't like any boy in the world as much as she does Tuck. I'd never let any boy or any thing make me act like she does. I'm not going to waste my time and try to make Sis be like she used to be. I get lonesome—sure—but I don't care. I know there's no way I can make myself stay thirteen all my life, but I know I'd never let anything really change me at all—no matter what it is.

I skate and ride my bike and go to the school football games every Friday. But when one afternoon the kids all got quiet in the gym basement and then started telling certain things—about being married and all—I got up quick so I wouldn't hear and went up and played basketball. And when some of the kids said they were going to start wearing lipstick and stockings I said I wouldn't for a hundred dollars.

You see I'd never be like Sis is now. I wouldn't. Anybody could know that if they knew me. I just wouldn't, that's all. I don't want to grow up—if it's like that.

DISCUSSION TOPICS

1. Have you ever wanted to stop time—to remain at a certain age forever? Discuss that age and that time.

SUGGESTED ACTIVITIES

1. Ask ten preschool girls and ten preschool boys to tell you what their ambition is. Then ask the same number of 10- or 12-year-olds the same question. If possible, tape all responses. Is there any discernible difference in the attitudes of the preschoolers and the ten-year-olds?

2. Volunteer to work in a nursery school or child-care center for a minimum of twenty hours. Observe the behavior of boys and girls. Are there differences according to sex or according to personality? Report on your findings.

25 Older Women

Many adult women spend their later years on their own as widows. Up until this time major decisions concerning their lifestyles and friends were determined by their husbands. The sudden and unlooked for independence of widowhood forces women to exist as solitary people. Some become active, independent people interested in everything around them. Others remain passive, reliving old memories and experiencing life through others, most frequently through their children.

In the two short stories that follow, you will see how some active and passive women live their lives.

Born into a comfortable New York family in 1862, Edith Wharton began her writing career after her marriage. Her works were a critical and popular success. Ethan Frome, *written in 1911, and* The Age of Innocence, *written in 1920, are considered by many critics to be two of her best works. She was the first woman to receive an honorary doctorate in letters from Yale University.*

In addition to her novels, Ms. Wharton wrote several volumes of short stories. In the following story, the two widows in "Roman Fever" spend their time reliving the past, which can sometimes be a dangerous thing to do.

Roman Fever

Edith Wharton

From the table at which they had been lunching, two American ladies of ripe but well-cared-for middle age moved across the lofty terrace of the Roman restaurant and, leaning on its parapet, looked first at each other, and then down on the outspread glories of the Palatine and the Forum, with the same expression of vague but benevolent approval.

As they leaned there a girlish voice echoed up gaily from the stairs leading to the court below.

"Well, come along, then," it cried, not to them but to an invisible companion, "and let's leave the young things to their knitting"; and a voice as fresh laughed back: "Oh, look here, Babs, not actually *knitting*—" "Well, I mean figuratively," rejoined the first. "After all, we haven't left our poor parents much else to do. . ." and at that point the turn of the stairs engulfed the dialogue.

The two ladies looked at each other again, this time with a tinge of smiling embarrassment, and the smaller and paler one shook her head and colored slightly.

"Barbara!" she murmured, sending an unheard rebuke after the mocking voice in the stairway.

The other lady, who was fuller, and higher in color, with a small determined nose supported by vigorous black eyebrows, gave a good-humored laugh. "That's what our daughters think of us!"

Her companion replied by a deprecating gesture. "Not of us individually. We must remember that. It's just the collective modern idea of Mothers. And you see—" Half guiltily she drew from her handsomely mounted black handbag a twist of crimson silk run through by two fine knitting needles. "One never knows," she murmured. "The new system has certainly given us a good deal of time to kill; and sometimes I get tired just looking—even at this." Her gesture was now addressed to the stupendous scene at their feet.

The dark lady laughed again, and they both relapsed upon the view, contemplating it in silence, with a sort of diffused serenity which might have been borrowed from the spring effulgence of the Roman skies. The luncheon hour was long past, and the two had their end of the vast terrace to themselves. At its opposite extremity a few groups, detained by a lingering look at the outspread city were gathering up guidebooks and fumbling for tips. The last of them scattered, and the two ladies were alone on the air-washed height.

"Well, I don't see why we shouldn't just stay here," said Mrs. Slade, the lady of the high color and energetic brows. Two derelict basket chairs stood near, and she pushed them into the angle of the parapet, and settled herself in one, her gaze upon the Palatine. "After all, it's still the most beautiful view in the world."

"It always will be, to me," assented her friend Mrs. Ansley, with so slight a stress on the "me" that Mrs. Slade, though she noticed it, wondered if it were not merely accidental, like the random underlinings of old-fashioned letter-writers.

"Grace Ansley was always old-fashioned," she thought; and added aloud, with a retrospective smile: "It's a view we've both been familiar with for a good many years. When we first met here we were younger than our girls are now. You remember?"

"Oh, yes, I remember," murmured Mrs. Ansley, with the same undefinable stress.— "There's that headwaiter wondering," she interpolated. She was evidently far less sure than her companion of herself and of her rights in the world.

"I'll cure him of wondering," said Mrs. Slade, stretching her hand toward a bag as discreetly opulent looking as Mrs. Ansley's. Signing to the headwaiter, she explained that she and her friend were old lovers of Rome, and would like to spend the end of the afternoon looking down on the view—that is, if it did not disturb the service? The headwaiter, bowing over her gratuity, assured her that the ladies were most welcome, and would be still more so if they would condescend to remain for dinner. A full moon night, they would remember. . .

Mrs. Slade's black brows drew together, as though references to the moon were out-of-place and even unwelcome. But she smiled away her frown as the headwaiter retreated. "Well, why not? We might do worse. There's no knowing, I suppose, when the girls will be back. Do you even know back from *where*? I don't!"

Mrs. Ansley again colored slightly. "I think those young Italian aviators we met at the Embassy invited them to fly to Tarquinia for tea. I suppose they'll want to wait and fly back by moonlight."

"Moonlight—moonlight! What a part it still

plays. Do you suppose they're as sentimental as we were?"

"I've come to the conclusion that I don't in the least know what they are," said Mrs. Ansley. "And perhaps we didn't know much more about each other."

"No; perhaps we didn't."

Her friend gave her a shy glance. "I never should have supposed you were sentimental, Alida."

"Well, perhaps I wasn't." Mrs. Slade drew her lids together in retrospect; and for a few moments the two ladies, who had been intimate since childhood, reflected how little they knew each other. Each one, of course, had a label ready to attach to the other's name; Mrs. Delphin Slade, for instance, would have told herself, or any one who asked her, that Mrs. Horace Ansley, twenty-five years ago, had been exquisitely lovely—no, you wouldn't believe it, would you? . . . though, of course, still charming, distinguished. . . Well, as a girl she had been exquisite; far more beautiful than her daughter Barbara, though certainly Babs, according to the new standards at any rate, was more effective—had more *edge*, as they say. Funny where she got it, with those two nullities as parents. Yes; Horace Ansley was—well, just the duplicate of his wife. Museum specimens of old New York. Good looking, irreproachable, exemplary. Mrs. Slade and Mrs. Ansley had lived opposite each other—actually as well as figuratively—for years. When the drawing room curtains in No. 20 East 73rd Street were renewed, No. 23, across the way, was always aware of it. And of all the movings, buyings, travels, anniversaries, illnesses—the tame chronicle of an estimable pair. Little of it escaped Mrs. Slade. But she had grown bored with it by the time her husband made his big *coup* in Wall Street and when they bought in upper Park Avenue had already begun to think: "I'd rather live opposite a speakeasy for a change; at least one might see it raided." The idea of seeing Grace raided was so amusing that (before the move) she launched it at a woman's lunch. It made a hit, and went the rounds—she sometimes wondered if it had

crossed the street, and reached Mrs. Ansley. She hoped not, but didn't much mind. Those were the days when respectability was at a discount, and it did the irreproachable no harm to laugh at them a little.

A few years later, and not many months apart, both ladies lost their husbands. There was an appropriate exchange of wreaths and condolences, and a brief renewal of intimacy in the half-shadow of their mourning; and now, after another interval, they had run across each other in Rome, at the same hotel, each of them the modest appendage of a salient daughter. The similarity of their lot had again drawn them together, lending itself to mild jokes, and the mutual confession that, if in old days it must have been tiring to "keep up" with daughters, it was now, at times, a little dull not to.

No doubt, Mrs. Slade reflected, she felt her unemployment more than poor Grace ever would. It was a big drop from being the wife of Delphin Slade to being his widow. She had always regarded herself (with a certain conjugal pride) as his equal in social gifts, as contributing her full share to the making of the exceptional couple they were: but the difference after his death was irremediable. As the wife of the famous corporation lawyer, always with an international case or two on hand, every day brought its exciting and unexpected obligation: the impromptu entertaining of eminent colleagues from abroad, the hurried dashes on legal business to London, Paris, or Rome, where the entertaining was so handsomely reciprocated; the amusement of hearing in her wake: "What, that handsome woman with the good clothes and the eyes is Mrs. Slade—*the* Slade's wife? Really? Generally the wives of celebrities are such frumps."

Yes; being *the* Slade's widow was a dullish business after that. In living up to such a husband all her faculties had been engaged; now she had only her daughter to live up to, for the son who seemed to have inherited his father's gifts had died suddenly in boyhood. She had fought through that agony because her husband was there, to be helped and to help; now, after the father's death, the thought of the boy had become unbearable. There was nothing left but to mother her daughter; and dear Jenny was such a perfect daughter that she needed no excessive mothering. "Now with Babs Ansley I don't know that I *should* be so quiet," Mrs. Slade sometimes half-enviously reflected; but Jenny, who was younger than her brilliant friend, was that rare accident, an extremely pretty girl who somehow made youth and prettiness seem as safe as their absence. It was all perplexing—and to Mrs. Slade a little boring. She wished that Jenny would fall in love—with the wrong man, even; that she might have to be watched, outmaneuvered, rescued. And instead it was Jenny who watched her mother, kept her out of drafts, made sure that she had taken her tonic. . .

Mrs. Ansley was much less articulate than her friend, and her mental portrait of Mrs. Slade was slighter, and drawn with fainter touches. "Alida Slade's awfully brilliant; but not as brilliant as she thinks," would have summed it up; though she would have added, for the enlightenment of strangers, that Mrs. Slade had been an extremely dashing girl; much more so than her daughter, who was pretty, of course, and clever in a way, but had none of her mother's—well, "vividness," some one had once called it. Mrs. Ansley would take up current words like this, and cite them in quotation marks, as unheard of audacities. No; Jenny was not like her mother. Sometimes Mrs. Ansley thought Alida Slade was disappointed; on the whole she had had a sad life. Full of failures and mistakes; Mrs. Ansley had always been rather sorry for her. . .

So these two ladies visualized each other, each through the wrong end of her little telescope.

For a long time they continued to sit side by side without speaking. It seemed as though, to both, there was a relief in laying down their somewhat futile activities in the presence of the vast Memento Mori which faced them. Mrs. Slade sat quite still, her eyes fixed on the golden slope of the Palace of the Caesars, and after a while Mrs. Ansley ceased to fidget with her bag, and she too sank into meditation. Like many intimate friends, the two ladies had never before had occasion to be silent together, and Mrs. Ansley was slightly embarrassed by what seemed, after so many years, a new stage in their intimacy, and one with which she did not yet know how to deal.

Suddenly the air was full of that deep clangor of bells which periodically covers Rome with a roof of silver. Mrs. Slade glanced at her wristwatch. "Five o'clock already," she said, as though surprised.

Mrs. Ansley suggested interrogatively: "There's bridge at the Embassy at five." For a long time Mrs. Slade did not answer. She appeared to be lost in contemplation, and Mrs. Ansley thought the remark had escaped her. But after a while she said, as if speaking out of a dream: "Bridge, did you say? Not unless you want to. . . But I don't think I will, you know."

"Oh, no," Mrs. Ansley hastened to assure her. "I don't care to at all. It's so lovely here; and so full of old memories, as you say." She settled herself in her chair, and almost furtively drew forth her knitting. Mrs. Slade took sideway note of this activity, but her own beautifully cared for hands remained motionless on her knee.

"I was just thinking," she said slowly, "what different things Rome stands for to each generation of travelers. To our grandmothers, Roman fever; to our mothers, sentimental dangers —how we used to be guarded!—to our daughters, no more dangers than the middle of Main Street. They don't know it—but how much they're missing."

The long golden light was beginning to pale, and Mrs. Ansley lifted her knitting a little closer to her eyes. "Yes; how we were guarded!"

"I always used to think," Mrs. Slade continued, "that our mothers had a much more difficult job than our grandmothers. When Roman fever stalked the streets it must have been comparatively easy to gather in the girls at the danger hour; but when you and I were young, with such beauty calling us, and the spice of disobedience thrown in, and no worse risk than catching cold during the one hour after sunset, the mothers used to be put to it to keep us in—didn't they?"

She turned again toward Mrs. Ansley, but the latter had reached a delicate point in her knitting. 'One, two, three—slip two; yes they must have been," she assented, without looking up.

Mrs. Slade's eyes rested on her with a deepened attention. "She can knit—in the face of *this!* How like her. . ."

Mrs. Slade leaned back, brooding, her eyes ranging from the ruins which faced her to the long green hollow of the Forum, the fading glow of the church fronts beyond it, and the outlying immensity of the Colosseum. Suddenly she thought: "It's all very well to say that our girls have done away with sentiment and moonlight. But if Babs Ansley isn't out to catch that young aviator—the one who's a Marchese—then I don't know anything. And Jenny has no chance beside her. I know that too. I wonder if that's why Grace Ansley likes the two girls to go everywhere together? My poor Jenny as a foil—!" Mrs. Slade gave a hardly audible laugh, and at the sound Mrs. Ansley dropped her knitting.

"Yes—?"

"I—oh, nothing. I was only thinking how your Babs carries everything before her. That Campolieri boy is one of the best matches in Rome. Don't look so innocent, my dear—you know he is. And I was wondering, ever so respectfully, you understand . . . wondering how two such exemplary characters as you and Horace had managed to produce anything quite so dynamic." Mrs. Slade laughed again, with a touch of asperity.

Mrs. Ansley's hands lay inert across her needles. She looked straight out at the great accumulated wreckage of passion and splendor at her feet. But her small profile was almost expressionless. At length she said: "I think you overrate Babs, my dear."

Mrs. Slade's tone grew easier. "No; I don't. I appreciate her. And perhaps envy you. Oh, my girl's perfect; if I were a chronic invalid I'd—well, I think I'd rather be in Jenny's hands. There must

be times . . . but there! I always wanted a brilliant daughter . . . and never quite understood why I got an angel instead."

Mrs. Ansley echoed her laugh in a faint murmur. "Babs is an angel too."

"Of course—of course! But she's got rainbow wings. Well, they're wandering by the sea with their young men; and here we sit . . . and it all brings back the past a little too acutely."

Mrs. Ansley had resumed her knitting. One might almost have imagined (if one had known her less well, Mrs. Slade reflected) that, for her also, too many memories rose from the lengthening shadows of those august ruins. But no; she was simply absorbed in her work. What was there for her to worry about? She knew that Babs would almost certainly come back engaged to the extremely eligible Campolieri. "And she'll sell the New York house, and settle down near them in Rome, and never be in their way . . . she's much too tactful. But she'll have an excellent cook, and just the right people in for bridge and cocktails . . . and a perfectly peaceful old age among her grandchildren."

Mrs. Slade broke off this prophetic flight with a recoil of self-disgust. There was no one of whom she had less right to think unkindly than of Grace Ansley. Would she never cure herself of envying her? Perhaps she had begun too long ago.

She stood up and leaned against the parapet, filling her troubled eyes with the tranquilizing magic of the hour. But instead of tranquilizing her the sight seemed to increase her exasperation. Her gaze turned toward the Colosseum. Already its golden flank was drowned in purple shadow, and above it the sky curved crystal clear, without light or color. It was the moment when afternoon and evening hang balanced in mid-heaven.

Mrs. Slade turned back and laid her hand on her friend's arm. The gesture was so abrupt that Mrs. Ansley looked up, startled.

"The sun's set. You're not afraid, my dear?"

"Afraid—?"

"Of Roman fever or pneumonia? I remember how ill you were that winter. As a girl you had a very delicate throat, hadn't you?"

"Oh, we're all right up here. Down below, in the Forum, it does get deathly cold, all of a sudden . . . but not here."

"Ah, of course you know because you had to be so careful." Mrs. Slade turned back to the parapet. She thought: "I must make one more effort not to hate her." Aloud she said: "Whenever I look at the Forum from up here, I remember that story about a great-aunt of yours, wasn't she? A dreadfully wicked great-aunt?"

"Oh, yes; Great-aunt Harriet. The one who was supposed to have sent her young sister out to the Forum after sunset to gather a night-blooming flower for her album. All our great-aunts and grandmothers used to have albums of dried flowers."

Mrs. Slade nodded. "But she really sent her because they were in love with the same man—"

"Well, that was the family tradition. They said Aunt Harriet confessed it years afterward. At any rate, the poor little sister caught the fever and died. Mother used to frighten us with the story when we were children."

"And you frightened *me* with it, that winter when you and I were here as girls. The winter I was engaged to Delphin."

Mrs. Ansley gave a faint laugh. "Oh, did I? Really frightened you? I don't believe you're easily frightened."

"Not often; but I was then. I was easily frightened because I was too happy. I wonder if you know what that means?"

"I—yes . . ." Mrs. Ansley faltered.

"Well, I suppose that was why the story of your wicked aunt made such an impression on me. And I thought: 'There's no more Roman fever, but the Forum is deathly cold after sunset—especially after a hot day. And the Colosseum's even colder and damper.'"

"The Colosseum—?"

"Yes. It wasn't easy to get in, after the gates were locked for the night. Far from easy. Still, in those days it could be managed; it was managed, often. Lovers met there who couldn't meet elsewhere. You knew that?"

"I—I daresay. I don't remember."

"You don't remember? You don't remember going to visit some ruins or other one evening, just after dark, and catching a bad chill? You were supposed to have gone to see the moon rise. People always said that expedition was what caused your illness."

There was a moment's silence; then Mrs. Ansley rejoined: "Did they? It was all so long ago."

"Yes. And you got well again—so it didn't matter. But I suppose it struck your friends—the reason given for your illness, I mean—because everybody knew you were so prudent on account of your throat, and your mother took such care of you. . . You *had* been out late sight-seeing, hadn't you, that night?"

"Perhaps I had. The most prudent girls aren't always prudent. What made you think of it now?"

Mrs. Slade seemed to have no answer ready. But after a moment she broke out: "Because I simply can't bear it any longer—!"

Mrs. Ansley lifted her head quickly. Her eyes were wide and very pale. "Can't bear what?"

"Why—your not knowing that I've always known why you went."

"Why I went—?"

"Yes. You think I'm bluffing, don't you? Well, you went to meet the man I was engaged to—and I can repeat every word of the letter that took you there."

While Mrs. Slade spoke Mrs. Ansley had risen unsteadily to her feet. Her bag, her knitting and gloves, slid in a panic-stricken heap to the ground. She looked at Mrs. Slade as though she were looking at a ghost.

"No, no—don't," she faltered out.

"Why not? Listen, if you don't believe me.

'My one darling, things can't go on like this. I must see you alone. Come to the Colosseum immediately after dark tomorrow. There will be somebody to let you in. No one whom you need fear will suspect'—but perhaps you've forgotten what the letter said?"

Mrs. Ansley met the challenge with an unexpected composure. Steadying herself against the chair she looked at her friend, and replied: "No; I know it by heart too."

"And the signature? 'Only *your* D.S.' Was that it? I'm right, am I? That was the letter that took you out that evening after dark?"

Mrs. Ansley was still looking at her. It seemed to Mrs. Slade that a slow struggle was going on behind the voluntarily controlled mask of her small quiet face. "I shouldn't have thought she had herself so well in hand," Mrs. Slade reflected, almost resentfully. But at this moment Mrs. Ansley spoke. "I don't know how you knew. I burnt that letter at once."

"Yes; you would, naturally—you're so prudent!" The sneer was open now. "And if you burnt the letter you're wondering how on earth I know what was in it. That's it, isn't it?"

Mrs. Slade waited, but Mrs. Ansley did not speak.

"Well, my dear, I know what was in that letter because I wrote it!"

"You wrote it?"

"Yes."

The two women stood for a minute staring at each other in the last golden light. Then Mrs. Ansley dropped back into her chair. "Oh," she murmured, and covered her face with her hands.

Mrs. Slade waited nervously for another word or movement. None came, and at length she broke out: "I horrify you."

Mrs. Ansley's hands dropped to her knee. The face they uncovered was streaked with tears. "I wasn't thinking of you. I was thinking—it was the only letter I ever had from him!"

"And I wrote it. Yes; I wrote it! But I was the girl he was engaged to. Did you happen to remember that?"

Mrs. Ansley's head drooped again. "I'm not trying to excuse myself. . . I remembered. . ."

"And still you went?"

"Still I went."

Mrs. Slade stood looking down on the small bowed figure at her side. The flame of her wrath her already sunk, and she wondered why she had ever thought there would be any satisfaction in inflicting so purposeless a wound on her friend. But she had to justify herself.

"You do understand? I'd found out—and I hated you, hated you. I knew you were in love with Delphin—and I was afraid; afraid of you, of your quiet ways, your sweetness . . . your . . . well, I wanted you out of the way, that's all. Just for a few weeks; just till I was sure of him. So in a blind fury I wrote that letter. . . I don't know why I'm telling you now."

"I suppose," said Mrs. Ansley slowly, "it's because you've always gone on hating me."

"Perhaps. Or because I wanted to get the whole thing off my mind." She paused. "I'm glad you destroyed the letter. Of course I never thought you'd die."

Mrs. Ansley relapsed into silence, and Mrs. Slade, . . . was conscious of a strange sense of isolation, of being cut off from the warm current of human communion. "You think me a monster!"

"I don't know. . . It was the only letter I had, and you say he didn't write it?"

"Ah, how you care for him still!"

"I cared for that memory," said Mrs. Ansley.

Mrs. Slade continued to look down on her. She seemed physically reduced by the blow—as if, when she got up, the wind might scatter her like a puff of dust. Mrs. Slade's jealousy suddenly leapt up again at the sight. All these years the woman had been living on that letter. How she must have loved him, to treasure the mere memory of its ashes! The letter of the man her friend was engaged to. Wasn't it she who was the monster?

"You tried your best to get him away from me, didn't you? But you failed; and I kept him. That's all."

"Yes. That's all."

"I wish now I hadn't told you. I'd no idea you'd feel about it as you do; I thought you'd be amused. It all happened so long ago as you say; and you must do me the justice to remember that I had no reason to think you'd ever taken it seriously. How could I, when you were married to Horace Ansley two months afterward? As soon as you could get out of bed your mother rushed you off to Florence and married you. People were rather surprised—they wondered at its being done so quickly; but I thought I knew. I had an idea you did it out of *pique*—to be able to say you'd got ahead of Delphin and me. Girls have such silly reasons for doing the most serious things. And your marrying so soon convinced me that you'd never really cared."

"Yes. I suppose it would," Mrs. Ansley assented.

The clear heaven overhead was emptied of all its gold. Dusk spread over it, abruptly darkening the Seven Hills. Here and there lights began to twinkle through the foliage at their feet. Steps were coming and going on the deserted terrace—waiters looking out of the doorway at the head of the stairs, then reappearing with trays and napkins and flasks of wine. Tables were moved, chairs straightened. A feeble string of electric lights flickered out. Some vases of faded flowers were carried away, and brought back replenished. A stout lady in a dust-coat suddenly appeared, asking in broken Italian if any one had seen the elastic band which held together her tattered Baedeker. She poked with her stick under the table at which she had lunched, the waiters assisting.

The corner where Mrs. Slade and Mrs. Ansley sat was still shadowy and deserted. For a long time neither of them spoke. At length Mrs. Slade began again: "I suppose I did it as a sort of joke—"

"A joke?"

"Well, girls are ferocious sometimes, you know. Girls in love especially. And I remember laughing to myself all that evening at the idea that you were waiting around there in the dark, dodg-ing out of sight, listening for every sound, trying to get in—. Of course I was upset when I heard you were so ill afterward."

Mrs. Ansley had not moved for a long time. But now she turned slowly toward her companion. "But I didn't wait. He'd arranged everything. He was there. We were let in at once," she said.

Mrs. Slade sprang up from her leaning position. "Delphin there? They let you in?—Ah, now you're lying!" she burst out with violence.

Mrs. Ansley's voice grew clearer, and full of surprise. "But of course he was there. Naturally he came—"

"Came? How did he know he'd find you there? You must be raving!"

Mrs. Ansley hesitated, as though reflecting. "But I answered the letter. I told him I'd be there. So he came."

Mrs. Slade flung her hands up to her face. "Oh, God—you answered! I never thought of your answering. . ."

"It's odd you never thought of it, if you wrote the letter."

"Yes. I was blind with rage."

Mrs. Ansley rose, and drew her fur scarf about her. "It is cool here. We'd better go. . . I'm sorry for you," she said, as she clasped the fur about her throat.

The unexpected words sent a pang through Mrs. Slade. "Yes, we'd better go." She gathered up her bag and cloak. "I don't know why you should be sorry for me," she muttered.

Mrs. Ansley stood looking away from her toward the dusky secret mass of the Colosseum. "Well—because I didn't have to wait that night."

Mrs. Slade gave an unquiet laugh. "Yes; I was beaten there. But I oughtn't to begrudge it to you, I suppose. At the end of all these years. After all, I had everything; I had him for twenty-five years. And you had nothing but that one letter that he didn't write."

Mrs. Ansley was again silent. At length she turned toward the door of the terrace. She took a step, and turned back, facing her companion.

"I had Barbara," she said, and began to move ahead of Mrs. Slade toward the stairway.

Among the works that have established Katherine Anne Porter as one of the finest writers of our time are Flowering Judas And Other Stories, Pale Horse, Pale Rider, *and* Ship of Fools. *Ms. Porter, who was born in Texas in 1894, has taught and lectured at many colleges and universities in the United States and Europe.*

The grandmother in "The Source" represents an active and, at times, overwhelming personality. She is surely the matriarch of her family, and we watch the way her presence dominates the story.

The Source

Katherine Anne Porter

Once a year, in early summer, after school was closed and the children were to be sent to the farm, the Grandmother began to long for the country. With an air of tenderness, as if she enquired after a favorite child, she would ask questions about the crops, wonder what kind of gardens the Negroes were making, how the animals were faring. She would remark now and then, "I begin to feel the need of a little change and relaxation, too," in a vague tone of reassurance, as if to say this did not mean that she intended for a moment really to relax her firm hold on family affairs. It was her favorite theory that change of occupation was one way, probably the best way, of resting. The three grandchildren would begin to feel the faint sure stirrings of departure in the house; her son, their father, would assume the air of careful patience which imperfectly masked his annoyance at the coming upsets and inconveniences to be endured at the farm. "Now, Harry, now, Harry!" his mother would warn him, for she was never deceived by his manner; indeed, he never meant her to be; and she would begin trying to placate him by wondering falsely if she could

possibly get away, after all, with so much yet to be done where she was. She looked forward with pleasure to a breath of country air. She always imagined herself as walking at leisure in the shade of the orchards watching the peaches ripen; she spoke with longing of clipping the rosebushes, or of tying up the trellised honeysuckle with her own hands. She would pack up her summer-weight black skirts, her thin black-and-white basques, and would get out a broad-brimmed, rather battered straw shepherdess hat she had woven for herself just after the war. Trying it on, turning her head critically this way and that before the mirror, she would decide that it might do nicely for the sun and she always took it along, but never wore it. She wore instead a stiffly starched white chambray bonnet, with a round crown buttoned on a narrow brim; it sat pertly on the top of her head with a fly-away look, the long strings hanging stiffly. Underneath this headdress, her pale, tightly drawn, very old face looked out with stately calm.

In the early spring, when the Indian cling peach tree against the wall of the town house began to bloom, she would say, "I have planted five orchards in three States, and now I see only one tree in bloom." A soft, enjoyable melancholy would come over her; she would stand quite still for a moment looking at the single tree, representing all her beloved trees still blooming, flourishing, and preparing to bring forth fruit in their separate places.

Leaving Aunt Nannie, who had been nurse to her children, in charge of the town house, she set out on her journey.

If departure was a delightful adventure for the children, arriving at the farm was an event for Grandmother. Hinry came running to open the gate, his coal-black face burst into a grin, his voice flying before him: "Howdy-do, Miss Sophia Jane!", simply not noticing that the carry-all was spilling over with other members of the family. The horses jogged in, their bellies jolting and churning, and Grandmother, calling out greetings in her feast-day voice, alighted, surrounded by her people, with the same flurry of travel that marked her journeys by train; but now with an indefinable sense of homecoming, not to the house but to the black, rich soft land and the human beings living on it. Without removing her long veiled widow's bonnet, she would walk straight through the house, observing instantly that everything was out of order; pass out into the yards and gardens, silently glancing, making instant plans for changes; down the narrow path past the barns, with a glance into and around them as she went, a glance of firm and purposeful censure; and on past the canebrake to the left, the hayfields to the right, until she arrived at the row of Negro huts that ran along the bois d'arc hedge.

Stepping up with a pleasant greeting to all, which in no way promised exemption from the wrath to come, she went into their kitchens, glanced into their meal barrels, their ovens, their cupboard shelves, into every smallest crevice and corner, with Littie and Dicey and Hinry and Bumper and Keg following, trying to explain that things was just a little out of shape right now because they'd had so much outside work they hadn't just been able to straighten out the way they meant to; but they were going to get at it right away.

Indeed they were, as Grandmother well knew. Within an hour someone would have driven away in the buckboard with an order for such lime for whitewash, so many gallons of kerosene oil, and so much carbolic acid and insect powder. Home-made lye soap would be produced from the washhouse, and the frenzy would begin. Every mattress cover was emptied of its corn husks and boiled, every little Negro on the place was set to work picking a fresh supply of husks, every hut was thickly whitewashed, bins and cupboards were scrubbed, every chair and bedstead was varnished, every filthy quilt was brought to light, boiled in a great iron washpot and stretched in the sun; and the uproar had all the special character of any annual occasion. The Negro women were put at making a fresh supply of shirts for the men and children, cotton dresses and aprons for themselves. Whoever wished to complain now seized his op-

portunity. Mister Harry had clean forgot to buy shoes for Hinry, look at Hinry: Hinry had been just like that, barefooted the live-long winter. Mister Miller (a red-whiskered man who occupied a dubious situation somewhere between overseer when Mister Harry was absent, and plain hired hand when he was present) had skimped them last winter on everything you could think of—not enough cornmeal, not half enough bacon, not enough wood, not enough of anything. Littie had needed a little sugar for her cawfy and do you think Mister Miller would let her have it? No. Mister Miller had said nobody needed sugar in their cawfy. Hinry said Mister Miller didn't even take sugar in his own cawfy because he was just too stingy. Boosker, the three-year-old baby, had earache in January and Miz Carleton had come down and put lodnum in it and Boosker was acting like she was deef ever since. The black horse Mister Harry bought last fall had gone clean wild and jumped a barbed wire fence and tore his chest almost off and hadn't been any good from that time on.

All these annoyances and dozens like them had to be soothed at once, then Grandmother's attention was turned to the main house, which must be overhauled completely. The big secretaries were opened and shabby old sets of Dickens, Scott, Thackeray, Dr. Johnson's dictionary, the volumes of Pope and Milton and Dante and Shakespeare were dusted off and closed up carefully again. Curtains came down in dingy heaps and went up again stiff and sweet-smelling; rugs were heaved forth in dusty confusion and returned flat and gay with flowers once more; the kitchen was no longer dingy and desolate but a place of heavenly order where it was tempting to linger.

Next the barns and smokehouses and the potato cellar, the gardens and every tree or vine or bush must have that restoring touch upon it. For two weeks this would go on, with the Grandmother a tireless, just, and efficent slave driver of every creature on the place. The children ran wild outside, but not as they did when she was not there. The hour came in each day when they were rounded up, captured, washed, dressed properly, made to eat what was set before them without giving battle, put to bed when the time came and no nonsense . . . They loved their Grandmother; she was the only reality to them in a world that seemed otherwise without fixed authority or refuge, since their mother had died so early that only the eldest girl remembered her vaguely: just the same they felt that Grandmother was tyrant, and they wished to be free of her; so they were always pleased, when on a certain day, as a sign that her visit was drawing to an end, she would go out to the pasture and call her old saddle horse, Fiddler.

He had been a fine, thorough-paced horse once, but he was now a weary, disheartened old hero, gray-haired on his jaw and chin, who spent his life nuzzling with pendulous lips for tender bits of grass or accepting sugar cautiously between his shaken teeth. He paid no attention to anyone but the Grandmother. Every summer when she went to his field and called him, he came doddering up with almost a gleam in his filmy eyes. The two old creatures would greet each other fondly. The Grandmother always treated her animal friends as if they were human beings temporarily metamorphosed, but not by this accident dispensed from those duties suitable to their condition. She would have Fiddler brought around under her old side-saddle—her little granddaughters rode astride and she saw no harm in it, for them—and mount with her foot in Uncle Jimbilly's curved hand. Fiddler would remember his youth and break into a stiff-legged gallop, and off she would go with her crepe bands and her old-fashioned riding skirt flying. They always returned at a walk, the Grandmother sitting straight as a sword, smiling, triumphant. Dismounting at the horse-block by herself, she would stroke Fiddler on the neck before turning him over to Uncle Jimbilly, and walk away carrying her train grandly over her arm.

This yearly gallop with Fiddler was important to her; it proved her strength, her unabated energy. Any time now Fiddler might drop in his tracks, but she would not. She would say, "He's getting stiff in the knees," or "He's pretty short-winded this year," but she herself walked lightly and breathed as easily as ever, or so she chose to believe.

That same afternoon or the next day, she would take her long-promised easy stroll in the orchards with nothing to do, her Grandchildren running before her and running back to her side: with nothing at all to do, her hands folded, her skirts trailing and picking up twigs, turning over little stones, sweeping a faint path behind her, her white bonnet askew over one eye, an absorbed fixed smile on her lips, her eyes missing nothing. This walk would usually end with Hinry or Jimbilly being dispatched to the orchards at once to make some trifling but indispensable improvement.

It would then come over her powerfully that she was staying on idling when there was so much to be done at home . . . There would be a last look at everything, instructions, advices, good-bys, blessings. She would set out with that strange look of leaving forever, and arrive at the place in town with the same air of homecoming she had worn on her arrival in the country in a gentle flurry of greeting and felicitations, as if she had been gone for half a year. At once she set to work restoring to order the place which no doubt had gone somewhat astray in her absence.

DISCUSSION TOPICS

1. Imagine yourself a middle-aged woman writing a letter of advice to a teenage child or grandchild. What subjects would you cover?

SUGGESTED ACTIVITIES

1. Prepare a report on a real matriarchal society. You will have to do library research in anthropology in order to find material. You might begin your research with the writings of Margaret Mead.

2. Write a series of short statements or ads designed to encourage senior citizens to join the feminist movement. Then visit a home for the elderly and tape responses to these statements or ads. Try to interview at least ten people.

What Is A Woman?

37

38

39

39A

40

41

44

45

47

48

49　　　　50

51

52

SOLIDARITY
WITH
Underground
SISTERS
FREE OUR
SISTERS
FREE OURSELVE

Sisters of the World Unite
SEXIS
WE Dem
immediate
medical C
for
PeggyHu

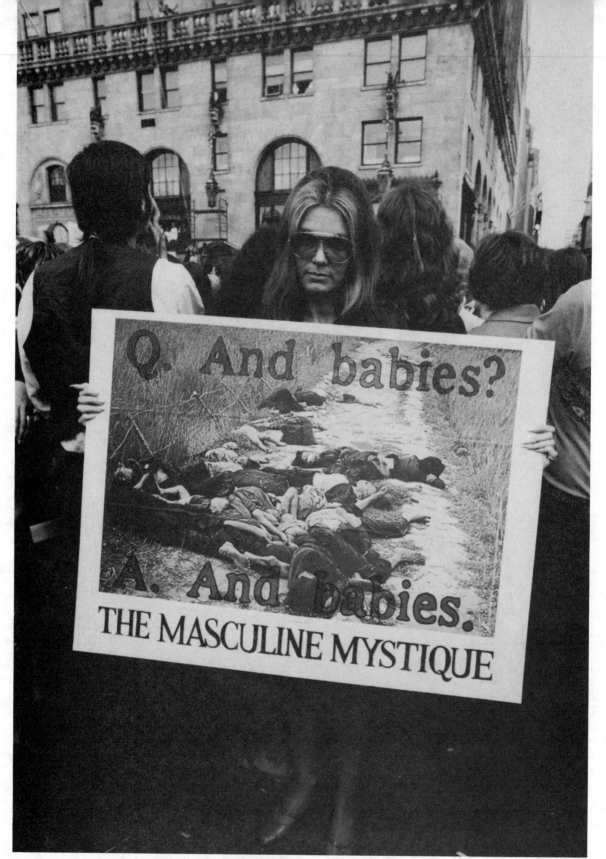

57–58

PART

Now Sisters...

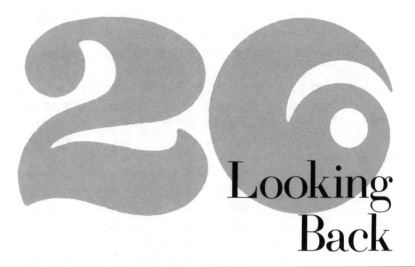

CHAPTER

26 Looking Back

In 1950, Eleanor Roosevelt wrote an essay called "Women Have Come A Long Way." By that time she had lived for sixty-six years and had seen many changes in the lifestyles of American women. Women were allowed to work, to be educated, and to dress in trousers if they chose. As a young woman from an upper class family at the turn of the century, Eleanor Roosevelt had been permitted none of these.

Unlike many of her female contemporaries, she overcame the lack of formal education and became one of the most influential women of the twentieth century. During her lifetime, Eleanor Roosevelt served in the United Nations as Chairman of the Commission on Human Rights, wrote a syndicated column, and exerted tremendous influence in the Democratic party. While her husband, Franklin Delano Roosevelt, was President, Mrs. Roosevelt actively campaigned for civil rights long before it was fashionable to do so.

As you read this essay, which originally appeared in <u>Harper's Magazine</u>, think about the progress women have made since 1950. At that time, Eleanor Roosevelt claimed they had come a long way. Have they come a long way since then?

Women Have Come A Long Way

Eleanor Roosevelt

As I look back over a rather long life, I am impressed with the great changes that I have witnessed in the status of women. I was brought up by my grandmother from the time I was eight years old, so perhaps I see the differences in a somewhat more exaggerated form than some of my contemporaries who were never under the direct influence of a member of that earlier generation. To my grandmother it was unthinkable that a girl should go to work unless she was destitute or at least really impoverished; and that she should wish to go to college seemed preposterous. But I imagine that most women who were brought up at the time I was, and in roughly the same sort of surroundings, will share my sense of the contrasts that have come about.

I learned to ride horseback, but I rode side-saddle. I can remember the excitement there was over girls who rode bicycles wearing bloomers, and how outrageous many people thought them. We went bathing in bathing suits with skirts, and long black stockings; propriety demanded that we be completely covered. And some girls even wore hats in bathing to shield them from the sun, for it was considered important to preserve the whiteness of one's skin; young ladies would have been dismayed at getting the healthy look of tan that today they deliberately acquire in the South in the winter, and wherever they are in the summer.

At eighteen I was introduced to New York Society. I was a frightened young girl who had spent three years at a finishing school in Europe and had practically no friends, either male or female, in this country. There was still a Four Hundred in New York Society. If you belonged you were asked to the "right parties" and if you didn't belong you were not asked. In those days it took not only money but a really concentrated campaign to get recognition if you came as an unknown to New York. I remember a few lovely girls who took the city by storm, arriving from other parts of the country, but either they were great beauties or had a reputation for having brains and knew some of the "right" people to introduce them. People were just beginning to accept the fact that a Miss Livingston could marry a Mr. Mills from California; but on the whole New York Society was compact and chary of outsiders.

It was conceded that girls of Society families had an obligation to do some kind of charitable work, but very, very few of them took money-earning jobs; and if they "had to work," as the phrase of the day went, they were largely limited to becoming teachers, trained nurses, social workers, or librarians. Miss Elizabeth Marbury once told me how horrified the New York Society of her young days was when she had to go to work and began to represent artists and build a talent office.

A girl whose family was on a lower income level could be a clerk in a store or work in an office, but generally speaking she did this only so long as it was an absolute economic necessity; male pride and general public opinion frowned on any woman who worked outside the home if she could manage to avoid it. Not many executive positions were held by women and they had hardly begun to be recognized in the professions. That has come only after a long, hard fight; and few young things today have any idea of what they owe to the women who pioneered in higher education and in working in the professional fields.

We still heard with amusement and horror in the early nineteen-hundreds of the early fighters for suffrage who had worn trousers and walked around the streets of New York in them. Women were doing a great many things for the first time, but most of them were content to be housekeepers and mothers who stayed in the home—where they often worked very hard indeed—and many became pretty Society butterflies, spoiled and ruled by their husbands.

A change came with World War I. For large numbers of women who had to go to work when their husbands were in the service found they liked the new freedom and continued in their jobs after the war was over; the percentage of women working for wages outside the home jumped upward.

My mother had been well educated for a girl of her generation and she took a great interest in my education, but in those days a solid foundation of learning and training in the ability to think were less highly regarded than the social graces which made you attractive and charming in Society. I learned to speak French fluently before I learned to speak English, but my arithmetic was learned by rote without the slightest understanding of why certain things produced certain answers. I learned the whole of the first four books of Euclid by heart, and I have never understood what use that was in preparation for the life that I was expected to live in the future. Of course, I have had quite a different life from the one that my mother and grandmother envisioned for me; I was certainly not consciously prepared for it.

I was fifteen when I came in contact, in Europe, with the first women I had ever known who were really intellectually emancipated, and I found this experience extremely stimulating. The Boer War was being fought and the Dreyfus case was still being argued. I heard the rights and wrongs of such public issues discussed at length and heatedly, in fact with passion—something I had never heard at home. In my grandmother's home politics were never mentioned and I think she was rather ashamed to acknowledge that even by marriage anything so contaminating as a government official was related to the family.

But if I was not brought up to be useful or to think of the obligations to society that must be recognized by a conscientious citizen of a democracy, I was nevertheless given a very free rein in my intellectual development along many lines. The library in our country house, as in the city house we lived in, was filled with books gathered by my grandfather, who had had a special bent toward theology, though apparently he never had any inclination to become a minister. I never wanted to read the books on theology (though I remember shedding tears over the illustrations in the Doré Bible); but other books on those shelves —the classics, biographies, travel, novels, stories about life anywhere of any kind—fed the interests of my childhood and helped to show me, eventually, why so many women were beginning to fight for equality in the political and social world, which up to that time had seemed of very little importance to me.

I had my first contact with the suffrage movement rather late, and consider myself lucky to have heard Anna Howard Shaw speak and to have known Carrie Chapman Catt before she was widely recognized as the great leader of women in the struggle for equal political rights.

As a result of the shift of public opinion which these women helped to bring about, there have been far-reaching amendments during the past fifty years of the laws which touch on the rights of women. These vary in different parts of the world and, for that matter, in different states in our own country. The old Blue Laws which were accepted throughout New England at one time may still be on the statute books, but even where such antiquated legislation remains it is completely ignored, and by and large women seem to be considered as equals before the law in the United States. Of late there has been a great agitation to pass an equal rights amendment; but I think that if one looks over the reforms of the past generation, one must decide that it would be easier in our particular situation to change such state laws as seem to discriminate against women than to pass a federal amendment.

Women have now become an integral part of nearly all the trade unions, and it is interesting to note that some of the unions in the industries which employ largely women are as good as any there are.

In family life, too, the change has been great. Fifty years ago women had to resort to subtlety if they wished to exert influence; now their influence is exerted openly and accepted by husband and children. Fifty years ago no young girl had an apartment of her own while she was single; "Mrs. Grundy" frowned on that. Today no one questions the right of an adult woman to have her own home.

In my lifetime I have seen women accepted as doctors, surgeons, psychiatrists, lawyers, architects, and even during the war as mechanics on the assembly line. I remember the day when John Golden said in the White House that women lacked the power to be creative and that there had never been any great creative women artists. I took that up seriously with him later, and contended that this might seem to be true in our time, but had not always been true in the past; and that if it was true now, this was not because women lacked ability but because they lacked opportunity. I think that today we must realize that in the past generation we have developed many very able writers and painters and some very able sculptors among the women of this country and other countries. Modern life moves very quickly and the distractions and multitudinous occupations that are thrust upon women tend to make the development of an artist's creative talents more difficult than in the past; but in spite of these outward circumstances, the urge to create is so strong that I think we are going to find more and more women expressing themselves not only through the bearing and rearing of children but through the creative arts.

One thing that strikes me particularly today is the way in which women are accepting responsibility in creating the pattern for the new states. Take India, for example. I have seen in the United Nations a woman delegate, Madame Pandit, the sister of the Prime Minister, lead her delegation —the only woman to occupy such a position.

I have been impressed, too, with the number of women of charm and ability who have come to the United Nations with good backgrounds of work in various fields that fit them for their duties in that body. I think at once of Madame Lefoucheaux of France, who was chairman of the last meeting of the Commission on the Status of Women; Miss Bowie, who represented the United Kingdom on the Human Rights Commission; Madame Hansa Mehta of India, also on this commission; and many women who have acted as advisers to the harried delegates and brought us the information without which some of us would have found it very difficult to carry on the work confronting us in fields in which we had had little or no experience. Even ten years ago, if there had been such a body as the United Nations, it would hardly have been possible to find women sitting as delegates, and certainly it would have been considered doubtful whether the United States would ever send a woman as a delegate. Now it sends a woman alternate as well!

Perhaps the position of women in the United Nations is the best example of the fact that they have graduated from exclusion from business and the professions to almost complete acceptance and equality, and that they are now generally treated as virtually on a par with men in the political world at home and abroad. Some nations are slower in granting this recognition than others, but the trend is unmistakable. It is toward complete equality.

I think it might still be said that if a woman wants really to succeed she must do better than a man, for she is under more careful scrutiny; but this is practically the only handicap under which women now labor in almost any field of endeavor.

DISCUSSION QUESTIONS

1. Refute the statement made by John Golden that women lack the power to be creative in the arts.

SUGGESTED ACTIVITIES

1. Do a statistical comparison of the kinds of jobs held by women before World War I and now.

CHAPTER

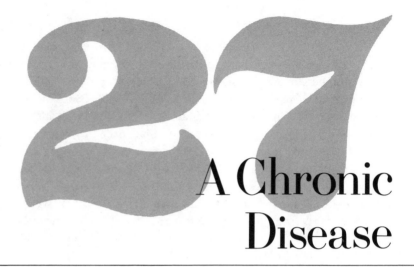

A Chronic Disease

The modern American woman has more material comforts and timesaving devices than any woman in the world has ever had. Yet in the opening chapter of <u>The Feminine Mystique</u>, Betty Friedan reports that these pampered women feel discontented, purposeless, and fatigued for no apparent reason. What is the matter with them? Is it that they are grasping, selfish women who are beyond ever being satisfied, who are bottomless pits of acquisitiveness?

"The Problem That Has No Name," the first chapter of <u>The Feminine Mystique</u>, examines the reasons for the discontent of the American housewife. Ms. Friedan, in her travels across the country and in her interviews with women from different income levels and educational backgrounds, discovered the problem to be almost universal. Unearthing this pervasive difficulty was no easy task; pinpointing reasons or causes for feeling unfulfilled cannot be done quickly. You, yourself, may have experienced this problem. But you don't talk about it through fear—fear that it means you are a personal failure, or fear that this experience is unique to you alone, or fear that the problem is morally and socially unacceptable.

This is exactly what was silencing the women Betty Friedan talked to. As they gradually realized they were not alone, the women began to discuss their attitudes. And all of them complained that spending all their time tending a husband, children, and a house left them incomplete. They wanted more responsibility and a sense of purpose outside the home.

Ms. Friedan's interviews finally resulted in <u>The Feminine Mystique</u>, which is partially responsible for the current feminist movement. In addition to writing the book, Ms. Friedan has taken an activist role in the drive for Women's Rights by founding the National Organization for Women, a group concerned with the position of women in America.

The Problem That Has No Name

Betty Friedan

The problem lay buried, unspoken, for many years in the minds of American women. It was a strange stirring, a sense of dissatisfaction, a yearning that women suffered in the middle of the twentieth century in the United States. Each suburban wife struggled with it alone. As she made the beds, shopped for groceries, matched slipcover material, ate peanut butter sandwiches with her children, chauffeured Cub Scouts and Brownies, lay beside her husband at night, she was afraid to ask even of herself the silent question: "Is this all?"

For over fifteen years there was no word of this yearning in the millions of words written about women, for women, in all the columns, books, and articles by experts telling women their role was to seek fulfillment as wives and mothers. Over and over women heard in voices of tradition and of Freudian sophistication that they could desire no greater destiny than to glory in their own femininity. Experts told them how to catch a man and keep him, how to breastfeed children and handle their toilet training, how to cope with sibling rivalry and adolescent rebellion; how to buy a dishwasher, bake bread, cook gourmet snails, and build a swimming pool with their own hands; how to dress, look, and act more feminine and make marriage more exciting; how to keep their husbands from dying young and their sons from growing into delinquents. They were taught to pity the neurotic, unfeminine, unhappy women who wanted to be poets or physicists or presidents. They learned that truly feminine women do not want careers, higher education, political rights— the independence and the opportunities that the old-fashioned feminists fought for. Some women, in their forties and fifties, still remembered painfully giving up those dreams, but most of the younger women no longer even thought about them. A thousand expert voices applauded their femininity, their adjustment, their new maturity.

All they had to do was devote their lives from earliest girlhood to finding a husband and bearing children.

By the end of the nineteen-fifties, the average marriage age of women in America dropped to 20, and was still dropping, into the teens. Fourteen million girls were engaged by 17. The proportion of women attending college in comparison with men dropping from 47 percent in 1920 to 35 percent in 1958. A century earlier, women had fought for higher education; now girls went to college to get a husband. By the mid-fifties, 60 percent dropped out of college to marry, or because they were afraid too much education would be a marriage bar. Colleges built dormitories for "married students," but the students were almost always the husbands. A new degree was instituted for the wives—"Ph.T." (Putting Husband Through).

Then American girls began getting married in high school. And the women's magazines, deploring the unhappy statistics about these young marriages, urged that courses on marriage, and marriage counselors, be installed in the high schools. Girls started going steady at twelve and thirteen, in junior high. Manufacturers put out brassieres with false bosoms of foam rubber for little girls of ten. And an advertisement for a child's dress, sizes 3–6x, in *The New York Times* in the fall of 1960, said: "She Too Can Join the Man-Trap Set."

By the end of the fifties, the United States birthrate was overtaking India's. The birth-control movement, renamed Planned Parenthood, was asked to find a method whereby women who had been advised that a third or fourth baby would be born dead or defective might have it anyhow. Statisticians were especially astounded at the fantastic increase in the number of babies among college women. Where once they had two children, now they had four, five, six. Women who had once wanted careers were now making careers out of having babies. So rejoiced *Life* magazine in a 1956 paean to the movement of American women back to the home.

In a New York hospital, a woman had a nervous breakdown when she found she could not breastfeed her baby. In other hospitals, women dying of cancer refused a drug which research had proved might save their lives: its side effects were said to be unfeminine. "If I have only one life, let me live it as a blonde," a larger-than-life-sized picture of a pretty, vacuous woman proclaimed from newspaper, magazine, and drugstore ads. And across America, three out of every ten women dyed their hair blonde. They ate a chalk called Metrecal, instead of food, to shrink to the size of the thin young models. Department-store buyers reported that American women, since 1939, had become three and four sizes smaller. "Women are out to fit the clothes, instead of vice-versa," one buyer said.

Interior decorators were designing kitchens with mosaic murals and original paintings, for kitchens were once again the center of women's lives. Home sewing became a million-dollar industry. Many women no longer left their homes, except to shop, chauffeur their children, or attend a social engagement with their husbands. Girls were growing up in America without ever having jobs outside the home. In the late fifties, a sociological phenomenon was suddenly remarked: a third of American women now worked, but most were no longer young and very few were pursuing careers. They were married women who held part-time jobs, selling or secretarial, to put their husbands through school, their sons through college, or to help pay the mortgage. Or they were widows supporting families. Fewer and fewer women were entering professional work. The shortages in the nursing, social work, and teaching professions caused crises in almost every American city. Concerned over the Soviet Union's lead in the space race, scientists noted that America's greatest source of unused brain-power was women. But girls would not study physics: it was "unfeminine." A girl refused a science fellowship at Johns Hopkins to take a job in a real-estate office. All she wanted, she said, was what every other American girl wanted—to get married, have four children, and live in a nice house in a nice suburb.

The suburban housewife—she was the dream image of the young American women and the envy, it was said, of women all over the world. The American housewife—freed by science and labor-saving appliances from the drudgery, the dangers of childbirth, and the illnesses of her grandmother. She was healthy, beautiful, educated, concerned only about her husband, her children, her home. She had found true feminine fulfillment. As a housewife and mother, she was respected as a full and equal partner to man in his world. She was free to choose automobiles, clothes, appliances, supermarkets; she had everything that women ever dreamed of.

In the fifteen years after World War II, this mystique of feminine fulfillment became the cherished and self-perpetuating core of contemporary American culture. Millions of women lived their lives in the image of those pretty pictures of American suburban housewives, kissing their husbands goodbye in front of the picture window, depositing their stationwagonsful of children at school, and smiling as they ran their new electric waxers over the spotless kitchen floors. They baked their own bread, sewed their own and their children's clothes, kept their new washing machines and dryers running all day. They changed the sheets on the beds twice a week instead of once, took the rug-hooking class in adult education, and pitied their poor frustrated mothers, who had dreamed of having a career. Their only dream was to be perfect wives and mothers; their highest ambition to have five children and a beautiful house, their only fight to get and keep their husbands. They had no thought for the unfeminine problems of the world outside the home; they wanted the men to make the major decisions. They gloried in their role as women, and wrote proudly on the census blank: "Occupation: housewife."

For over fifteen years, the words written for women, and the words women used when they talked to each other, while their husbands sat on the other side of the room and talked shop or politics or septic tanks, were about problems with their children, or how to keep their husbands happy, or improve their children's school, or cook chicken, or make slipcovers. Nobody argued whether women were inferior or superior to men; they were simply different. Words like "emancipation" and "career" sounded strange and embarrassing; no one had used them for years. When a Frenchwoman named Simone de Beauvoir wrote a book called *The Second Sex*, an American critic commented that she obviously "didn't know what life was all about," and besides, she was talking about French women. The "woman problem" in America no longer existed.

If a woman had a problem in the 1950s and 1960s, she knew that something must be wrong with her marriage, or with herself. Other women were satisfied with their lives, she thought. What kind of a woman was she if she did not feel this mysterious fulfillment waxing the kitchen floor? She was so ashamed to admit her dissatisfaction that she never knew how many other women shared it. If she tried to tell her husband, he didn't understand what she was talking about. She did not really understand it herself. For over fifteen years women in America found it harder to talk about this problem than about sex. Even the psychoanalysts had no name for it. When a woman went to a psychiatrist for help, as many women did, she would say, "I'm so ashamed," or "I must be hopelessly neurotic." "I don't know what's wrong with women today," a suburban psychiatrist said uneasily. "I only know something is wrong because most of my patients happen to be women. And their problem isn't sexual." Most women with this problem did not go to see a psychoanalyst, however. "There's nothing wrong really," they kept telling themselves. "There isn't any problem."

But on an April morning in 1959, I heard a mother of four, having coffee with four other mothers in a suburban development fifteen miles from New York, say in a tone of quiet desperation, "the problem." And the others knew, without words, that she was not talking about a problem with her husband, or her children, or her home. Suddenly they realized they all shared the same problem, the problem that has no name. They began, hesitantly, to talk about it. Later, after they had picked up their children at nursery school and taken them home to nap, two of the women cried, in sheer relief, just to know they were not alone.

Gradually I came to realize that the problem that has no name was shared by countless women in America. As a magazine writer I often interviewed women about problems with their children, or their marriages, or their houses, or their communities. But after a while I began to recognize the telltale signs of this other problem. I saw the same signs in suburban ranch houses and split-levels on Long Island and in New Jersey and Westchester County; in colonial houses in a small Massachusetts town; on patios in Memphis; in suburban and city apartments; in living rooms in the Midwest. Sometimes I sensed the problem, not as reporter, but as a suburban housewife, for during this time I was also bringing up my own three children in Rockland County, New York. I heard echoes of the problem in college dormitories and semi-private maternity wards, at PTA meetings and luncheons of the League of Women Voters, at suburban cocktail parties, in station wagons waiting for trains, and in snatches of conversation overheard at Schrafft's. The groping words I heard from other women, on quiet afternoons when children were at school or on quiet evenings when husbands worked late, I think I understood first as a woman long before I understood their larger social and psychological implications.

Just what was this problem that has no name? What were the words women used when they tried to express it? Sometimes a woman would say "I feel empty somehow . . . incomplete." Or she would say "I feel as if I don't exist." Sometimes she blotted out the feeling with a tranquilizer. Sometimes she thought the problem was with her husband, or her children, or that what she really needed was to redecorate her house, or move to a better neighborhood, or have an affair, or another baby. Sometimes, she went to a doctor with symptoms she could hardly describe: "A tired feeling . . . I get so angry with the children it scares me . . . I feel like crying without any reason." (A Cleveland doctor called it "the housewife's syndrome.") A number of women told me about great bleeding blisters that break out on their hands and arms. "I call it the housewife's blight," said a family doctor in Pennsylvania. "I see it so often lately in these young women with four, five, and six children who bury themselves in their dishpans. But it isn't caused by detergent and it isn't cured by cortisone."

Sometimes a woman would tell me that the feeling gets so strong she runs out of the house and walks through the streets. Or she stays inside her house and cries. Or her children tell her a joke, and she doesn't laugh because she doesn't hear it. I talked to women who had spent years on the analyst's couch, working out their "adjustment to the feminine role," their blocks to "fulfillment as a wife and mother." But the desperate tone in these women's voices, and the look in their eyes, was the same as the tone and the look of other women, who were sure they had no problem, even though they did have a strange feeling of desperation. . . .

In 1960, the problem that has no name burst like a boil through the image of the happy American housewife. In the television commercials the pretty housewives still beamed over their foaming dishpans and *Time's* cover story on "The Suburban Wife, an American Phenomenon" protested: "Having too good a time . . . to believe that they should be unhappy." But the actual unhappiness of the American housewife was suddenly being reported—from *The New York Times* and *Newsweek* to *Good Housekeeping* and CBS Television ("The Trapped Housewife"), although almost everybody who talked about it found some superficial reason to dismiss it. It was attributed to incompetent appliance repairmen (*New York Times*), or the distances children must be chauffeured in the suburbs (*Time*), or too much PTA (*Redbook*). Some said it was the old problem—education: more and more women had education,

which naturally made them unhappy in their role as housewives. "The road from Freud to Frigidaire, from Sophocles to Spock, has turned out to be a bumpy one," reported *The New York Times* (June 28, 1960). "Many young women—certainly not all —whose education plunged them into a world of ideas feel stifled in their homes. They find their routine lives out of joint with their training. Like shut-ins, they feel left out. In the last year, the problem of the educated housewife has provided the meat of dozens of speeches made by troubled presidents of women's colleges who maintain, in the face of complaints, that sixteen years of academic training is realistic preparation for wifehood and motherhood."

There was much sympathy for the educated housewife. ("Like a two-headed schizophrenic . . . once she wrote a paper on the Graveyard poets; now she writes notes to the milkman. Once she determined the boiling point of sulphuric acid; now she determines her boiling point with the overdue repairman. . . . The housewife often is reduced to screams and tears. . . . No one, it seems, is appreciative, least of all herself, of the kind of person she becomes in the process of turning from poetress into shrew.")

Home economists suggested more realistic preparation for housewives such as high-school workshops in home appliances. College educators suggested more discussion groups on home management and the family, to prepare women for the adjustment to domestic life. A spate of articles appeared in the mass magazines offering "Fifty-eight Ways to Make Your Marriage More Exciting." No month went by without a new book by a psychiatrist or sexologist offering technical advice or finding greater fulfillment through sex.

A male humorist joked in *Harper's Bazaar* (July, 1960) that the problem could be solved by taking away woman's right to vote. ("In the pre-19th Amendment era, the American woman was placid, sheltered, and sure of her role in American society. She left all the political decisions to her husband and he, in turn, left all the family decisions to her. Today a woman has to make both the family *and* the political decisions, and it's too much for her.")

A number of educators suggested seriously that women no longer be admitted to the four-year colleges and universities: in the growing college crisis, the education which girls could not use as housewives was more urgently needed than ever by boys to do the work of the atomic age.

The problem was also dismissed with drastic solutions no one could take seriously. (A woman writer proposed in *Harper's* that women be drafted for compulsory service as nurses' aides and baby-sitters.) And it was smoothed over with the age-old panaceas: "love is their answer," "the only answer is inner help," "the secret of completeness—children," "a private means of intellectual fulfillment," "to cure this toothache of the spirit—the simple formula of handing one's self and one's will over to God."

The problem was dismissed by telling the housewife she doesn't realize how lucky she is—her own boss, no time clock, no junior executive gunning for her job. What if she isn't happy—does she think men are happy in this world? Does she really, secretly, still want to be a man? Doesn't she know yet how lucky she is to be a woman?

The problem was also, and finally, dismissed by shrugging that there are no solutions: this is what being a woman means, and what is wrong with American women that they can't accept their role gracefully? As *Newsweek* put it (March 7, 1960):

> *She is dissatisfied with a lot that women of other lands can only dream of. Her discontent is deep, pervasive, and impervious to the superficial remedies which are offered at every hand. . . . An army of professional explorers have already charted the major sources of trouble. . . . From the beginning of time, the female cycle has defined and confined woman's role. As Freud was credited with saying: "Anatomy is destiny." Though no group of women has ever pushed these natural restrictions as far as the American wife, it seems that she still cannot accept them with good grace. . . . A young*

> *mother with a beautiful family, charm, talent, and brains is apt to dismiss her role apologetically. "What do I do?" you hear her say. "Why nothing. I'm just a housewife." A good education, it seems, has given this paragon among women an understanding of the value of everything except her own worth . . .*

And so she must accept the fact that "American women's unhappiness is merely the most recently won of women's rights," and adjust and say with the happy housewife found by *Newsweek*: "We ought to salute the wonderful freedom we all have and be proud of our lives today. I have had college and I've worked, but being a housewife is the most rewarding and satisfying role. . . . My mother was never included in my father's business affairs . . . she couldn't get out of the house and away from us children. But I am an equal to my husband; I can go along with him on business trips and to social business affairs."

The alternative offered was a choice that few women would contemplate. In the sympathetic words of *The New York Times:* "All admit to being deeply frustrated at times by the lack of privacy, the physical burden, the routine of family life, the confinement of it. However, none would give up her home and family if she had the choice to make again." *Redbook* commented: "Few women would want to thumb their noses at husbands, children, and community and go off on their own. Those who do may be talented individuals, but they rarely are successful women."

The year American women's discontent boiled over, it was also reported (*Look*) that the more than 21 million American women who are single, widowed, or divorced do not cease even after fifty their frenzied, desperate search for a man. And the search begins early—for seventy percent of all American women now marry before they are twenty-four. A pretty twenty-five-year-old secretary took thirty-five different jobs in six months in the futile hope of finding a husband. Women were moving from one political club to another, taking evening courses in accounting or sailing, learning to play golf or ski, joining a number of churches in succession, going to bars alone, in their ceaseless search for a man.

Of the growing thousands of women currently getting private psychiatric help in the United States the married ones were reported dissatisfied with their marriages, the unmarried ones suffering from anxiety and, finally, depression. Strangely, a number of psychiatrists stated that in their experience, unmarried women patients were happier than married ones. So the door of all those pretty suburban houses opened a crack to permit a glimpse of uncounted thousands of American housewives who suffered alone from a problem that suddenly everyone was talking about, and beginning to take for granted, as one of those unreal problems in American life that can never be solved—like the hydrogen bomb. By 1962 the plight of the trapped American housewife had become a national parlor game. Whole issues of magazines, newspaper columns, books learned and frivolous, educational conferences, and television panels were devoted to the problem.

Even so, most men, and some women, still did not know that this problem was real. But those who had faced it honestly knew that all the superficial remedies, the sympathetic advice, the scolding words, and the cheering words were somehow drowning the problem in unreality. A bitter laugh was beginning to be heard from American women. They were admired, envied, pitied, theorized over until they were sick of it, offered drastic solutions or silly choices that no one could take seriously. They got all kinds of advice from the growing armies of marriage and child-guidance counselors psychotherapists, and armchair psychologists, on how to adjust to their role as housewives. No other road to fulfillment was offered to American women in the middle of the twentieth century. Most adjusted to their role and suffered or ignored the problem that has no name. It can be less painful for a woman, not to hear the strange, dissatisfied voice stirring within her.

It is no longer possible to ignore that voice, to dismiss the desperation of so many American women. This is not what being a woman means, no matter what the experts say. For human suffering there is a reason; perhaps the reason has not been found because the right questions have not been asked, or pressed far enough. I do not accept the answer that there is no problem because American women have luxuries that women in other times and lands never dreamed of; part of the strange newness of the problem is that it cannot be understood in terms of the age-old material problems of man: poverty, sickness, hunger, cold. The women who suffer this problem have a hunger that food cannot fill. It persists in women whose husbands are struggling internes and law clerks, or prosperous doctors and lawyers; in wives of workers and executives who make $5,000 a year or $50,000. It is not caused by lack of material advantages; it may not even be felt by women preoccupied with desperate problems of hunger, poverty, or illness. And women who think it will be solved by more money, a bigger house, a second car, moving to a better suburb, often discover it gets worse.

It is no longer possible today to blame the problem on loss of femininity: to say that education and independence and equality with men have made American women unfeminine. I have heard so many women try to deny this dissatisfied voice within themselves because it does not fit the pretty picture of femininity the experts have given them. I think, in fact, that this is the first clue to the mystery: the problem cannot be understood in the generally accepted terms by which scientists have studied women, doctors have treated them, counselors have advised them, and writers have written about them. Women who suffer this problem, in whom this voice is stirring, have lived their whole lives in the pursuit of feminine fulfillment. They are not career women (although career women may have other problems); they are women whose greatest ambition has been marriage and children. For the oldest of these women, these daughters of the American middle class, no other dream was possible. The ones in their forties and fifties who once had other dreams gave them up and threw themselves joyously into life as housewives. For the youngest, the new wives and mothers, this was the only dream. They are the ones who quit high school and college to marry, or marked time in some job in which they had no real interest until they married. These women are very "feminine" in the usual sense, and yet they still suffer the problem. . . .

Can the problem that has no name be somehow related to the domestic routine of the housewife? When a woman tries to put the problem into words, she often merely describes the daily life she leads. What is there in this recital of comfortable domestic detail that could possibly cause a feeling of desperation? Is she trapped simply by the enormous demands of her role as modern housewife: wife, mistress, mother, nurse, consumer, cook, chauffeur, expert on interior decoration, child care, appliance repair, furniture refinishing, nutrition, and education? Her day is fragmented as she rushes from dishwasher to washing machine to telephone to dryer to station wagon to supermarket, and delivers Johnny to the Little League field, takes Janey to dancing class, gets the lawn mower fixed and meets the 6:45. She can never spend more than 15 minutes on any one thing; she has no time to read books, only magazines; even if she had time, she has lost the power to concentrate. At the end of the day, she is so terribly tired that sometimes her husband has to take over and put the children to bed.

This terrible tiredness took so many women to doctors in the 1960's that one decided to investigate it. He found, surprisingly, that his patients suffering from "housewife's fatigue" slept more than an adult needed to sleep—as much as ten hours a day—and that the actual energy they expended on housework did not tax their capacity. The real problem must be something else, he de-cided—perhaps boredom. Some doctors told their women patients they must get out of the house for a day, treat themselves to a movie in town. Others prescribed tranquilizers. Many suburban housewives were taking tranquilizers like cough drops. "You wake up in the morning, and you feel as if there's no point in going on another day like this. So you take a tranquilizer because it makes you not care so much that it's pointless."

It is easy to see the concrete details that trap the suburban housewife, the continual demands on her time. But the chains that bind her in her trap are chains in her own mind and spirit. They are chains made up of mistaken ideas and misinterpreted facts, of incomplete truths and unreal choices. They are not easily seen and not easily shaken off.

How can any woman see the whole truth within the bounds of her own life? How can she believe that voice inside herself, when it denies the conventional, accepted truths by which she has been living? And yet the women I have talked to, who are finally listening to that inner voice, seem in some incredible way to be groping through to a truth that has defied the experts. . . .

If I am right, the problem that has no name stirring in the minds of so many American women today is not a matter of loss of femininity or too much education, or the demands of domesticity. It is far more important than anyone recognizes. It is the key to these other new and old problems which have been torturing women and their husbands and children, and puzzling their doctors and educators for years. It may well be the key to our future as a nation and a culture. We can no longer ignore that voice within women that says: "I want something more than my husband and my children and my home."

DISCUSSION TOPICS

1. Relate the problem of the women Betty Frieden describes in *The Feminine Mystique* to the problem of women you know.

2. Discuss the actions a housewife can take to relieve her dissatisfaction. The theme of your discussion should be "A Realistic Alternative."

SUGGESTED ACTIVITIES

1. Do a statistical comparison of the American woman of 1960 with the American woman of 1970. Include such things as marital status, income, education, age, age of marriage, and number of children.

2. Interview twenty women of different ages who have completed their schooling. Ask them to describe what their ambitions had been when they were younger, what their feelings are about their present situation, and what their chief hope for the future is. If possible, tape the responses.

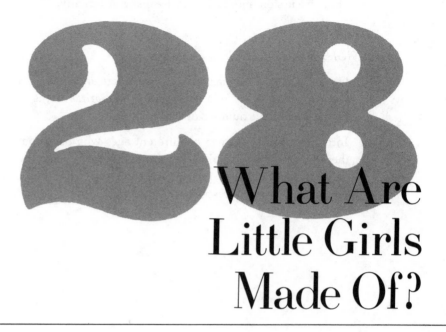

CHAPTER

28

What Are Little Girls Made Of?

What separate characteristics of human males and females are inborn and what characteristics are acquired through training? The nature vs. nurture debate is an old one indeed. More and more frequently, evidence seems to be pointing to the fact the traits of one sex that were thought to be innate are probably the result of learned behavior. For example, boys were—and still are—considered to be more aggressive than girls. Therefore, rough playing was encouraged in young males and frowned upon, if not absolutely forbidden, in girls.

In "Sexual Stereotypes Start Early," which originally appeared in Saturday Review, Florence Howe examines the question of sex roles and how children learn them. According to her, children begin to learn when they see the different ways in which very young boys and girls are treated by adults. Stereotyping continues in the formal educational process through the way males and females are described in textbooks. Perhaps even worse, history books ignore the role of women in American history, and literary anthologies choose Henry James over Edith Wharton.

The author, a college professor and co-author with Paul Lauter of Conspiracy of the Young, maintains reform is beginning in some small areas of education, but real change can occur only when society changes.

Sexual Stereotypes Start Early

Florence Howe

"I remember quite clearly a day in sixth grade," a college freshman told me a year ago,

"when the class was discussing an article from a weekly supplementary reader. The story was about a chef, and someone in the class ventured the opinion that cooking was women's work, that a man was a 'sissy' to work in the kitchen. The teacher's response surprised us all. She informed us calmly that men make the best cooks, just as they make the best dress designers, singers, and laundry workers. 'Yes,' she said, 'anything a woman can do a man can do better.' There were no male students present; my teacher was a woman."

Children learn about sex roles very early in their lives, probably before they are eighteen months old, certainly long before they enter school. They learn these roles through relatively simple patterns that most of us take for granted. We throw boy babies up in the air and roughhouse with them. We coo over girl babies and handle them delicately. We choose sex-related colors and toys for our children from their earliest days. We encourage the energy and physical activity of our sons, just as we expect girls to be quieter and more docile. We love both our sons and daughters with equal fervor, we protest, and yet we are disappointed when there is no male child to carry on the family name.

A hundred fifty years ago, Elizabeth Cady Stanton learned to master a horse and the Greek language in an attempt to comfort her father who had lost his only son and heir. No matter what evidence of brilliance Cady Stanton displayed, her father could only shake his head and murmur, "If only you were a boy, Elizabeth," much to the bafflement of the girl who had discerned that riding horses and studying Greek were the activities that had distinguished her dead brother from her living sisters. Only thirty years ago, at family gatherings, I remember hearing whispers directed at my brother and me: "Isn't it a pity that he has all the looks while she has all the brains." Others could contribute similar anecdotes today.

The truth of it is that while we in the West have professed to believe in "liberty, equality, and fraternity," we have also taken quite literally the term "fraternity." We have continued to maintain, relatively undisturbed, all the ancient edicts about the superiority of males, the inferiority of females. Assumptions current today about woman's alleged "nature" are disguised psychological versions of physiological premises in the Old Testament, in the doctrines of the early church fathers, and in the

thinking of male philosophers, writers, educators—including some who founded women's colleges or opened men's colleges to women. In short, what we today call the "women's liberation movement" is only the most recent aspect of the struggle that began with Mary Wollstonecraft's *Vindication of the Rights of Women* in 1795—a piece of theory that drew for courage and example on the fathers of the French and American revolutions. It is, of course, only one hundred years since higher education was really opened up to women in this country, and many people know how dismal is the record of progress for professional women, especially during the past fifty years.

How much blame should be placed on public education? A substantial portion, although it is true that schools reflect the society they serve. Indeed, schools function to reinforce the sexual stereotypes that children have been taught by their parents, friends, and the mass culture we live in. It is also perfectly understandable that sexual stereotypes demeaning to women are also perpetuated by women—mothers in the first place, and teachers in the second—as well as by men—fathers, the few male teachers in elementary schools, high school teachers, and many male administrators and educators at the top of the school's hierarchy.

Sexual stereotypes are not to be identified with sexual or innate differences, for we know nothing about these matters. John Stuart Mill was the first man (since Plato) to affirm that we could know nothing about innate sexual differences, since we have never known of a society in which either men or women lived wholly separately. Therefore, he reasoned, we can't "know" what the pure "nature" of either sex might be: What we see as female behavior, he maintained, is the result of what he called the education of "willing slaves." There is still no "hard" scientific evidence of innate sexual differences, though there are new experiments in progress on male hormones of mice and monkeys. Other hormonal experiments, especially those using adrenaline, have indicated that, for human beings at least, social factors and pressures are more important than physiological ones.

Sexual stereotypes are assumed differences, social conventions or norms, learned behavior, attitudes, and expectations. Most stereotypes are well-known to all of us, for they are simple—not to say simple-minded. Men are smart, women are dumb but beautiful, etc. A recent annotated catalogue of children's books (distributed by the National Council of Teachers of English to thousands of teachers and used for ordering books with federal funds) lists titles under the headings "Especially for Girls" and "Especially for Boys." Verbs and adjectives are remarkably predictable through the listings. Boys "decipher and discover," "earn and train," or "foil" someone; girls "struggle," "overcome difficulties," "feel lost," "help solve," or "help [someone] out." One boy's story has "strange power," another moves "from truancy to triumph." A girl, on the other hand, "learns to face the real world" or makes a "difficult adjustment." Late or early, in catalogues or on shelves, the boys of children's books are active and capable, the girls passive and in trouble. All studies of children's literature—and there have been many besides my own—support this conclusion.

Ask yourself whether you would be surprised to find the following social contexts in a fifth-grade arithmetic textbook:

1. girls playing marbles; boys sewing;

2. girls earning money, building things, and going places; boys buying ribbons for a sewing project;

3. girls working at physical activities; boys baby-sitting and, you guessed it, sewing.

Of course you would be surprised—so would I. What I have done here is to reverse the sexes as found in a fifth-grade arithmetic text. I was not surprised, since several years ago an intrepid freshman offered to report on third-grade arithmetic texts for me and found similar types of sexual roles prescribed: Boys were generally making things or earning money; girls were cooking or spending money on such things as sewing equipment.

The verification of sexual stereotypes is a special area of interest to psychologists and sociologists. An important series of studies was done in 1968 by Inge K. Broverman and others at Worcester State Hospital in Massachusetts. These scientists established a "sex-stereotype questionnaire" consisting of "122 bipolar items"—characteristics socially known or socially tested as male or female. Studies by these scientists and others established what common sense will verify: that those traits "stereotypically masculine . . . are more often perceived as socially desirable" than those known to be feminine. Here are some "male-valued items" as listed on the questionnaire:

> very aggressive
> very independent
> not at all emotional
> very logical
> very direct
> very adventurous
> very self-confident
> very ambitious

These and other characteristics describe the stereotypic male. To describe the female, you need only reverse those traits and add "female-valued" ones, some of which follow:

> very talkative
> very tactful
> very gentle
> very aware of feelings of others
> very religious
> very quiet
> very strong need for security

and the one I am particularly fond of citing to men who control my field—"enjoys art and literature very much."

The Worcester scientists used their 122 items to test the assumptions of clinical psychologists about mental health. Three matched groups of male and female clinical psychologists were given three identical lists of the 122 items unlabeled and printed in random order. Each group was given a different set of instructions: One was told to choose those traits that characterize the healthy adult male; another to choose those of the healthy adult female;

the third, to choose those of the healthy adult—a person. The result: The clinically healthy male and the clinically healthy adult were identical—and totally divergent from the clinically healthy female. The authors of the study concluded that "a double standard of health exists for men and women." That is, the general standard of health applies only to men. Women are perceived as "less healthy" by those standards called "adult." At the same time, however, if a woman deviates from the sexual stereotypes prescribed for her—if she grows more "active" or "aggressive," for example—she doesn't grow healthier; she may, in fact, if her psychiatrist is a Freudian, be perceived as "sicker." Either way, therefore, women lose or fail, and so it is not surprising to find psychologist Phyllis Chesler reporting that proportionately many more women than men are declared "sick" by psychologists and psychiatrists.

The idea of a "double standard" for men and women is a familiar one and helps to clarify how severely sexual stereotypes constrict the personal and social development of women. Studies by child psychologists reveal that while boys of all ages clearly identify with male figures and activities, girls are less likely to make the same sort of identification with female stereotypes. With whom do girls and women identify? My guess is that there is a good deal of confusion in their heads and hearts in this respect, and that what develops is a pattern that might be compared to schizophrenia: The schoolgirl knows that, for her, life is one thing, learning another. This is like the Worcester study's "double standard"—the schoolgirl cannot find herself in history texts or as she would like to see herself in literature; yet she knows she is not a male. Many women may ultimately discount the question of female identity as unimportant, claiming other descriptions preferable—as a parent, for example, or a black person, or a college professor.

Children learn sexual stereotypes at an early age, and, by the time they get to fifth grade, it may be terribly difficult, perhaps hardly possible by traditional means, to change their attitudes about sex roles—whether they are male or female. For more than a decade, Paul Torrance, a psychologist particularly interested in creativity, has been conducting interesting and useful experiments with young children. Using a Products Improvement Test, for example, Torrance asked first-grade boys and girls to "make toys more fun to play with." Many six-year-old boys refused to try the nurse's kit, "protesting," Torrance reports, "I'm a boy! I don't play with things like that." Several creative boys turned the nurse's kit into a doctor's kit and were then "quite free to think of improvements." By the third grade, however, "boys excelled girls even on the nurse's kit, probably because," Torrance explains, "girls have been conditioned by this time to accept toys as they are and not to manipulate or change them."

Later experiments with third-, fourth-, and fifth-graders using science toys further verify what Torrance calls "the inhibiting effects of sex-role conditioning." "Girls were quite reluctant," he reports, "to work with these science toys and frequently protested: 'I'm a girl; I'm not supposed to know anything about things like that!'" Boys, even in these early grades, were about twice as good as girls at explaining ideas about toys. In 1959, Torrance reported his findings to parents and teachers in one school and asked for their cooperation in attempting to change the attitudes of the girls. In 1960, when he retested them, using similar science toys, the girls participated willingly and even with apparent enjoyment. And they performed as well as the boys. But in one significant respect nothing had changed: The boys' contributions were more highly valued—both by other boys and by girls—than the girls' contributions, regardless of the fact that, in terms of sex, boys and girls had scored equally. "Apparently," Torrance writes, "the school climate has helped to make it more acceptable for girls to play around with science things, but boys' ideas about science things are still supposed to be better than those of girls."

Torrance's experiments tell us both how useful and how limited education may be for women in a culture in which assumptions about their inferiority run deep in their own consciousness as well as in the consciousness of men. While it is encouraging to note that a year's effort had changed behavior patterns significantly, it is also clear that attitudes of nine-, ten-, and eleven-year-olds are not so easily modifiable, at least not through the means Torrance used.

Torrance's experiments also make clear that, whatever most of us have hitherto assumed, boys and girls are *not* treated alike in elementary school. If we consider those noncurricular aspects of the school environment that the late anthropologist Jules Henry labeled the "noise" of schools, chief among them is the general attitude of teachers, whatever their sex, that girls are likely to "love" reading and to "hate" mathematics and science. As we know from the Rosenthal study of teacher expectations, *Pygmalion in the Classroom*, such expectations significantly determine student behavior and attitudes. Girls are not expected to think logically or to understand scientific principles; they accept that estimate internally and give up on mathematics and science relatively early. And what encouragement awaits the interested few in high school? For example, in six high school science texts published since 1966 and used in the Baltimore city public schools—all of the books rich in illustrations —I found photographs of one female lab assistant, one woman doctor, one woman scientist, and Rachel Carson. It is no wonder that the percentage of women doctors and engineers in the United States has remained constant at 6 percent and 1 percent respectively for the past fifty years.

Though there is no evidence that their early physical needs are different from or less than boys', girls are offered fewer activities even in kindergarten. They may sit and watch while boys, at the request of the female teacher, change the seating arrangement in the room. Of course, it's not simply a matter of physical exercise or ability: Boys are learning how to behave as males, and girls are learning to be "ladies" who enjoy being "waited on." If there are student-organized activities to be arranged, boys are typically in charge, with girls assisting, perhaps in the stereotyped role of secretary. Boys are allowed and expected to be noisy and aggressive, even on occasion to express anger; girls must learn "to control themselves" and behave like "young ladies." On the other hand, boys are expected not to cry, though there are perfectly good reasons why children of both sexes ought to be allowed that avenue of expression. Surprisingly early, boys and girls are separated for physical education and hygiene, and all the reports now being published indicate preferential treatment for boys and nearly total neglect of girls.

In junior high schools, sexual stereotyping becomes, if anything, more overt. Curricular sex-typing continues and is extended to such "shop" subjects as cooking and sewing, on the one hand, and metal- and woodworking, printing, ceramics, on the other. In vocational high schools, the stereotyping becomes outright channeling, and here the legal battles have begun for equality of opportunity. Recently, the testimony of junior high and high school girls in New York has become available in a pamphlet prepared by the New York City chapter of NOW. Here are a few items:

> Well, within my physics class last year, our teacher asked if there was anybody interested in being a lab assistant, in the physics lab, and when I raised my hand, he told all the girls to put their hands down because he was only interested in working with boys.
>
> There is an Honor Guard . . . students who, instead of participating in gym for the term, are monitors in the hall, and I asked my gym teacher if I could be on the Honor Guard Squad. She said it was only open to boys. I then went to the head of the Honor Guard . . . who said that he thought girls were much too nasty to be Honor Guards. He thought they would be too mean in working on the job, and I left it at that.
>
> We asked for basketball. They said there wasn't enough equipment. The boys prefer to have it first. Then we will have what is left over. We haven't really gotten anywhere.

Finally, I quote more extensively from one case:

MOTHER: *I asked Miss Jonas if my daughter could take metalworking or mechanics, and she said there is no freedom of choice. That is what she said.*

THE COURT: *That is it?*

ANSWER: *I also asked her whose decision this was, that there was no freedom of choice. And she told me it was the decision of the board of education. I didn't ask her anything else because she clearly showed me that it was against the school policy for girls to be in the class. She said it was a board of education decision.*

QUESTION: *Did she use that phrase, "no freedom of choice"?*

ANSWER: *Exactly that phrase—no freedom of choice. That is what made me so angry that I wanted to start this whole thing.*

* * *

THE COURT: *Now, after this lawsuit was filed, they then permitted you to take the course; is that correct?*

DAUGHTER: *No, we had to fight about it for quite a while.*

QUESTION: *But eventually they did let you in the second semester?*

ANSWER: *They only let me in there.*

Q: *You are the only girl?*

A: *Yes.*

Q: *How did you do in the course?*

A: *I got the medal for it from all the boys there.*

Q: *Will you show the court?*

A: *Yes (indicating).*

Q: *And what does the medal say?*

A: *Metal 1970 Van Wyck.*

Q: *And why did they give you that medal?*

A: *Because I was the best one out of all the boys.*

THE COURT: *I do not want any giggling or noises in the courtroom. Just do the best you can to control yourself or else I will have to ask you to leave the courtroom. This is no picnic, you know. These are serious lawsuits.*

Such "serious lawsuits" will, no doubt, continue, but they are not the only routes to change. There are others to be initiated by school systems themselves.

One route lies through the analysis of texts and attitudes. So long as those responsible for the education of children believe in the stereotypes as givens, rather than as hypothetical constructs that a patriarchal society has established as desired norms—so long as the belief continues, so will the condition. These beliefs are transmitted in the forms we call literature and history, either on the printed page or in other media.

Elementary school readers are meant for both sexes. Primers used in the first three grades offer children a view of a "typical" American family: a mother who does not work, a father who does, two children—a brother who is always older than a sister—and two pets—a dog and sometimes a cat—whose sexes and ages mirror those of the brother and sister. In these books boys build or paint things; they also pull girls in wagons and push merry-go-rounds. Girls carry purses when they go shopping; they help mother cook or pretend that they are cooking; and they play with their dolls. When they are not making messes, they are cleaning up their rooms or other people's messes. Plots in which girls are involved usually depend on their inability to do something—to manage their own roller skates or to ride a pony. Or in another typical role, a girl named Sue admires a parachute jumper: "What a jump!" said Sue. "What a jump for a man to make!" When her brother puts on a show for the rest of the neighborhood, Sue, whose name appears as the title of the chapter, is part of his admiring audience.

The absence of adventurous heroines may shock the innocent; the absence of even a few stories about women doctors, lawyers, or professors thwarts reality; but the consistent presence of one female stereotype is the most troublesome matter:

Primrose was playing house. Just as she finished pouring tea for her dolls she began to think. She thought and thought and she thought some more: "Whom shall I marry? Whomever shall I marry?

"I think I shall marry a mailman. Then I could go over to everybody's house and give them their mail.

"Or I might marry a policeman. I could help him take the children across the street."

Primrose thinks her way through ten more categories of employment and concludes, "But now that I think it over, maybe I'll just marry somebody I love." Love is the opiate designated to help Primrose forget to think about what she would like to do or be. With love as reinforcer, she can imagine herself helping some man in his work. In another children's book, Johnny says, "I think I will be a dentist when I grow up," and later, to Betsy, he offers generously, "You can be a dentist's nurse." And, of course, Betsy accepts gratefully, since girls are not expected to have work identity other than as servants or helpers. In short, the books that schoolgirls read prepare them early for the goal of marriage, hardly ever for work, and never for independence.

If a child's reader can be pardoned for stereotyping because it is "only" fiction, a social studies text has no excuse for denying reality to its readers. After all, social studies texts ought to describe "what is," if not "what should be." And yet, such texts for the youngest grades are no different from readers. They focus on families and hence on sex roles and works. Sisters are still younger than brothers; brothers remain the doers, questioners, and knowers who explain things to their poor, timid sisters. In a study of five widely used texts, Jamie Kelem Frisof finds that energetic boys think about "working on a train or in a broom factory" or about being President. They grow up to be doctors or factory workers or (in five texts combined) to do some hundred different jobs, as opposed to thirty for women.

Consider for a moment the real work world of women. Most women (at least for some portion of their lives) work, and if we include "token" women—the occasional engineer, for instance—they probably do as many different kinds of work as men. Even without improving the status of working women, the reality is distinctly different from the content of school texts and literature written for children. Schools usually at least reflect the society they serve; but the treatment of working women is one clear instance in which the reflection is distorted by a patriarchal attitude about who *should* work and the maleness of work. For example, there are women doctors—there have been women doctors in this country, in fact, for a hundred years or so. And yet, until the publication this month of two new children's books by the Feminist Press, there were no children's books about women doctors.

In a novel experiment conducted recently by an undergraduate at Towson State College in Maryland, fourth-grade students answered "yes" or "no" to a series of twenty questions, eight of which asked, in various ways, whether "girls were smarter than boys" or whether "daddies were smarter than mommies." The results indicated that boys and girls were agreed that 1) boys were not smarter than girls, nor girls smarter than boys; but 2) that daddies were indeed smarter than mommies! One possible explanation of this finding depends on the knowledge that daddies, in school texts and on television (as well as in real life), work, and that people who work know things. Mommies, on the other hand, in books and on television, rarely stir out of the house except to go to the store—and how can someone like that know anything? Of course, *we* know that half of all mothers in the United States work at some kind of job, but children whose mommies do work can only assume—on the basis of evidence offered in school books and on television—that their mommies must be "different," perhaps even not quite "real" mommies.

If children's readers deny the reality of working women, high school history texts deny women their full historical role. A recent study by Janice Law Trecker of thirteen popular texts concludes with what by now must seem a refrain: Women in such texts are "passive, incapable of sustained organization or work, satisfied with [their] role in society, and well supplied with material blessings." Women, in the grip of economic and political forces, rarely fighting for anything, occasionally receive some "rights," especially suffrage in 1920, which, of course, solves all *their* problems. There is no discussion of the struggle by women to gain entrance into higher education, of their efforts to organize or join labor unions, of other battles for working rights, or of the many different aspects of the hundred-year-long multi-issue effort that ended, temporarily, in the suffrage act of 1920. Here is Dr. Trecker's summary of the history and contributions of American women as garnered from the thirteen texts combined:

> *Women arrived in 1619 (a curious choice if meant to be their first acquaintance with the New World). They held the Seneca Falls Convention on Women's Right in 1848. During the rest of the nineteenth century, they participated in reform movements, chiefly temperance, and were exploited in factories. In 1920, they were given the vote. They joined the armed forces for the first time during the Second World War and thereafter have enjoyed the good life in America. Add the names of the women who are invariably mentioned: Harriet Beecher Stowe, Jane Addams, Dorothea Dix, and Frances Perkins, with perhaps Susan B. Anthony, Elizabeth Cady Stanton . . . [and you have the story].*

Where efforts have been made in recent years to incorporate black history, again it is without attention to black women, either with respect to their role in abolitionist or civil rights movements, for example, or with respect to intellectual or cultural achievements.

Just as high school history texts rely on male spokesmen and rarely quote female leaders of the feminist movement—even when they were also articulate writers such as Charlotte Perkins Gilman, or speakers such as Sojourner Truth—so, too, literary anthologies will include Henry James or Stephen Crane rather than Edith Wharton or Kate Chopin. Students are offered James Joyce's *Portrait of the Artist as a Young Man* or the *Autobiography of Malcolm X*, rather than Doris Lessing's *Martha Quest* or Anne Moody's *Coming of Age in Mississippi*. As a number of studies have indicated, the literary curriculum, both in high school and college, is a male-centered one. That is, either male authors dominate the syllabus or the central characters of the books are consistently male. There is also usually no compensating effort to test the fictional portraits—of women and men—against the reality of life experience. Allegedly "relevant" textbooks for senior high school or freshman college composition courses continue to appear, such as Macmillan's *Representative Men: Heroes of Our Time*. There are two women featured in this book: Elizabeth Taylor, the actress, and Jacqueline Onassis, the Existential Heroine. Thirty-five or forty men—representing a range of racial, political, occupational, and intellectual interests—fill the bulk of a book meant, of course, for both men and women. And some teachers are still ordering such texts.

It's not a question of malice, I assume, but of thoughtlessness or ignorance. Six or seven years ago I too was teaching from a standard male-dominated curriculum—and at a women's college at that. But I speak from more than my own experience. Last fall at this time I knew of some fifty college courses in what has come to be known as women's studies. This fall, I know of more than 500, about half of which are in literature and history. I know also of many high school teachers who have already begun to invent comparable courses.

School systems can and should begin to encourage new curricular developments, especially in literature and social studies, and at the elementary as well as the high school level. Such changes, of course, must include the education and re-education of teachers, and I know of no better way to re-educate them than to ask for analyses of the texts they use, as well as of their assumptions and attitudes. The images we pick up, consciously or unconsciously, from literature and history significantly control our sense of identity, and our identity—our sense of ourselves as powerful or powerless, for example—controls our behavior. As teachers read new materials and organize and teach new courses, they will change their views. That is the story of most of the women I know who, like me, have become involved in women's studies. The images we have in our heads about ourselves come out of literature and history; before we can change those images, we must see them clearly enough to exorcise them and, in the process, to raise others from the past we are learning to see.

That is why black educators have grown insistent upon their students' learning black history —slave history, in fact. That is also why some religious groups, Jews for example, emphasize their history as a people, even though part of that history is also slave history. For slave history has two virtues: Not only does it offer a picture of servitude against which one can measure the present; it offers also a vision of struggle and courage. When I asked a group of young women at the University of Pittsburgh last year whether they were depressed by the early nineteenth century women's history they were studying, their replies were instructive: "Certainly not," one woman said, "we're angry that we had to wait until now—after so many years of U.S. history in high school—to learn the truth about some

things." And another added, "But it makes you feel good to read about those tremendous women way back then. They felt some of the same things we do now."

Will public education begin to change the images of women in texts and the lives of women students in schools? There will probably be some movement in this direction, at least in response to the pressures from students, parents, and individual teachers. I expect that parents, for example, will continue to win legal battles for their daughters' equal rights and opportunities. I expect that individual teachers will alter their courses and texts and grow more sensitive to stereotypic expectations and behavior in the classroom. But so far there are no signs of larger, more inclusive reforms: no remedial program for counselors, no major effort to de-stereotype vocational programs or kindergarten classrooms, no centers for curricular reform. Frankly, I don't expect this to happen without a struggle. I don't expect that public school systems will take the initiative here. There is too much at stake in a society as patriarchal as this one. And schools, after all, tend to follow society, not lead it.

DISCUSSION TOPICS

1. Describe the first time in your life that you were sex-typed. Be sure to include your age, the situation, and the person who made you aware of what society considers appropriate for your sex.

2. Continue the list begun by Florence Howe on reversing the roles of the sexes as found in elementary school textbooks. Think of as many as you can even if some of them seem silly to you at first. After your list is complete, have a discussion on the results.

SUGGESTED ACTIVITIES

1. Florence Howe mentions Elizabeth Cady Stanton. Compile a list of at least 20 other American women important in history, literature, science, the arts. Then poll twenty people over thirty and twenty people of high school or college age to check their familiarity with the names on your list. Divide the people you poll equally according to sex.

2. Write a short story for young children that avoids sexual stereotyping. If possible, illustrate it.

3. Go to your local library. Choose three books written for children who cannot read and evaluate them for sexual stereotyping.

29

The Womanly Image: Character Assassination Through The Ages

Being asked if you are in love is not one of the usual questions in a job interview. But that was asked of Paula Stern, a free-lance writer and a doctoral candidate, as well as the author of "The Womanly Image." The interviewer, a man, was worried that Ms. Stern would not be able to cope with love, perhaps marriage, and a job simultaneously.

The myth of male superiority is not a phenomenon of this generation, this century, or even the last ten centuries. It started thousands of years ago when Adam blamed the fall of man on Eve. Eve is not the only woman in the Bible, but she certainly is the most notorious one. The story of Eve may have been the birth of the notion of female inferiority. Certainly Jewish and Christian religions have regarded woman as something less than man. This idea of female inferiority persists in literature and philosophy. Any woman who attempted to rise above the role of housekeeper was discouraged by men like Samuel Johnson who claimed "man is in general better pleased when he has a good dinner upon his table, than when his wife talks Greek." Apparently no woman can do both, and if something must be sacrificed, let it be her mind.

More recently, Sigmund Freud maintained that women have deep seated feelings of inadequacy and are naturally passive.

In Paula Stern's view, the womanly image of the inferior, inadequate, passive female is constantly reinforced in girl's and woman's magazines whose articles and advertising stress the image of the desirable woman. Being desirable, of course, means never, never being assertive or aggressive. Submission is the natural way to a successful relationship with a man.

The Womanly Image

Paula Stern

I had a job interview several weeks ago. Friends warned me not to be too aggressive. During the interview, I tried to present myself as a competent candidate, able to "think like a man" and yet not to be a "masculine" female. After fielding several questions relevant to the job, I suddenly heard, "Miss Stern, are you in love?"

Do you think they asked my competition—seven men—the same question? No, for a cultureful of reasons. Jacqueline Onassis was quoted once as saying, "There are two kinds of women: those who want power in the world and those who want power in bed." And the majority seem to agree with Jackie that the latter is socially more acceptable. That's how many women in America have been taught to think. And that's how many men think women ought to think.

Children are taught sexual stereotypes early, as well as the appropriate behavior for a sex-determined role in life. Asking a little boy, "What do you want to be when you grow up?" implies to him unlimited possibilities in his future. But most often we ask a little girl, "Where did you get that pretty dress?" suggesting she has only one real option open to her. If we do ask her what she wants to be, she's likely to give the conditioned female response—"A mother." Why? So she can replace her dolls with real babies.

The inspiration for teaching girls to expect less than boys comes from a range of cultural sources, religious, literary, psychiatric, and pop. Even in the Bible, exceptional, independent women like Rebecca, Sarah, Deborah, or Ruth are practically "unknowns" compared with infamous Eve or Delilah.

Eve was made from one of Adam's spare parts, almost as an afterthought, to help him out on earth: "And the Lord God said: 'It is not good that the man should be alone; I will make him a helpmeet for him.'"

There is a contrary legend of the first female, Lilith, who was created equal to man.

> When the Lord created the world and the first man, he saw that man was alone, and quickly created a woman for him, made like him from the earth, and her name was Lilith. Right away, they began to quarrel. He would say "You sleep on the bottom," and she would say "No, you sleep on the bottom, since we are equals and both formed from the earth. . . ." When Lilith saw what the situation was, she pronounced the Ineffable Name and disappeared into thin air.

But Eve, not Lilith, is the prototypal woman —man's little helper, and his temptress.

Today the heirs to the Bible in America— Jews and Christians—have formalized biblical biases in laws and ceremonies and thereby elevated folklore to religious truths. Among the Orthodox Jews, for example, discrimination against women is so blatant that they are forced to sit segregated behind a curtain or in a balcony. The rationale is that women will distract men from their prayers. It is no wonder that men thank God every morning in their ritual prayer "that Thou has not made me a woman."

The majority of Jews have modified most traditional formalities, but independent female expression is still discouraged if outside the confines of the home or not channeled through husband and children.

A Jewish wife is less subservient to her husband than a gentile wife; so say comparative studies on the subject. That's somewhat understandable since Christianity owes much to a prominent classical heritage, that held the second sex in even lower esteem. Utopia for the male chauvinist is Demosthenes' description of Hellenic male-female arrangements: "We have hetairae for the pleasure of the spirit, concubines for sensual pleasure, and wives to bear our sons."

Aristotle's definition of feminity was "a certain lack of qualities; we should regard the female nature as afflicted with a natural defectiveness."

And his disciple Saint Thomas Aquinas echoed him religiously: ". . . a female is something deficient and by chance."

Contempt for women helps explain why they can't become Catholic priests, and why theologians, religious education courses, and Catholic marriage manuals highlight the supposedly inferior and passive qualities of women who "naturally" subordinate themselves to men.

Traditional Protestant marriage services also perpetuate the attitude that the female is a second-class human being. Like a piece of property, the bride is "given" by her father to the groom, whom she promises to "obey." (Although formally removed from the liturgy, this vow still persists in the popular image of the wedding ceremony.) The clergyman reminds her of her proper place when he says, "I pronounce that they are man and wife." Not husband and wife. Not man and woman. The man keeps his status, while she takes on a new one. Her identity vanishes when she sheds her maiden name for his identification. (Blackstone's *Commentaries* on the law strips a married woman of her rights altogether as she legally dies on her wedding day and becomes "incorporated and consolidate with her husband." Accordingly, "A man cannot grant anything to his wife for the grant would be to suppose her separate existence.")

Although reputedly "progressing" beyond the attitudes of antiquity and the Middle Ages, our enlightened European ancestors continued furnishing us some not too enlightened guidelines on a woman's place—or lack of it—in the world.

High school English students learn from Shakespeare that "Frailty, thy name is woman." Rousseau's contribution to the ideas of man's equality and natural goodness makes one exception: "Woman was made to yield to man and put up with his injustice."

Samuel Johnson's word to the wise woman is that "a man is in general better pleased when he has a good dinner upon his table, than when his wife talks Greek." Honoré de Balzac adds, "A woman who is guided by the head and not the heart is a social pestilence: she has all the defects of a passionate and affectionate woman with none of her compensations: she is without pity, without love, without virtue, without sex."

When in 1776 in America, Abigail Adams asked her husband, John Adams, to "be more generous and favorable to them [women] than your ancestors" and to see to it that the new government not "put such unlimited power into the hands of the husbands," John reportedly chuckled. The Continental Congress ignored her. Two hundred years later Spiro Agnew said: "Three things have been difficult to tame—the ocean, fools, and women. We may soon be able to tame the ocean; fools and women will take a little longer."

The myths of marriage counselor G. C. Payetter (from his book *How To Get and Hold a Woman*) have been praised by a number of psychiatrists, and he is consulted in earnest by troubled people. Payetter counsels:

> *Feelings, moods, and attitude . . . rule a woman, not facts, reason, nor logic.*
>
> *By herself woman is all mixed-up but superb as an auxiliary (Genesis: helper).*
>
> *Woman is inanimate or on the defensive until you create a feeling such as a praise. Then she goes all out.*
>
> *Never scold or explain when she is angry, remember she is feeling not thinking. . . .*
>
> *Stop bossing; just manipulate her in her feelings. . . .*
>
> *The acquisition of knowledge or responsibilities does not lessen women's need for support, guidance, and control. Quite the contrary.*
>
> *Why ask women when they only need to be told? Why ask women when they hope to be taken?*

America's twentieth century gospel is the work of Freud. Although Freud supposedly has altered the entire course of Western intellectual history, many of his ideas about women are simply male chauvinism. Letters he wrote his fiancée reveal that he, too, wanted his woman kept relatively docile and ignorant so she couldn't compete with him.

His theories have given scientific status to prejudice. The Freudians—psychiatrists, clinical psychologists, psychiatric social workers, marriage counselors, pastoral counselors, educators, writers, literary critics, historians, anthropologists, sociologists, criminologists, and just plain subway psychiatrists in the newspapers, magazines, and on TV —all subscribe to the belief that "anatomy is destiny." In other words, biological differences between the sexes determine personality differences; standards of mental health depend on the sex of the sick.

How? Dr. Judd Marmor, clinical professor of psychiatry at UCLA, has summarized Freud's views on feminine psychology:

> The most significant of the biological factors . . . is the lack of the penis, which inevitably leads to "penis envy" in the woman. Freud considered penis envy to be a dominant theme in all feminine life, and one that inevitably causes women to feel inferior to men. These deep seated feelings of inadequacy can be compensated for only partially by giving birth to a male child. . . .

> Masochism and passivity . . . are natural aspects of normal femininity and whenever a woman behaves in non-passive or aggresive ways or competes with men, she is being neurotically unfeminine. . . .

> The most complicated sequence of personality development that women are subject to . . . leads inevitably . . . to less adequate superego formation than in men. This presumably is reflected in women having a poorer sense of justice and weaker social interests than men have.

Any resemblance between women and pet dogs or mute concubines is purely coincidental. No doubt, Payetter's model woman is the runner-up to this year's Miss America, who said women shouldn't try to run things "because they are more emotional and men can overcome their emotions with logic."

Even more objectionable are psychiatrist-authors who pronounce final judgment on the men-

tal health of thousands of women reading books like *The Power of Sexual Surrender*. Featured in the book, which has had at least ten paperback printings and been excerpted in *Pageant* magazine, is "The Masculine Woman." (Doctor, how can a woman be a female and be masculine simultaneously?) She's "frigid"—"a driving, competitive woman who was very successful in the business world, having graduated from a leading woman's college." "Clear thinking and logical mind, her emotionless almost masculine forthrightness in expressing herself belied her softly feminine appearance." Surrendering to her "real nature," the doctor's cure, is the only way she can be mentally healthy. Then miraculously

> . . . those details of life that once seemed so difficult become simple. And because they are feminine tasks, household work, planning, and getting dinners, keeping the children busy or in line—whatever life demands—soon lose their irksome and irritating quality and become easy, even joyful. . . . At this juncture, or closely following on it, a woman begins to feel her full power, the power that comes to her for her surrender to her destiny.

The spuriously Freudian vision of a truly "feminine" female serves the purposes of admen who woo women to spend millions on clothes and cosmetics in vain pursuit of their "real nature." To sell a new product, industry need only simultaneously make the product and manufacture anxiety in gals, pressing them to consume or be consumed in a female identity crisis. For example, featured in every women's magazine, including those for teen-agers, are the latest advertising campaigns for vaginal deodorants, a "female necessity." One called Cupid's Quiver comes in four flavors—Orange Blossom, Raspberry, Champagne, or Jasmine. Madison Avenue courts the female, even seducing minors. Teenform, Inc., manufacturers of bras for teen-agers, estimates that nine-year-olds spend $2 million on bras annually.

Ingenue magazine pushes teen-agers into adult posturing. The format is peppered with advertisements for engagement rings, pictures of desirable adolescent boys, and occasionally a plan of attack such as dinners for two. The ads for cosmetics and clothes are practically identical to those in magazines designed for their mothers. Typical of women's magazines, *Ingenue* includes at least one psychologically centered article. Recently, it explained in "The Hardest Thing About Growing Up" that "inevitably, relationships with boys affect relationships with girls." It condoned the statement, "I don't trust other girls in the same way anymore. They become rivals." This is how girls learn the platitudes: women can't work with other women when men are around, and never work for a woman.

If a girl manages to survive *Ingenue* without succumbing to marriage, *Glamour* picks her up. ("How Five Groovy Men Would Make You Over Into Their Dream Girls") Where the boys are is where it's at for the reader who is shunted from high school to college to career to marriage to motherhood—"Find Your New Look. College Into Career Make-over. Job Into Mother Make-over."

The lucky gal who's made the grade by landing a man is promoted to *Modern Bride*, which induces her to buy "utterly feminine" wedding gowns, bride-and-groom matching wedding rings, silver, china, furniture, ad nauseam. The wedding itself is big business; Wediquette International, Inc., offers total planning—the place, time, invitations, gown, caterers, florist, photographer . . .

Ah, then conjugal bliss—and of course, a magazine for mothers. *Redbook* boasts its biggest year because it knows "Young Mamas Spend More Than Big Daddies" and so talks "to that 18–34 year-old the way she wants to be talked to," which means in baby talk or kitchen chatter.

McCall's claims 16 million matrons who "buy more than the readers of any other woman's service magazine." Its reader "buys more cosmetics and toiletries, more prepared foods, owns more life insurance, more automobiles . . ."

Although *Cosmopolitan* says its reader is the career woman who desires success in her own right, it is pitched to the gal who missed the marriage boat the first time around. Female passivity is still the accepted mode of behavior. She can be assertive in the office, but when man-hunting after five, she must be seductively submissive. Who knows? She might hook a divorced man or married man looking for an affair.

Cosmo repeats an old tip from Jackie and Delilah—sex is a woman's hidden arsenal. Under a pseudonym, "a well-known American gynecologist" instructs readers "How to Love Like a Real Woman." "If your man bawls at you and you know you are in the right, what should you do?" "You should take your clothes off. Sex is a woman's strongest weapon. It is her proper weapon."

Taking a cue from *The Power of Sexual Surrender*, the expert explains, "Women must give and give and give again because it is their one and only way to obtain happiness for themselves." Further, "To argue is a male activity. To fight is a male activity. I say to women: 'Don't become a man in skirts. Don't fight. Don't argue. . . .'" Any female who would practice this advice must be masochistic —typical of a "normal" female, according to Freudian thought.

A popular misconception is that in time education will erase all the ill effects of thinking in stereotypes. But the educational system takes over where cultural myths, Freudian folklore, and the media leave off in depressing a girl's aspirations and motivations. All along, she's taught to accept a double standard for success and self-esteem: It's marriage and motherhood for girls, while it's education and career for boys. She's pushed to be popular, date, and marry young (more than half of all American women are married before the age of twenty-one). Success in school only inhibits her social life. Intellectual striving, a necessity for academic success, is considered competitively aggressive; that is unnatural and unladylike behavior, since the essence of femininity, she has learned, is repressing aggressiveness. Telling her she thinks like a man is a backhanded compliment, which is discouraging if she has tried to be a woman using her brains, not sex, in the classroom and office.

While girls outperform boys intellectually

in prepuberty, attrition in IQ sets in during adolescence when they learn from new, extracurricular lessons that looks, not brains, are what counts. After high school, achievement in terms of productivity and accomplishment drops off even more. More than 75 percent (some say as high as 95 percent) of all qualified high schoolers not entering college are girls. Those who go attend more for husband-hunting than for educational self-advancement; one study at a Midwestern university revealed 70 percent of the freshmen women were there for an MRS. Women BA's are less than half as likely to try for a graduate degree as equally qualified men.

Women should not be given an even break in education and careers, says a clichéd argument, because they will get married and quit anyway. But that's because they are given an arbitrary, unfair option which men aren't forced to accept—either career or marriage. Career opportunities and salary levels for women are so poor that a calculating female would figure marriage is a better bargain. Once married, she can stop fighting the stereotypes and start teaching them to her children.

DISCUSSION TOPICS

1. Explain in what ways, if any, the religious bodies in your community have changed in their attitudes toward women. For example, have the words of the marriage vows changed in recent years? What parts do women take in religious ceremonies? May women become part of the clergy?

SUGGESTED ACTIVITIES

1. Read a biography of Sigmund Freud and analyze his relationships with the women close to him.

2. Select current and back issues of *Ingenue*, *Glamour*, *Modern Bride*, *Redbook*, *McCalls* and *Cosmopolitan*. Try to find back issues that are at least three years old. Compare the current and back issues of each magazine for their change in attitudes toward the roles of girls and women. Report your findings to the group.

Catherine Drinker Bowen has written biographies of important people in law, politics, and music. Two of her most outstanding works are <u>Yankee From Olympus</u>, a biography of Associate Justice Oliver Wendell Holmes of the United States Supreme Court, and <u>The Lion and the Throne</u>, about the English jurist Sir Edward Coke. In addition, she has written her own family's story, <u>A Family Portrait</u>.

Long ago Ms. Bowen had to choose between her desire to write and society's idea of the place for a woman. Obviously, she wanted to be more than a wife and a mother.

In this article, which originally appeared in <u>The Atlantic</u>, Ms. Bowen writes about the artist-woman in contemporary society. She answers the question of why there have been no female Shakespeares or Dantes and discusses the resentment that women artists feel at being put in a category separate from male artists. Perhaps Catherine Drinker Bowen's success as an author lies in her family's treatment of her as a child, which she also discusses in the article.

We've Never Asked A Woman Before

Catherine Drinker Bowen

For thirty years I have been writing about lawyers and the law. And for almost as many years I have been the recipient of invitations to stand on platforms and address large assemblies of legal experts. I enjoy receiving these invitations; it shows that people are reading my books. Yet I often hesitate; the program means serious preparation. A non-lawyer—and a non-man—cannot stand up and talk drivel for thirty minutes or fifty (as specified) to a hall bristling with five hundred or so hard-minded professional gentlemen. Therefore I hold off, saying into the telephone that I haven't the time; I am writing a new book and must stay home by myself, where writers belong. Perhaps the committee will send a letter, giving details? "Mrs. Bowen!" says an urgent voice from Houston or San Francisco. "This is our law society's big annual celebration. We've had Senator Fulbright as speaker, and Wechsler of Columbia, and the Lord Chief Justice of England [and God and Santa Claus]. But we've never asked a woman before."

At this moment all my latent feminism rises up. Why haven't they asked a woman before —aren't there any women lawyers? Impossible to refuse this challenge! In Washington there exists a prestigious group called the American Law Institute. The cream of the profession belongs to it; the work they do is significant to the country at large. After I spoke at the Institute's annual dinner, women lawyers crowded to shake my hand. They said they had sat for years watching those men at the head table; they wanted me to know what it meant to see a woman sitting there. It made me very glad that I had come.

The word feminism is outmoded. "The movement," young women call it today. We know of the ferocity with which the goal is pursued. We have heard of the extremists—ten thousand strong —called Women's Liberation; how they crop their hair short, wear baggy trousers and loose sweaters to conceal the more notable evidences of sex. "Abolish sexism!" is their slogan. Brassieres must go, and beauty contests. "Miss America!" say their banners. "Men make money off *your* body too. Pornography, Bunnies, *Playboy* Magazine are as degrading to women as racism is to blacks."

But of course! And why, one asks oneself, has it taken the sisters so long to find this out, so long to proclaim that for women sex is neither cute nor funny and can result in pain, disgrace, or years of virtual—though respectable—servitude? Sex jokes are a male invention. It is indeed a naïve girl who grows up in our society unaware of what her world considers the primary function of women. To suggest that women don't have to be beautiful is the worst kind of heresy; it means women have more important functions than pleasing men.

How does all this affect women writers? The answer is, profoundly. Nobody writes from a vacuum; writers compose from their life experience. They use what they know and feel in the environment round about, the stuff of life as it has been handed out or as they have been able to grasp it, hold it up and look at it with courage and with truth. For many centuries girls have been told

that their business is wifehood, motherhood—and nothing else. "When children cease to be altogether desirable, women cease to be altogether necessary," said John Langdon Davis in *A Short History of Women.* I once had a husband who liked to say that nothing is expected of a wife-and-mother but respectability. Yet writers, male and female, belong in the category artist. (Muriel Rukeyser, the poet, puts women into four classes: whores, saints, wives, and artists). No artist can operate lacking belief in her mission. *His* mission; the very pronoun confesses an age-old situation. I hope the young activists in the movement wipe out that generalized pronoun, so bland, so denigrating to the woman professional in any field.

Without a clear view of their capabilities, men and women cannot function. Convince a two-legged man that he has but one leg, and he will not be able to walk. A writer must know her horizon, how wide is the circle within which she, as artist, extends. The world still professes to wonder why there has been no female Shakespeare or Dante, no woman Plato or Isaiah. Yet people do what society looks for them to do. The Quaker Meeting House has existed for centuries, but it has produced no Bach and no B Minor Mass. Music was not desired by Quakers, it was frowned on. Poetry, fiction, playwriting have been expected from women only recently, as history counts time. Of the brilliant, erratic Margaret Cavendish, her husband, the Duke of Newcastle, remarked, circa 1660, "A very wise woman is a very foolish thing." As lately as 1922, Christina Rossetti's biographer wrote of her, that "like most poetesses, she was purely subjective, and in no sense creative." What a beautiful triple sneer, and how it encompasses the entire second sex! One recalls the fiery poetess, Lady Winchelsea, born 1661, said to be "lost in melancholy"—and small wonder:

> *Debarred from all improvements of the mind*
> *[she wrote],*
> *And to be dull, expected and designed....*
> *Alas! a woman that attempts the pen,*
> *Such a presumptuous creature is esteemed,*
> *The fault can by no virtue be redeemed.*

Good breeding, fashion, dancing, dressing,
  play,
Are the accomplishments we should desire;
To write, or read, or think, or to enquire,
Would cloud our beauty, and exhaust our time,
And interrupt the conquests of our prime,
Whilst the dull manage of a servile house
Is held by some our utmost art and use.

Because I write about the law and the Constitution I am often asked why I entered "a man's field." Men tell me I write like a man. "Mrs. Bowen," they say with pleased smiles, "you *think* like a man." No, gentlemen, thank you, I do not, I write like a woman. I enjoy being a woman and thinking like a woman, which means using my mind and using it hard. Women have an advantage as writers because they are trained from childhood to notice the relationships between people. Upon such perceptions all their later welfare can depend. Is it not a mother's business, a wife's business to soothe hurt feelings, pacify the male, keep peace within her household? She is vitally concerned therefore with human motivation, what trial lawyers call *intent*. In my own field, intent lies at the base of the entire structure; the motivation of mankind makes up the plot of every biography that is written.

Women writers do not think like men. It is when I am told so that I remember Lady Winchelsea, remember also the ladies who had to use men's names on their books: George Eliot, George Sand, Currer Bell and her sisters, the Brontës.

I have used the word ladies in speaking of artists. I ask their forgiveness. No writer, no artist, is a lady. She can't afford to be. The novelist, biographer, historian, looks bleakly at life, lingers to squint at its sorrier aspects, reaches out to touch the dirty places, and raises the hand to the nostrils to make sure. Charles Beard [the American historian] once told me, "You have to have a strong stomach to study history." Happily, I was early indoctrinated against being a lady. At sixteen, the family decided to send me to boarding school, in order to correct certain provincialisms of speech

and deportment picked up from schoolmates in the Lehigh Valley town where we lived. I didn't want to go, and protested furiously. A brother, Cecil, ten years my senior, protested also. "That place," he told me morosely, "is called a finishing school. They want to make a lady of you, Katz. But you're born for something better, and don't you ever forget it."

I did not forget it. I was the youngest of six; the four brothers were considerably older. They taught me their skills; in fact, they insisted that I learn. "Push out, Katz, with that right skate. *Don't be scared!* Get your whole body into it." I grew up believing that girls were supposed to compete with boys, not just compete *for* boys. Our mother devoted herself wholly to domesticity. Yet she told my sister and me that a girl could be just as independent and well educated as a boy, there was no reason why not. My Aunt Cecilia Beaux was earning a living painting portraits by the time she was twenty-five, though Cecilia, my mother said, resented being referred to in the newspapers as a woman painter. "They don't talk about a *man* painter," Cecilia Beaux said. Aunt Beaux made money enough to buy six acres in Gloucester, Massachusetts, and build a house and studio there called Green Alley.

It would be hard to exaggerate the effect this had on a girl of twelve, fourteen, eighteen. I have been told that women feel guilty competing intellectually with men. Anaïs Nin, the writer, so confesses in her diary, and I have seen graphs drawn by psychologists, showing that girls do badly in what the professors call "achievement-oriented situations vis-à-vis boys." Guilt at competing? To me it is a contradiction in terms. I would have thought myself guilty in *not* competing. My parents expected high marks at school examinations, and if I brought home a bad paper, "What's wrong?" my brother Cecil would ask, "lose your nerve this time, Katz, or just lazy?" As for Beaux's Green Alley, it has become the family summer place. I have written four books there, in Aunt Beaux's studio by the bay; her spirit sustained me while I wrote. "We think back through our mothers if we are women." It was Virginia Woolf who said it.

Nevertheless, the female brain does not reside in the uterus, though women as well as men try their best so to persuade us. A recent newspaper showed Grace Kelly on a platform receiving an award from the YWCA. Glittering in sequins, she announced complacently that today's women, pushing into a man's world, were sacrificing their femininity. (Nothing was said about the twenty-nine million American women who work for their living.) A day or so later, a woman newspaper columnist eagerly affirmed this by recounting at length the joys of motherhood, ending with the dictum that once the children grow up and depart the scene, mothers never again experience a like happiness and sense of fulfillment. Wives too come forward with proud claims: the self-sacrifice, the best years given. "There is no career more exciting or exacting for a woman than marriage to a great man." So writes a recent biographer of Mrs. Gladstone [wife of English Prime Minister William Gladstone], and a female biographer at that.

Against this flood of bilge water I am fortified by a line in my great-great-grandmother's diary. Elizabeth Drinker, having given birth to nine and reared five, wrote in the year 1790 that she had often thought a woman's best years came after she left off bearing and rearing. I myself happen to be the mother of two and grandmother of four. I always expected to be married and looked forward to it—but not as sole career; never, never as sole career. It is not the maternal chores that oppress but the looming of that altar which has been erected to motherhood, its sacro-sanctity, the assumption that nothing but motherhood is important. For the woman artist this ideal can prove as bewildering as the onset of a national war. Nothing matters but this patriotism, this motherhood. One is praised and petted for being a mother, all other values put in the discard. When the baby comes: "You have joined the human race!" women cry, bringing gifts, adding gleefully that you won't have time *now* for writing (or sculpting or painting or playing the violin). When

my two children, a girl and then a boy, came along, I had already published two small books and twelve magazine articles. A local newspaper, the Easton *Daily Express*, paid me a dollar a day for a three-hundred-word column, handsomely boxed in. I looked on the pay as munificent and was terrified that I wouldn't be worth it. When time came for the first baby to be born I wrote two weeks' columns ahead, told the editor, a red-headed Irishman, that I'd be back in a fortnight, received his blessing, and never wrote another line until both children were in nursery school, five years later, and the mornings were once more my own. It was about this time that I came on Katherine Mansfield's thrice-blessed words: "Mothers of children grow on every bush."

A writer's regimen can reduce certain nagging moralisms to dust—the notion, for instance, that housework is ennobling to women, or at least instinctive to them as scuffing leaves to clean his bed is instinctive to a dog. Love of cooking is thought by many to be a secondary female sex characteristic. So is the exercise of following little children interminably about the yard. If I had not been a writer, these moralistic conceptions would have defeated me before I reached the age of thirty. Writing saved me. The housework still had to be done and done cheerfully. The children still had to be followed around the yard. But these activities, repeated day after day for years, were no longer defeating because they were no longer the be-all and end-all of existence.

"How fortunate, dear, that you have this hobby of writing to occupy you while your husband is away!" Thus my mother-in-law in September of the year 1941. I was two years along with *Yankee from Olympus*. My husband, a surgeon and member of the Naval Reserve, had gone to Honolulu on a hospital ship. By this time I had published six books and become inured to married women's attitudes toward the professional writer, so I merely told my mother-in-law, yes, it *was* lucky, and I had better get upstairs to my typewriter. Back and forth in the family the question raged: Should I take our daughter out of college, our son from school, and migrate to Honolulu? Hawaii was paradise! people said. We'd all love it, and what an opportunity! I could do my Holmes research in the Honolulu University's splendid library. Palm trees and warm sea—a paradise!

The notion of Oliver Wendell Holmes of New England revealing himself at the University of Honolulu belonged, of course, in the realms of fantasy. Also, my daughter loved Radcliffe and my son Haverford School. I listened to women spelling out my duty (what today they call a husband-supportive program), and I developed stomachaches, a pain in the lower back. Then one night I had a dream that settled everything, so vivid I can see it today. I sat in a room filled with people; my father, white-haired, white-whiskered, and long since dead, stood across the carpet. He raised an arm and pointed at me. "Thou shalt not go to Paradise!" he said.

Next morning I announced we were staying home and went on with *Yankee from Olympus*. Nor did I suffer further qualms, Dr. Freud notwithstanding.

Subject A, young women call it today, bringing me the age-old query: How to manage a career, a husband, and children. Despite "the movement" and the liberation fronts, the problem is still here, sharp and demanding. I am likely to give a twofold answer. "You manage it by doing double work, using twice the energy other wives use: housework *and* writing. Or you do what Mrs. Eleanor Roosevelt told me. I quote her, verbatim: 'If a woman wants to pursue her own interests after marriage, she must choose the right husband. Franklin stood back of me in everything I wanted to do.'"

Competition was bred in my bones. Yet I never wrote to rival men; such a thing would not have occurred to me. Actually it was a man—my first husband—who started me writing, in my twenties. And once I saw my product in print, nothing mattered but to get on with the work, get on with studying history and with learning how to write sentences that said what I wanted to say.

Many writers hate writing. I happen to love it. With my hands on the typewriter I feel like the war-horse in the Bible that smells the battle far off and saith among the trumpets, Ha, ha. Writers have in them a vast ambition . . . hunger . . . egotism—call it what you will. A writer wants to be read, wants to be known. If there is talent, it must come out or it will choke its host, be she three times wife-and-mother. Scholarship also is a hungry thing, the urge to know. A great legal historian, Maitland, spoke of "the blessing which awaits all those who have honestly taught themselves anything."

A woman biographer must, like anybody else, earn her place in the sun. When I turned from writing about musical subjects to legal subjects, I entered a man's world with a vengeance, though some time passed before I was fully aware of it. The Holmes' Papers were guarded by two literary executors, John Gorham Palfrey (father of the tennis champion) and Felix Frankfurter, of the United States Supreme Court. In the six years since Holmes's death, quite evidently the executors had expected hordes of hungry biographers to descend. It came as a shock that the first to approach was a non-Bostonian, a non-lawyer, and a non-man. Nevertheless, Mr. Palfrey handed me five hundred of Holmes's letters, neatly copied in typescript, saying I could take all the notes I wished. I procured four court stenographers—this was before the days of Xerox—who copied profusely. In Washington I saw Felix Frankfurter, who greeted me jovially (he was an old friend), said of course I didn't plan to present the big cases, the Lochner dissent, Rosika Schwimmer, the Gitlow—the great issues of free speech, the ten-hour day, and so on? I said of course I did, why else would I be writing the book?

I went home and back to work. Two months later a letter came from Mr. Palfrey, enclosing what he called "some of the more unfavorable replies" to his queries among Holmes's legal friends and associates. Nothing in Mrs. Bowen's previous experience, these said, qualified her to write about a lawyer, a New Englander, or indeed an American. In short, the executors had decided to deny access to all unpublished material, even for the purpose of establishing chronology or telling me where Holmes had been at a given time. My work and my Boston visits, Mr. Palfrey said, had spurred the executors to appoint the "definitive biographer," Mark Howe of the Harvard Law School, secretary to the Justice the year before he died.

Plainly, the executors hoped to stop me from writing the book. I let the initial shock wear off and laid plans. Scores of men and women existed who had known Holmes. Whatever I needed from those letters I must get by legwork—even when letters had been sent me by recipients, like Rosika Schwimmer and others. I must persuade the writers to tell me what the Justice had said and done on the occasions their letters described. This exercise took perhaps an added year, but was well worth it. Meanwhile, Frankfurter wrote from time to time. He heard I had been at the Supreme Court building and had left some unsolved questions with the Marshal. Was I actually making an effort to attain accuracy, ceasing to be an artist and becoming merely a thinker? The letters were wonderful and awful. They kindled the anger that sends one on ever harder quests; Frankfurter could be a formidable antagonist. I talked with Irving Olds of United States Steel, Attorney General Francis Biddle, and ten other legal secretaries of Holmes's, choosing them not because of their worldly prominence but because their particular secretarial year coincided with an important Supreme Court case. I think my book benefited from the program, rigorous though it was, and by the denial of those hundreds of letters. A biography can smother under too much quoted material.

When finally the Book-of-the-Month chose my manuscript, Frankfurter sent me a long congratulatory telegram: "I always knew you could do it." I did not see him, however, until ten years and several biographies later. After my book on Sir Edward Coke was published, the director of the Folger Shakespeare Library, Louis Wright, invited me to speak in their Washington theater. He said Justice Frankfurter had telephoned, asking to introduce me, and why was this? Frankfurter never made such requests, Louis said.

On the appointed evening, the Justice sat on the platform with me; I had no notion of his intentions. He got up and told the audience that he had done all he could to stop Mrs. Bowen from writing *Yankee from Olympus,* but there were people who worked better under difficulties and I was one of them. He had not read the book, he would never read it, though he had read my other biographies. But he wished to make public apology, public amends. Then he bowed, grinned at me where I sat, and returned to his chair.

It was handsome of Frankfurter. Yet I had wondered how much of the entire feud, and its climax, could be laid to the fact of my sex. I do not know. But as time passed and I proceeded to other legal biographies—John Adams, Sir Edward Coke, Francis Bacon, *Miracle at Philadelphia*—I know that the rigors I underwent with *Yankee* stood me in good stead, toughened me, made me ready for whatever might come. With John Adams I was again refused unpublished material and again went on my quest, though this time it had to be in research libraries and took five years. Sir Edward Coke's college was Trinity, at Cambridge University. And even Bluebeard did not consider women more expendable than does a Cambridge don [a don is a teacher at an English university]. All but one of the law and history professors I met there brushed aside my project and did it smiling, with the careless skill of the knowledgeable Englishman. "Are you planning to write a popular book about Coke?" they asked. I smiled in turn, and said by popular they no doubt meant cheap, and that only the finished manuscript could answer their question. "At least," remarked another, "Mrs. Bowen has been shrewd enough to see that a book about Edward Coke will sell. And a person has to begin to learn *somewhere.*" After inquiring how many copies my other biographies had sold, one history professor looked glum. "Someday," he said, snapping his fingers, "I'm going to take a year off and write a popular book."

Seven years later the Acting Master of Trinity wrote to me in Philadelphia, saying he had read the English edition of my Coke biography, *The Lion and the Throne*. Did I recall how he had not, initially, been enthusiastic about the project? He went on to say kind things about the book, acknowledging that he had been mistaken. And next time I was in Cambridge, would I permit him to give a small celebration in my honor?

Again, I cannot know how much of the battle—the defeats and the victories—can be laid to my being a woman. I know only that I spent days of anger, of outrage, and that I enjoyed the challenge. How could one not enjoy it? *"We never invited a woman before . . ."*

One honors those who march in the streets for a cause; one knows that social liberation does not come peacefully. I have not taken part in the movement, though feminine activists greet me as a sister. I think they know that the woman writer who stays outside the movement by no means dodges the issue. She takes a risk too, though of another kind. Instead of the dangers of marching, she assumes the risks of lifelong dedication to her profession—a program that runs counter to many cherished slogans. As a young woman conversing with young men, I learned to caution myself: "Let him win! When a woman wins she loses." Yet even as I said it I knew that such capitulation was merely for the purposes of flirtation, where a woman can afford the delicious indulgence of yielding. Only when men—or women—block and balk her progress in the professions must a woman strike back, and then she must use every weapon in her artillery.

To bear and rear a child is all that it is said to be; it is joy and sorrow, the very heart of living. There is no comparing it with a woman's profession beyond the home. Simply, the two things do not bear comparison. It is false to say the home comes first, the career second. For the woman writer, there can be no first or second about these matters; even to think it is an offense. For myself I enjoy housekeeping, by which I mean I like living in an attractive house and entertaining my friends. I look on house-and-garden as the most delightful toys, and take pleasure in every facet. But I know also that if house-and-garden should interfere seriously with work, with writing, house-and-garden would go.

Women in the professions must make their choices. That many refuse, sidestepping to easy pursuits, is a reason why American women have not kept pace with their sisters in India and Russia. The United States Senate of 100 has one woman member.

Perhaps the real turn in the road will come —and I predict it is coming soon—when more than two children to a family will seem bad taste, like wearing mink in a starving village. No woman can devote a life to the rearing of two, she cannot even make a pretense of it. When the mother image loses its sanctity, something will take its place on the altar. And any writer knows that when the image of the heroine changes, the plot changes with her. Such an event could alter, for both men and women, the whole picture of American life.

DISCUSSION TOPICS

1. Analyze three dirty jokes.

SUGGESTED ACTIVITIES

1. Read *A Family Portrait* and evaluate the influence of Ms. Bowen's upbringing on her as an adult.

2. Do background reading about and prepare a report on a woman who became prominent after the death of her husband. In your report, be sure to include an analysis of why she was not as prominent before her husband died as well as an evaluation of her rise to prominence after his death.

31

The Black Woman and Women's Liberation

No group, organization, or movement can hope to survive long unless it represents the people it claims to. This is true for the Women's Movement also. If it intends to be a powerful, vibrant force, it must represent all women from all economic levels and ethnic backgrounds.

Before the Women's March in August 1970, many women believed the new wave of feminism was the domain of the more highly educated white, middle-class American female. Many people thought the various women's groups were primarily connected with doubling the salary of the very small percentage of women whose incomes were above ten thousand dollars a year. Of course, most women's groups are concerned with equal pay for equal work—but for everybody—not only for women professionals. With the possible exception of the low paying service jobs, such as domestic help, minority group women are the last hired and first fired.

Margaret Sloan, an editor of <u>Ms</u>. magazine, who has been active in the Black Movement and the Women's Movement, wrote the following article in <u>The New York Times</u> in defense of the black woman's role in the Women's Movement. Ms. Sloan believes that only when all women can control their own destinies will they then begin to know their potential as human beings.

What We Should Be Doing, Sister

Margaret Sloan

As a black woman who has been actively involved and still is in the black movement, part of my frustration has been that—after risking my life in sit-ins, pickets, marches; you name it—I was allowed to make coffee, not decisions. And so from there came the realization that I was going to help the brothers realize that as black women we cannot allow black men to do to us what white men have been doing to their women all these years. I decided to point out, as Bobby Seale said in *Seize the Time*, that real manhood doesn't depend on the subjugation of anyone; to remind him that the racist Patrick Moynihan lied when he said that the problem with black men is black women.

Because we know that the problem with black men is white racism and no amount of going back to the kitchen is going to give a black man a job. It is an insult to black men to say that black women must be behind them pushing them into their manhood. Sister, I want to make sure that, comes the revolution, I will be able to use all my talents and creativity and energies, which has nothing to do with cooking grits for the revolutionaries.

Black women do work. In fact, most women in this country work, and yet a black female with a bachelor's degree earns slightly less than a high school-educated black male. It is incorrect to assume that all black women are living at home with a man and depending on a man's income. The reality is that a large percentage of the black workforce is women. We are often heads of household, and supporting children as well. That's why black women are concerned about equal pay for equal work, and decent day care for their children.

As many women die each year from botched, illegal abortions as American men die in Vietnam—and a disproportionate number of these are black and brown women. That is why we want repeal of all abortion laws. It is a fact that black women are having abortions, and if the brothers are concerned about genocide, then they will fight with us to establish community-controlled health clinics. We know that once the black warrior has planted his revolutionary seed in our black (or white) womb, we're the ones who often face the reality of raising, clothing, feeding that child by ourselves, while he is sowing oats in other fields. If we can't get equal pay for equal work, how can we survive? How can the children survive? To assume that black women are not concerned about themselves as women is really a putdown. Because we do get raped, we do get sterilized against our will, we do get left with unwanted pregnancies, we do get worse treatment in jails, the courts, the schools, in fact in every institution in this country, than men. We are on the welfare rolls in infinitely greater numbers than men, for sexist reasons. We do, in fact, suffer from a dual stigma in this racist and sexist society. We must have liberation—not for half a race but for the entire black nation, women as well as men.

DISCUSSION TOPICS

1. Support or refute the statement that the positions of blacks and women in America are parallel.

2. In what ways are the aims of the feminist movement desirable for all women, not just for white middle-class females?

SUGGESTED ACTIVITIES

1. Organize a research team to determine how organizations representing different minority groups (Mexican American, Indian, black, etc.) stand on the feminist movement. Once you have their statements, analyze them and report your findings to the group.

2. Write and tape a radio commercial aimed at attracting minority group women to the Women's Movement.

3. Arrange a panel discussion with women members of minority group organizations to speak on the topic, *Minority Group Women and Women's Liberation.* Try to invite women with a broad range of opinion on the subject.

32 Fringe Benefits

There are many women in the Feminist Movement who speak out against the injustices, both social and economic, suffered by millions of women throughout this country. Some of these women are known only to small groups of people; others are national symbols. Of the women in the Movement who are universally recognized none is more well known than Gloria Steinem.

As a writer and editor, as well as president of Ms. Magazine Corporation, Ms. Steinem has never been content to be a neutral observer of events. For years she has raised her voice for the peace movement and liberal politics. Most recently, advancing the cause of women—one of the many groups she believes to be outside the power structure in America—has taken all of her energies.

The following article is excerpted from a commencement address Ms. Steinem delivered at Vassar in 1970, and it clearly indicates her commitment to a revolution that is currently taking place in America.

Women's Liberation Aims to Free Men, Too

Gloria Steinem

This is the year of Women's Liberation. Or at least, it's the year the press has discovered a movement that has been strong for several years now, and reported it as a small, privileged, rather lunatic event instead of the major revolution in consciousness—in everyone's consciousness, male or female—that I believe it truly is.

It is a movement that some call feminist but should more accurately be called humanist; a movement that is an integral part of rescuing this country from its old, expensive patterns of elitism, racism, and violence.

The first problem for all of us, men and women, is not to learn, but to unlearn. We are filled with the popular wisdom of several centuries just past, and we are terrified to give it up. Patriotism means obedience, age means wisdom, woman means submission, black means inferior: these are preconceptions imbedded so deeply in our thinking that we honestly may not know that they are there.

Unfortunately, authorities who write textbooks are sometimes subject to the same popular wisdom as the rest of us. They gather their proof around it, and end by becoming the theoreticians of the status quo. Using the most respectable of scholarly methods, for instance, English scientists proved definitively that the English were descended from the angels while the Irish were descended from the apes.

It was beautifully done, complete with comparative skull measurements, and it was a rationale for the English domination of the Irish for more than 100 years. I try to remember that when I'm reading Arthur Jensen's current and very impressive work on the limitations of black intelligence, or when I'm reading Lionel Tiger on the inability of women to act in groups.

It wasn't easy for the English to give up their mystic superiority. Indeed, there are quite a few Irish who doubt that they have done it yet. Clearing our minds and government policies of outdated myths is proving to be at least as difficult, but it is also inevitable. Whether it's woman's secondary role in society or the paternalistic role of the United States in the world, the old assumptions just don't work any more.

Part of living this revolution is having the scales fall from our eyes. Every day, we see small obvious truths that we had missed before. Our histories, for instance, have generally been written for and about white men. Inhabited countries were "discovered" when the first white male set foot there, and most of us learned more about any one European country than we did about Africa and Asia combined.

I confess that, before some consciousness-changing of my own, I would have thought that the women's history courses springing up around the country belonged in the same cultural ghetto as home economics. The truth is that we need Women's Studies almost as much as we need Black Studies, and for exactly the same reason: too many of us have completed a "good" education believing

that everything from political power to scientific discovery was the province of white males.

We believe, for instance, that the vote had been "given" to women in some whimsical, benevolent fashion. We never learned about the long desperation of the women's struggle, or about the strength and wisdom of the women who led it. We knew a great deal more about the outdated, male supremacist theories of Sigmund Freud than we did about societies where women had equal responsibility, or even ruled.

"Anonymous," Virginia Woolf once said sadly, "was a woman."

A Black Parallel

I don't mean to equate our problems of identity with those that flowed from slavery. But, as Gunnar Myrdal pointed out in his classic study *An American Dilemma*, "In drawing a parallel between the position of, and feeling toward, women and Negroes, we are uncovering a fundamental basis of our culture."

Blacks and women suffer from the same myths of childlike natures; smaller brains; inability to govern themselves, much less white men; limited job skills; identity as sex objects, and so on. Ever since slaves arrived on these shores and were given the legal status of wives——that is, chattel——our legal reforms have followed on each other's heels—with women, I might add, still lagging considerably behind.

President Nixon's Commission on Women concluded that the Supreme Court sanctions discrimination against women—discrimination that it long ago ruled unconstitutional in the case of blacks —but the commission report remains mysteriously unreleased by the White House. . . . Neither blacks nor women have role-models in history: models of individuals who have been honored in authority outside the home.

As Margaret Mead has noted, the only women allowed to be dominant and respectable at the same time are widows. You have to do what society wants you to do, have a husband who dies, and then have power thrust upon you through no fault of your own. The whole thing seems very hard on the men.

Before we go on to other reasons why Women's Liberation is Men's Liberation, too—and why this incarnation of the Women's Movement is inseparable from the larger revolution—perhaps we should clear the air of a few more myths—the myth that women are biologically inferior, for instance. In fact, an equally good case could be made for the reverse.

Women live longer than men. That's when the groups being studied are always being cited as proof that we work them to death, but the truth is that women live longer than men even when the groups being studied are monks and nuns. We survived Nazi concentration camps better, are protected against heart attacks by our female hormones, are less subject to many diseases, withstand surgery better and are so much more durable at every stage of life that nature conceives 20 to 50 percent more males just to keep the balance going.

The Auto Safety Committee of the American Medical Association has come to the conclusion that women are better drivers because they're less emotional than men.(I never thought I would hear myself quoting the AMA, but that one was too good to resist.)

I don't want to prove the superiority of one sex to another; that would only be repeating a male mistake. The truth is that we're just not sure how many of our differences are biological and how many are societal. What we do know is that the differences between the two sexes, like the differences between races, are much less great than the differences to be found within each group.

Chains of Mink

A second myth is that women are already being treated equally in this society. We ourselves have been guilty of perpetuating this myth, especially at upper economic levels where women have grown fond of being lavishly maintained as ornaments and children. The chains may be made of

mink and wall-to-wall carpeting, but they are still chains.

The truth is that a woman with a college degree working full time makes less than a black man with a high school degree working full time. And black women make least of all. In many parts of the country—New York City, for instance—a woman has no legally guaranteed right to rent an apartment, buy a house, get accommodations in a hotel, or be served in a public restaurant. She can be refused simply because of her sex.

In some states, women get longer jail sentences for the same crime. Women on welfare must routinely answer humiliating personal questions; male welfare recipients do not. A woman is the last to be hired, the first to be fired. Equal pay for equal work is the exception. Equal chance for advancement, especially at upper levels or at any level with authority over men, is rare enough to be displayed in a museum.

As for our much-touted economic power, we make up only 5 percent of the Americans receiving $10,000 a year or more, and that includes all the famous rich widows. We are 51 percent of all stockholders, a dubious honor these days, but we hold only 18 percent of the stock—and that is generally controlled by men.

In fact, the myth of economic matriarchy in this country is less testimony to our power than to resentment of the little power we do have.

You may wonder why we have submitted to such humiliations all these years; why, indeed, women will sometimes deny that they are second-class citizens at all. The answer lies in the psychology of second-classness. Like all such groups, we come to accept what society says about us. We believe that we can make it in the world only by "Uncle Tom-ing," by a real or pretended subservience to white males.

Even when we come to understand that we, as individuals, are not second-class, we still accept society's assessment of our group—a phenomenon psychologists refer to as internalized aggression. From this stems the desire to be the only woman in an office, an academic department, or any other part of the man's world. From this also stems women who put down their sisters—and my own profession of journalism has some of them.

Inhumanity to Man

I don't want to give the impression, though, that we want to join society exactly as it is. I don't think most women want to pick up briefcases and march off to meaningless, depersonalized jobs. Nor do we want to be drafted—and women certainly should be drafted; even the readers of *Seventeen* magazine were recently polled as being overwhelmingly in favor of women in national service—to serve in a war like the one in Indochina.

We want to liberate men from those inhuman roles as well. We want to share the work and responsibility, and to have men share equal responsibility for the children. Probably the ultimate myth is that children must have full-time mothers, and that liberated women make bad ones. The truth is that most American children seem to be suffering from too much mother and too little father.

Women now spend more time with their homes and families than in any other or present society we know about. To get back to the sanity of the agrarian or joint family system, we need free universal day care. With that aid, as in Scandinavian countries, and with laws that permit women equal work and equal pay, man will be relieved of his role as sole breadwinner and stranger to his own children.

No more alimony. Fewer boring wives. Fewer childlike wives. No more so-called "Jewish mothers," who are simply normally ambitious human beings with all their ambitiousness confined to the house. No more wives who fall apart with the first wrinkle because they've been taught that their total identity depends on their outsides. No more responsibility for another adult human being who has never been told she is responsible for her own life, and who sooner or later says some version of, "If I hadn't married you, I could have been a star."

Women's Liberation really is Men's Liberation, too.

The family system that will emerge is a great subject of anxiety. Probably there will be a variety of choices. Colleague marriages, such as young people have now, with both partners going to law school or the Peace Corps together, is one alternative. At least they share more than the kitchen and the bedroom. Communes; marriages that are valid for the child-rearing years only—there are many possibilities.

The point is that Women's Liberation is not destroying the American family. It is trying to build a human, compassionate alternative out of its ruins.

Simply Incorruptible

One final myth: that women are more moral than men. We are not more moral; we are only uncorrupted by power. But until the old generation of male chauvinists is out of office, women in positions of power can increase our chances of peace a great deal.

I personally would rather have had Margaret Mead as President during the past six years of Vietnam than either Lyndon Johnson or Richard Nixon. At least, she wouldn't have had her masculinity to prove. Much of the trouble this country is in has to do with the masculine mystique: The idea that manhood somehow depends on the subjugation of other people. It's a bipartisan problem.

The challenge to all of us is to live a revolution, not to die for one. There has been too much killing, and the weapons are now far too terrible. This revolution has to change consciousness, to upset the injustice of our current hierarchy by refusing to honor it. And it must be a life that enforces a new social justice.

Because the truth is that none of us can be liberated if other groups are not. Women's Liberation is a bridge between black and white women, but also between the construction workers and the suburbanites, between Mr. Nixon's Silent Majority and the young people it fears. Indeed, there's much more injustice and rage among working-class women than among the much publicized white radicals.

Women are sisters; they have many of the same problems, and they can communicate with each other. "You only get radicalized," as black activists always told us, "on your own thing." Then we make the connection to other injustices in society. The Women's Movement is an important revolutionary bridge, and we are building it.

DISCUSSION TOPICS

1. Rate your local, state, and nationally elected officials on their positions on the Women's Movement. Devise your own rating system.

2. Prepare your own marriage contract.

SUGGESTED ACTIVITIES

1. Prepare a panel on the *Need for the Liberation of Women* to present to a school or community group.

2. Write a speech for a woman announcing her candidacy for the Presidency of the United States. Include a description of her qualifications, the specific locale of the announcement, and her reasons for running for office.

3. Write and perform a skit on one of the following topics:
   a. A man speaking to a group of women on the topic, *Woman Means Submission.*
   b. An automobile salesman delivering a sales pitch on a particular model to a man and then to a woman.
   c. The only female executive working in an office.

PHOTO CREDITS